Policing and Security in Practice

Crime Prevention and Security Management series

Series Editor: **Martin Gill**

Titles include:

Joshua Bamfield
SHOPPING AND CRIME

Mark Button
DOING SECURITY
Critical Reflections and an Agenda for Change

Paul Ekblom
CRIME PREVENTION, SECURITY AND COMMUNITY SAFETY USING THE
5IS FRAMEWORK

Janice Goldstraw-White
WHITE COLLAR CRIME
Accounts of Offending Behaviour

Bob Hoogenboom
THE GOVERNANCE OF POLICING AND SECURITY
Ironies, Myths and Paradoxes

Kate Moss
BALANCING LIBERTY AND SECURITY
Human Rights, Human Wrongs

Kate Moss
SECURITY AND LIBERTY
Restriction by Stealth

Tim Prenzler
POLICING AND SECURITY IN PRACTICE
Challenges and Achievements

Adam White
THE POLITICS OF PRIVATE SECURITY
Regulation, Reform and Re-Legitimation

Crime Prevention and Security Management
Series Standing Order ISBN 978–0–230–01355–1 hardback
978–0–230–01356–8 paperback
(*outside North America only*)

You can receive future titles in this series as they are published by placing a standing order. Please contact your bookseller or, in case of difficulty, write to us at the address below with your name and address, the title of the series and the ISBN quoted above.

Customer Services Department, Macmillan Distribution Ltd, Houndmills, Basingstoke, Hampshire RG21 6XS, England

---

Policing and Security in Practice

Challenges and Achievements

Edited by

Tim Prenzler

Professor and Chief Investigator, Australian Research Council Centre of Excellence in Policing and Security, Griffith University, Australia

palgrave
macmillan

First published 2012 by
PALGRAVE MACMILLAN

Palgrave Macmillan in the UK is an imprint of Macmillan Publishers Limited,
registered in England, company number 785998, of Houndmills, Basingstoke,
Hampshire RG21 6XS.

Palgrave Macmillan in the US is a division of St Martin's Press LLC,
175 Fifth Avenue, New York, NY 10010.

Palgrave Macmillan is the global academic imprint of the above companies
and has companies and representatives throughout the world.

Palgrave® and Macmillan® are registered trademarks in the United States,
the United Kingdom, Europe and other countries.

ISBN 978–0–230–30056–9

This book is printed on paper suitable for recycling and made from fully
managed and sustained forest sources. Logging, pulping and manufacturing
processes are expected to conform to the environmental regulations of the
country of origin.

A catalogue record for this book is available from the British Library.

A catalog record for this book is available from the Library of Congress.

10   9   8   7   6   5   4   3   2   1
21   20   19   18   17   16   15   14   13   12

Printed and bound in the United States of America
by Edwards Brothers Malloy, Inc.

*This book is dedicated to the memory of Michael Selleck,
1940–2010. He was a great teacher, a believer and a cynic*

Contents

Tables and Figures

Tables

Figures

Preface

A major feature of the current international political landscape is mass uprisings by citizens seeking to depose oppressive regimes and establish democratic governments. Central to this project is the replacement of policing agencies that were the tools of despots with professional police departments that serve the people and are accountable to elected parliaments. Police have a key role to play in establishing the rule of law and creating a safe environment in which people can enjoy liberty and build prosperity. The spread of democratic freedoms and market freedoms in the last few decades has also stimulated growth in private security, providing a supplementary and, sometimes, a primary source of security for businesses and households. But what are the best forms of policing and security? Is it possible for these agencies to minimize crime while protecting individual freedoms and human rights? Many emerging democracies look to established democracies, mainly in Europe and North America, for examples of good practice. However, these countries also struggle to ensure that policing and security services are free from misconduct and are as efficient and effective as possible.

This book is designed to address these crucial questions by focusing on the international evidence concerning appropriate standards and effective strategies across key domains in police and security work. It develops the lessons from the scientific literature in short chapters in an easy-to-read format and with attention to practical means of implementation. The book is unique in recognizing the co-contribution of police and security to crime prevention and community safety, with attention to key points of strategic cooperation. It is also designed to appeal to a wide readership, including academics, students of policing and security, managers and operational officers in both fields and legislators and policy makers. The book is a valuable and convenient guide for busy practitioners and managers, but it also advances academic theory and knowledge about problems and solutions in law enforcement and crime prevention across the public and private sectors.

Many of the chapter authors are members of the Australian Research Council Centre of Excellence in Policing and Security (ARC CEPS), established in 2007, located at Griffith University and the University of Queensland in Brisbane, the Australian National University in Canberra and Charles Sturt University in Sydney. Although the book is designed in part to showcase work being undertaken in CEPS, the primary focus is on the international dimensions of a wide range of topics. Consequently, the authors are joined by a number of other subject experts recruited to provide further depth and breadth across the field.

The chapter topics were selected on the basis of relevance, both in terms of contemporary challenges, where work needs to be done, and areas of achievement, where demonstrated improvements have been made and lessons can be drawn. The first chapter establishes key principles for subsequent chapters, by emphasizing the need for police to account for their use of taxpayers' funds through performance indicators and impact data, while at the same time questioning the relevance of many traditional performance measures. This is followed by a chapter that makes an empirical assessment of what counts as legitimacy in policing. Chapter 2 shows that, while limited by numerous political and social constraints, there is a great deal that police can do to obtain public acceptance and support and to engage more closely and effectively with their varied constituencies.

The next group of chapters shifts the focus to specific crime problems. Chapter 3 considers the problem of organized crime and the challenge of increased internationalization of criminal networks. This is an area where knowledge about 'what works' is still developing, and the authors outline a number of promising strategies and provisional evidence of success. The policing of mass demonstrations and other forms of protest presents police with another challenge. Chapter 4 provides examples of good and bad practice in different approaches to managing protest with a view to minimizing harm while allowing the exercise of basic rights of freedom of speech and assembly.

Police are making increasing use of criminal intelligence methods and intelligence databases in solving and preventing crime. This is an area of emerging academic interest. However, as the authors of Chapter 5 point out, measures of what counts as good or effective intelligence are still in development, and there is a clear need, which the chapter addresses, for better protocols to ensure the most advantageous uptake of intelligence capacity in law enforcement. One area where we can see policing making a large difference is in traffic law enforcement. Chapter 6 examines the many successes of improved policing in crash reduction. At the same time, many more lives could be saved and more injuries prevented if the findings from this chapter were consistently put into practice.

Addressing the challenges identified in the book requires visionary leadership and effective human resource management. Chapter 7 reviews current knowledge on management strategies in policing and sets out a coherent programme for developing and selecting the best leaders. Deficient leadership has been identified as a major factor behind the problems of corruption and misconduct that have plagued modern police services and continue to undermine police legitimacy and effectiveness. Chapter 8 examines the destructive effects of unethical policing and identifies the lessons from the literature about the need for complex and overlapping systems to proactively prevent corruption and ensure the highest ethical standards in police work.

At this juncture the book turns back to an examination of the core crime prevention and control tasks of police, but this time by examining the potential for police to work with the business sector, including security businesses, in cooperative projects. Chapter 9 makes use of a series of studies of different types of public–private partnerships to demonstrate the potential in this area as long as accountability and public interest criteria are met. The logic of police and private security working together is reflected in partially overlapping work profiles and, unfortunately, high-risk profiles for fatalities and injuries to officers, suspects and members of the public. Chapter 10 reviews the limited literature on this topic and shows what can be done through upgraded procedures and training to reduce physical harm in law enforcement.

Growth in the number of security personnel has been accompanied by rapid growth in the uptake of security technology – which is often criticized as ineffective, inconvenient and a threat to privacy. Chapter 11 provides examples of the successful application of security devices in the fight against crime and describes a security risk management framework for the selection and effective management of security technology. The security industry is also subject to many of the ethical risks associated with policing and has a parallel history of corruption, human rights violations, excessive force and failed accountability. With this in mind, Chapter 12 explores international experience with the regulation of the industry through occupational licensing regimes that include mandated training and disqualifying offences. The chapter argues that adequate government regulation is required if the private security industry is to realize its enormous potential in crime prevention.

The chapters in this book cover a diverse set of topics. The unifying theme is the potential for continuous improvement. The book shows how this can be done, by using research to identify problems, developing tailor-made interventions, evaluating the impacts and making modifications where necessary. Much has been done in this area, but the book also presents evidence that there is still some way to go to optimize best practice in policing and security.

I would like to thank all the authors for their time and cooperation in fitting their work to the aims and parameters of the book. And I would like to say a special 'thank you' to Geoff Alpert for advice on Chapter 10.

I hope that all readers will find the book enjoyable, useful and inspiring.

Tim Prenzler

Series Editor's Introduction

There are a range of security threats that face modern society, and the response will inevitably involve the police but also other policing groups. Some concerns are the result of emerging or developing crime patterns or concerns, such as organized crime, violent protest or terrorism; some concerns are the result of the way that police agencies respond (or do not do so properly), and focus on issues of legitimacy and managing complaints, measuring performance, establishing agreed best practices and techniques, developing partnerships and engaging with technology. This book incorporates a discussion about all of these concerns.

At least part of Professor Tim Prenzler's aims in bringing these authors and these papers together in one volume is to highlight the importance of both the police and private security in tackling crime. An emphasis is placed on reviewing current approaches and at the same time on highlighting innovative and progressive ways in which strategy and practice may develop.

At least part of the difficulty is that problems or threats are often poorly defined, as Julie Ayling and Roderic Broadhurst note in their discussion of organized crime. And similarly there are weaknesses in the way performance (of the police) is measured. As Tim Legrand and Simon Bronitt note, it is far from clear that the right things are being measured. It is perhaps not surprising then that Jacqueline Drew should argue that police leadership is less developed than is leadership in other organizations, and she laments the lack of a clear link between leadership qualities and police performance. At the same time there is increasing awareness that paying attention to causes lends credence to the need for a varied response to crime so that actions taken are fit for their purpose and are more likely to have an effect. For example, Lyndel Bates and colleagues highlight the need to avoid the 'one-size-fits-all' approach to tackling traffic offences. In a different way David Baker, in his discussion of policing protest, invites a focus on facilitating peaceful protest as the main priority rather than on readying to tackle confrontation at an early stage.

The need for improved practices in the security world is tackled too. Tim Prenzler and Rick Sarre present an insightful chapter on the benefits and drawbacks of different types of crime partnerships between the police and other agencies and generate a list of key ingredients which underpin success and provide an important reference point for the future. All too often 'partnership' is presented as an unqualified good, when in practice many are dogged by problems or otherwise fail to reach their potential.

Similarly discussion about making security effective rarely strays far from the need for effective regulatory regimes. Mark Button helpfully outlines why security work is a special case for regulation, representing as it does, a thin blue line in protecting parties in private space, a thinner blue line than the police play perhaps in protecting the public, but still a blue line.

Importantly, Rick Draper and colleagues summarize and highlight the growing body of research which reports that security has been successful and a key component in crime drops witnessed across the western world. Clearly building on good approaches is as important as eliminating weak ones in improving the response to crime, whether that be in the private or public sector.

Tim Prenzler has provided a more comprehensive overview of all the chapters and of how they inform our understanding of police and security. In doing so he highlights the crucial aim of this book series – to better inform the theory and practice of tackling crime, wherever it occurs, be that in organizations or in the community. Moreover, Tim highlights the potential of the public and private sectors to learn from each other and the ways in which they may do so.

Martin Gill

Notes on Contributors

Julie Ayling is a research associate in the Regulatory Institutions Network at the Australian National University (ANU), Canberra, Australia. As an associate investigator at the Centre of Excellence in Policing and Security (CEPS) she is working on Illicit Organizations, a project focusing on gangs, organized crime and terrorist groups that aims to generate insights about the characteristics, the rise and decline of these organizations and the recruitment, commitment and desistance of their members. Prior to joining RegNet, she was a senior lawyer in the Australian Public Service working on issues of international law and communications law. In RegNet she has researched areas as diverse as the governance of illicit synthetic drugs and the resourcing of police organizations. Her research interests include policing, criminalization, transnational crime (especially transnational environmental crime) and the global diffusion of criminal justice law and policies. She is an author, with Professors Peter Grabosky and Clifford Shearing, of *Lengthening the Arm of the Law* (2009).

David Baker is Head of Criminal Justice at Monash University, Gippsland, Australia. His main research interest is public order policing, especially the policing of industrial, social and political protests. He is the author of *Batons and Blockades: Policing Industrial Disputes in Australasia* (2005). He has also written interdisciplinary articles and chapters in relation to police history and reform, policing dissent, police unionism, labour history, South Pacific policing, the Australian Federal Police, industrial relations and politics. He is a member of the International Policing Research Consortium on the Police Use of Force and is an associate investigator for the Australian Research Council Centre of Excellence in Policing and Security (ARC CEPS).

Lyndel Bates is Research Director with the Queensland Parliamentary Service and a PhD student with the Centre for Accident Research and Road Safety – Queensland (CARRS-Q) at the Queensland University of Technology, Australia. She has over seven years of experience in road safety research. Her main research interests include graduated driver licensing and the use of road safety research to develop best practice policy. Lyndel is qualified in commerce and behavioural science.

Roderic Broadhurst is Chief Investigator (designate) for the Australian Research Council Centre of Excellence in Policing and Security (ARC CEPS), RegNet ANU College of Asia and the Pacific, Australia. He is also a professor in the School of Regulation, Justice and Diplomacy in the ANU College of Asia and the Pacific. He is Chief Investigator (designate) engaged in CEPS projects, including Illicit Organizations and Investigative Practices, with Victoria Police and other agencies. Professor Broadhurst is a graduate of the University of Western Australia, Perth, Australia, and Cambridge, UK, and has served in corrections (1974–1985) and public health (1986–1989) in Western Australia. He has extensive experience in criminal justice as a practitioner and researcher. His earlier research has focused on criminal behaviour, lethal violence, victimization and cyber crime, and has involved longitudinal research applying risk analysis methodologies to problems of recidivism, persistent offending, sex offending and dangerous offending. Current research also includes projects on crime and modernization in Cambodia, homicide in Hong Kong and China, UN surveys of crimes against business in China and omnibus UN crime victimization studies in Hong Kong and Cambodia, monitoring serious crime in cyberspace and a national survey of attitudes to sentencing in Australia.

Simon Bronitt is Director of the Australian Research Council Centre of Excellence in Policing and Security (ARC CEPS). He was previously Professor of Law at the Australian National University College of Law and Associate Director of the Australian Centre for Military Law and Justice, ANU. Between 2006 and 2009 he served as Director of the National Europe Centre, Research School of Humanities, ANU. Drawing on comparative and interdisciplinary perspectives, Simon has published widely on criminal justice issues, including counter-terrorism law and human rights, covert policing, telecommunications interception and international criminal law. His publications include *Principles of Criminal Law* (2nd ed, 2005) and *Law in Context* (3rd ed, 2006).

Mark Button is Reader in Criminology and Associate Head Curriculum at the Institute of Criminal Justice Studies, University of Portsmouth, UK. There he has also recently founded the Centre for Counter Fraud Studies (CCFS), of which he is Director. Mark has written extensively on counter-fraud and private policing issues, publishing many articles and chapters and completing four books, with one forthcoming. Mark was also Director of the Security Institute and chaired its Academic Board. He is Head of Secretariat of the Counter Fraud Professional Accreditation Board. Before joining the University of Portsmouth he was a research assistant to the Rt Hon Bruce George, MP, specializing in policing, security and Home affairs issues. Mark completed his undergraduate studies at the University of Exeter, UK, his masters at the University of Warwick, UK, and his doctorate at the London School of Economics, UK. Mark has just completed the largest study of fraud victims to date in the United Kingdom, funded by the National Fraud Authority and the Association of Chief Police Officers (ACPO).

Jacqueline Davis is a research assistant working with the Australian Research Council Centre of Excellence in Policing and Security (ARC CEPS) at the University of Queensland, Australia. Her educational background is in psychology and quantitative business research techniques. She has experience in systematic reviews and meta-analysis, and is especially interested in the application of these methods to the evaluation of social policy interventions.

Rick Draper is a career crime prevention and security risk management professional, with over 25 years of local and international experience. He is also Adjunct Senior Lecturer in the School of Criminology and Criminal Justice at Griffith University in Brisbane, Australia. Rick holds a degree in education, with major studies in security and justice. Prior to earning his degree, he obtained electrical trade and electronics qualifications and worked extensively in the installation, commissioning and servicing of electronic security systems, including large-scale access control and closed-circuit television systems. Rick is also a forensic security consultant and has served as an expert witness in civil litigation cases involving security, with a number of cases involving matters related to crime prevention through environmental design (CPTED). Rick has written and presented numerous papers and articles on a diverse range of topics in the areas of crime prevention and security. He wrote chapters for both the third and fourth editions of the highly regarded *Handbook of Loss Prevention and Crime Prevention* (edited by Lawrence J. Fennelly).

Jacqueline M. Drew is Lecturer in the School of Criminology and Criminal Justice at Griffith University, Australia, and a member of the

Australian Research Council Centre of Excellence in Policing and Security (ARC CEPS). Dr Drew trained as a psychologist and received her PhD in organizational psychology from Griffith University. Her research interests include the attraction and retention of police personnel, performance management within police organizations and organizational structure and systems, as they relate to innovative police strategies and operational practice.

Janet Evans is a senior research assistant in the Centre of Excellence in Policing and Security (CEPS), Australia, where she is Project Manager of the Intelligence Methods Project. Janet holds an M.Sc. in investigative psychology from the University of Liverpool, UK. Janet began her career as a crime and intelligence analyst in England, working for Lancashire Constabulary, and she later worked as Principal Intelligence Analyst/Analytical Coordinator at West Midlands Police, where she managed crime and intelligence analysts whose expertise covered strategic, tactical and operational intelligence. Janet has also worked in Australia in research for the Queensland Police Service and as Manager of Intelligence in Police Misconduct for the Queensland Crime and Misconduct Commission.

Mark Kebbell is Chief Investigator with the Australian CEPS. His expertise and research is in the area of investigative psychology, particularly with regard to the investigation and prosecution of serious crime. Within the Centre he is Lead Chief Investigator on the Risky People and Intelligence Methods projects. His previous work has included writing the guidelines for police officers in England and Wales (with Graham Wagstaff) for the assessment of eyewitness evidence and a review of factors associated with violent extremism for the National Policing Improvement Agency commissioned by the Office for Security and Counter Terrorism in the United Kingdom (with colleagues). He has worked on more than 70 criminal cases, principally involving murder or serious sexual assault, and has given expert evidence on numerous occasions, including uncontested psychological evidence in an Old Bailey appeal case. Academically, the quality of his work has been recognized by the award of a British Academy Postdoctoral Fellowship for Outstanding Younger Scholars. He is Editor, with Professor Graham Davies, of *Practical Psychology for Forensic Investigations and Prosecutions* (2006).

Tim Legrand is a post-doctoral research fellow in the Australian Research Council Centre of Excellence in Policing and Security (ARC

CEPS), Griffith University, Brisbane, Australia. He completed his PhD in political science at the University of Birmingham, UK, in 2008. He is currently Head of Research for a government consultancy in the United Kingdom and works with the UK Home Office, Department of Children, Schools and Families, Ministry of Justice and with the Department of Health as a specialist policy adviser. His current research focuses on developing drug, alcohol and policing policy for the Home Office and local governments. His academic work focuses on the value that policy makers place on overseas policy learning and on the economy of knowledge in the policy process.

Lorraine Mazerolle is Research Professor in the Institute for Social Science Research (ISSR) at the University of Queensland, Australia. She is also Foundation Director and Chief Investigator at the Australian Research Council Centre of Excellence in Policing and Security (ARC CEPS), Chief Investigator in the Drug Policing Modeling Program and the ISSR's 'Policing and Security' Program Director. Professor Mazerolle leads a team of research scholars with expertise in experimental criminology, urban criminological theories, survey methods, advanced multi-level statistics and spatial statistics. She is the recipient of numerous US and Australian national competitive research grants on topics such as community regulation, problem-oriented policing, police technologies, civil remedies, street-level drug enforcement and the policing of public housing sites. Professor Mazerolle is a fellow of the Academy of Experimental Criminology, current President of the same Academy, Foundation Vice President of the American Society of Criminology Division of Experimental Criminology and author of scholarly books and articles on policing, drug law enforcement, third-party policing, regulatory crime control, displacement of crime and crime prevention.

Kristina Murphy is Associate Professor at Griffith University's School of Criminology and Criminal Justice, Australia. She is also Associate Investigator at Griffith University's Australian Research Council Centre of Excellence in Policing and Security (ARC CEPS). Kristina is a leading Australian scholar in the field of procedural justice and legitimacy research. She has undertaken procedural justice and legitimacy research in law enforcement, taxation and welfare contexts. In her research, she has found that widespread resistance to authorities can partially be explained by a lack of procedural justice and a breakdown in trust between individuals.

Louise Porter is a research fellow in the Australian Research Council Centre of Excellence in Policing and Security (ARC CEPS), where she works in the Integrity Systems and Risky People projects. Louise joined CEPS from the United Kingdom, where she was Lecturer in Forensic Psychology at the University of Liverpool. Her research interests centre on interpersonal processes, specifically leadership and peer influence in forensic contexts. She began by examining the criminogenic environment of juvenile crime, drug use and the desistance process, primarily through work with Professor Shadd Maruna on the Liverpool Desistance Study. Since this early work, Louise has explored social and organizational features of group crime, specifically with regard to rape and robbery groups and, more recently, police corruption. Much of Louise's work in this area has involved a behavioural approach, examining the actions of offenders in their crimes, as taken from archival accounts such as police statements, law reports and media sources. She has also worked on a number of criminal cases, aiding the preparation of psychological reports for both the courts and the police.

Tim Prenzler is Chief Investigator at the Centre of Excellence in Policing and Security (CEPS) and Professor in the School of Criminology and Criminal Justice, Griffith University, Brisbane, Australia. He teaches courses in professional ethics and corruption prevention and in situational crime prevention and security management. At CEPS he manages the Police Integrity research project and is a member of the Frontline Policing project. Tim's research has a strong focus on the application of crime prevention principles to corruption and misconduct, especially misconduct amongst police and security providers. He also has a broader sociological interest in issues associated with the development of the private security industry and specialist police agencies and in safety issues for police and security officers. He is the co-author of *The Law of Private Security in Australia* (2009, with Rick Sarre), which won an Award for Excellence from the Australian Security Industry Association, and is the author of *Police Corruption: Preventing Misconduct and Maintaining Integrity* (2009) and *Ethics and Accountability in Criminal Justice* (2009).

Jessica Ritchie has degrees in criminology and law, and works as Security and Crime Prevention Support Officer with Amtac Professional Services, Australia. She also works as a tutor in the School of Criminology and Criminal Justice at Griffith University, Australia. Jessica's professional interests include litigation relating to the security industry and the development of strategies to mitigate the range of consequential risks arising from security-related incidents. She is a member of the Safer Places project team (developing online resources for crime prevention) and is responsible for developing the Amtac clearing house for security risk management and crime prevention resources.

Elise Sargeant is a PhD candidate in the School of Social Science at the University of Queensland (UQ), Australia, which is affiliated with the Australian Research Council Centre of Excellence in Policing and Security (ARC CEPS). Elise also works as a senior research assistant at the Institute for Social Science Research at UQ. Elise has experience in survey design and interview research, using both quantitative and qualitative methods. She currently works on the Community Capacity Study, a large-scale community survey of 298 suburbs in Brisbane and Melbourne, Australia. Her key areas of interest include policing and the ecology of crime.

Rick Sarre is Professor of Law and Criminal Justice at the University of South Australia. He was, from 1992 to 1998, Head of the School of Law and Legal Practice, University of South Australia. He currently lectures in criminal justice, policing, media law, sport law and commercial law with the School of Commerce. He received a Citation from the Australian Learning and Teaching Council in 2008. He has published widely on issues to do with policing, private security and criminal justice. His books include *The Law of Private Security in Australia* (2nd ed, 2009, with Tim Prenzler) and *Key Issues in Criminal Justice* (2005, edited with J. Tomaino).

David Soole joined the Centre for Accident Research & Road Safety – Queensland (CARRS-Q), Australia, as a research assistant in 2006. He graduated from Griffith University, Australia, in 2004 with qualifications in behavioural science and criminology and criminal justice, and is currently completing his master's degree in applied science (research), investigating driver perceptions of police speed enforcement in Queensland. Since joining CARRS-Q, David has worked on numerous projects covering a range of topics, including speed enforcement, drink-driving, driver aggression, novice driver safety, traffic enforcement sanctions, intelligent transportation systems, older drivers and pedestrian safety.

Barry Watson is Director of the Centre for Accident Research & Road Safety – Queensland (CARRS-Q), which is based at the Queensland

University of Technology, Brisbane, Australia. Barry has over 25 years of experience in road safety and has been involved in the development and delivery of courses in road safety and traffic psychology for both undergraduate and postgraduate students, as well as in leading research teams examining a range of road-user behaviour issues, including drink-driving, speeding, driver licensing, driver education, traffic law enforcement and international drivers.

1
Policing to a Different Beat: Measuring Police Performance

Tim Legrand and Simon Bronitt

The objectives of policing in a modern democracy are to uphold the rule of law and safeguard human rights (albeit the simplicity of these objectives belies the enormous political, normative, financial and administrative challenges the police face on a daily basis). In meeting these objectives, the police must constantly engage in a complex series of administrative manoeuvres to meet the evolving social, political, economic, demographic and technological demands of the state and the public. Against this imperative, it has become ever more important to refine and improve service delivery in terms of efficiency (which denotes the ratio of resources used to outcomes delivered) and – this is paramount – effectiveness (which describes how well the rule of law and human rights are upheld). The greater transparency that is ostensibly delivered by measuring police efficiency and effectiveness has been widely welcomed by the public and governments. In the most part, this is because, firstly, the public's experience of crime is seen as the litmus test of the success of policing strategies, while, secondly, performance metrics provide some measure of the value or burden to the public purse. Yet efficiency and effectiveness are not comfortable bedfellows. A police force dedicated entirely to efficiency is not likely to be a wholly effective one, and *vice versa*. Thus, policing is a series of ongoing trade-offs between tackling priorities and resource management. Importantly, there is little to gauge how well the police perform their public duties in regard to, *inter alia*, policing protests and events, community consultation, knowledge and appropriate application of the law and human rights and use of procedural justice.

In this chapter, we seek to address some of the limitations associated with the use of efficiency and effectiveness metrics. In particular, we are concerned with the competing incentives produced by the two sorts of measures. We will explore this issue with reference to the use of metrics across, particularly, the United Kingdom and Australia. It is our intention to explore the different policing dynamics induced by performance regimes and to propose additional measures of policing that act as a corrective to the unwelcome trade-offs that often arise under these performance regimes. In so doing, we seek to address two pressing questions of measuring contemporary policing:

1. What tensions arise between the use of effective and efficient measures of policing in performance management regimes?
2. Are there alternative measures of policing that can better reflect the range of police duties and their interaction with the public?

To address these questions we will first undertake an examination of the evolution of police performance measurement, where we will briefly unpack the impact of New Public Management (NPM) on efficiency metrics. Second, we will engage with contemporary notions of police effectiveness. In so doing, we will draw out the tensions and unintended consequences that result from the use of efficiency and effectiveness measures. Here we make the claim that these measures can distract the police from their core goals of upholding law and order and human rights. Third, we conclude with an expression of support for broader measures of police effectiveness that incorporate clear tests of public interest.

Measuring up: The rise of new public management and police performance metrics

The use of efficiency and effectiveness metrics is now a familiar reality for police forces in developed and, more recently, in developing countries. The growing sophistication of digitized record-keeping in particular has contributed to the amassing of statistical datasets on police activities, outputs and outcomes. However, the development of measures of policing performance and outcomes has not been without methodological and normative problems. Initiatives to improve the efficiency of police forces have met with resistance by the rank-and-file officers and attracted criticism from academic commentators for their crudity, at least in their initial forms (see de Bruijn, 2002). This is by no means a recent issue. Parrat, writing in 1938, asks the same methodological questions of measuring police effectiveness that scholars pose today:

First, it is necessary to determine what the standard of approvals and disapprovals of police practices and behaviors is at a particular time. Second, it is necessary to devise some methodology permitting determination of the difference between what actually exists and what is desired or approved by an effective sector of citizen opinion.

(Parratt, 1938, p. 739)

The saliency of these imperatives remains relevant. Indeed, since the 1990s there has been widespread adoption of public sector management tools to measure the effectiveness of policing and criminal justice agencies and policies more generally (see Fleming, 2009). The watershed for modern policing arrived with the introduction of performance measurement and its corollary: 'objective-setting'. These two levers – descriptive and prescriptive respectively – are operated by the government to direct police efforts (at the operational street level and broadly strategic level) to meet the outcomes defined by the elected government and are executed through the offices of the relevant minister. Together, these levers constitute performance management: an ethos of public administration that has percolated across governments of almost all political creeds worldwide under the auspices of NPM (see Kaboolian, 1998).

The principles of NPM took root in the mentality of public officials in Western democracies in the 1970s and 1980s. These were eras in which deregulation and privatization were seen as the corrective to bloated and costly government. The 'New Right' ideology of the Reagan–Thatcher administrations trusted the private sector to deliver effective public services at better value for money with the bare minimum of government intervention. NPM owes its philosophy broadly to the instincts of the corporate sphere. It places the philosophies and techniques of business management at the forefront, including market-based solutions of cost-saving, resource-maximizing, performance incentives and rewards. Market forces in the government domain, it is claimed, privilege the measurement of tangible outcomes, drive down superfluous costs and deliver services that match the expectations of taxpayers. In his influential overview of the inexorable march towards NPM standards in government, Hood argues that it entailed the following:

A move towards more explicit and measurable (or at least checkable) standards of performance for public sector organizations, in terms of the range, level and content of services to be provided, as against trust in professional standards and expertise across the public sector.

(1995, p. 97)

The demand for NPM accountability in the 1990s however confronted a muddied legal framework for policing, largely unchanged for more than a century. This position was particularly apparent in the United Kingdom and Australia where, under the common law, the position of the constable (which *a fortiori* includes the office of Chief Constable or Commissioner) is that of an officer *but not servant* of the Crown (*Enever v R* (1906) 3 CLR 969). In a series of leading cases in the twentieth century in the United Kingdom and Australia, the doctrine of constabulary independence established that the office of police constable confers an original rather than delegated discretion that ordinarily would not be amenable to judicial review (Bronitt and Stenning, 2011). Moreover, in the absence of the master–servant relationship that characterizes other civil servants and public officials, the state was not vicariously liable for civil wrongs committed by the police (though this particular implication of the common law doctrine was ultimately reversed by statute). In a practical sense, it also meant that the power of the executive (exercised though the relevant minister) to give directions to police was limited to policy rather than operational decision-making. Admittedly, the boundary between operational and policy matters is notoriously blurry, inviting not infrequent political controversy about police independence and accountability (Bersten, 1990). Although Australian Police Acts adopted in the nineteenth and twentieth centuries made state police organizations and their commissioners accountable to the executive and parliament (typically through the police or justice minister), this development did not fundamentally alter the common law doctrine of constabulary independence (Bersten, 1990, p. 309). The British model, by contrast, has always been more decentralized, with responsibility for policing shared between local authorities and the central government. The trend in the last 30 years has favoured increased centralization of powers in the office of Home Secretary. The newly reformed local police authorities, introduced in the Police Act 1996 (UK), were tasked with maintaining an 'efficient and effective' force which signalled that they were 'to be local watch-dogs of the managerialist, value-for-money ethos that successive governments have injected into the whole public sector' (Reiner & Newburn, 2007, p. 925).

Allegations of the political misuse of police surfaced in the 1980s and 1990s, prompted by the police role in industrial disputes in the United Kingdom and surveillance of government critics in several Australian states (see Chan & Dixon, 2007; Sullivan, 1998). Coupled with growing public concern over police corruption, there were calls for fundamental reappraisal of the models of police accountability based on traditional notions of constabulary independence (Bersten, 1990). Rather than responding by reasserting or indeed strengthening the ideal of constabulary independence, the state began to impose new forms of public oversight and accountability for policing. In Australia, accountability was pursued largely through enhanced political and institutional oversight through the establishment of independent anti-corruption agencies and Police Integrity Commissions. The United Kingdom pursued a similar strategy, though with greater emphasis placed on reforming the management structure of the police force and tying, for the first time, policing performance with its funding (Reiner & Newburn, 2007, p. 926). The *White Paper on Police Reform* (1993) in the United Kingdom called for better internal management of police forces and closer monitoring of performance through national benchmarking. Managerial accountability and performance measurement, it was reasoned, would induce the police to make better use of their human and technical resources to increase crime clear-up rates and lower public perceptions of crime. Crucially, these proposals withdrew the discretion that local police forces had to determine local priorities as part of a broader effort by the then Conservative government to claw back power from local authorities to Whitehall. This was not just limited to law enforcement, but extended across government services, as Winstanley and Stuart-Smith noted:

> The influence of central Government is endemic in the systems of rewards and penalties, operating in the use of appraisal systems in universities, IPR [individual performance review]and clinical audit in the health service, and PRP [performance-related pay] in local government, and in the use of league tables to evaluate performance in health and education.
>
> (1996, p. 67)

Senior police management (as in other sectors such as health and education) saw the opportunity to institute efficiency and cost-effectiveness as important measures of performance for police. The effect of NPM has been to prioritize the goals (or 'goods') of policing as crime prevention, order maintenance and bringing offenders to justice. On this model, the rates of reported crime in regions, arrests and 'clearances' (as measured by the number of cautions, infringement notices issued and convictions) are the markers of effective policing.

However, the development of the policing management model has not been without criticism. Fleming (2009) points out that the quantitative measures in existing performance management tools 'are not good at capturing the quality and effectiveness of the work involved and the many contributions that police make to a community's quality of life' (p. 225). Put crudely, it is argued that the danger of applying NPM to policing, as presently conceived, is that the proverbial 'tail wags the dog': those things most easy to quantify and measure through key performance indicators (KPIs) are made the core objects of policing. The effect is that the evaluative element of policing inscribes a set of normative objectives that essentially determines what can be measured is not only what should be measured but is also what should constitute the normative aims of the police. Skogan and Frydl argue that this issue is an artifact of the broader attitude of governments to image management:

> governments are more inclined to accept what police do (outputs) as a measure of effectiveness than what they achieve (outcomes). Police are, after all, part of government, and therefore they share an interest in shaping appearances. It is also easier and cheaper to document output activity than outcome accomplishments.
>
> (2004, pp. 34–35)

It is vitally important to realize that the way society and police managers conceive the objects of policing fundamentally affects the 'measures' being applied to police performance. The normative aims of modern policing, and more specifically the priorities accorded to competing objects (which range through crime prevention, public order, bringing offenders to justice, as well as newer roles such as protection of human rights and emergency management), affect what is measured and how. This is self-evidently not simply an empirical or sociological issue but also a political and moral one.

In the current financial climate, many police forces (indeed, public sector services) are required to operate with diminishing or finite resources. In the United Kingdom, the Inspectorate of the Constabulary has found that, on average, police forces intend to cut their expenditure by 14 per cent over the two years to 2014/15 (HMIC, 2011). More trade-offs between efficiency and effectiveness are, it seems, inevitable. It is clear that the measurement of efficiency is wrought with methodological, political and, indeed, moral questions. Notwithstanding these problems, determining the efficiency of the police remains a crucial challenge. Yet, without a set of overarching objectives, or awareness of the appropriate effects of policing, any measures of efficiency are redundant. Thus next we turn our attention to how effectiveness in policing has evolved.

Measuring effectiveness in policing

Political figures in recent years have reasoned that if the ultimate objective of a police force is to uphold the laws and values of the community, then policing effectiveness should be gauged from how civil society perceives its success in so doing. From the outset of its administration in 1997, New Labour in the United Kingdom sought to achieve popular consent for its radical agenda by way of 'managerial methods of promotion and forms of consultation (e.g. in focus groups) which it [could] control' (Fairclough, 2000, p. 12). A similar trend manifested in Australia in 2008, with the Rudd Government's 2020 Summit, and more relevantly in this context, the Federal Criminal Justice Forum, both of which aimed to assist in developing reform priorities for the incoming Labor Government (Attorney-General's Department, 2008). This approach to policy development in the United Kingdom and Australia contrasted sharply with that of the previous Conservative administrations, or indeed any administration, and demonstrated their commitment to placing the public's sense of security at the heart of police effectiveness. In the United Kingdom in particular, this commitment resulted in a series of performance frameworks, set out in legislation, that incorporated local perceptions of policing (viz. effectiveness) with efficiency. In Australia, it is less clear that these forums have functioned as anything but public relations exercises, at least in the context of criminal justice reform, which continue to be dominated by local state law and order agendas and moral panics about crime and disorder.

We now turn to a brief examination of how these principles of performance measurement sit together in this framework.

Effectiveness: A matter of (public) perspective

The notion that a community's personal experience of crime was implicitly linked to its perception of policing was underlined clearly in a policing initiative in New Jersey in the 1970s. The 'Safe and Clean Neighborhoods Program' intended to enhance the security of neighbourhoods by increasing the number of police officers on foot patrol. Five years after its inception, the Police Foundation (Washington DC) ran an evaluation of the project and found that although the project did not reduce crime rates, surveys of the local population found that residents tended to 'feel' more secure and believed that crime had been reduced in their area. The empirical basis of the evaluation was subsequently contested by the 'broken windows' theory. Kelling and Wilson (1982) propounded the simple hypothesis that a failure to address public disorder on the streets is a sign that no one cares and that this neglect invites further disorder and crime: '[t]he basic plot is simple: fighting minor disorder deters serious crime' (Harcourt, 2001, p. 27). Broken windows, in this view, become 'a metaphor for the deterioration of a neighbourhood' (Walker, 1984, p. 76).

While widely credited by senior police, politicians, media and some academics for solving crime problems in large cities, including New York and Chicago, there is a lack of empirical data to support the 'broken windows' hypothesis or zero-tolerance policing more generally (Harcourt, 2001, p. 8; Weatherburn, 2009, p. 186). Indeed, the danger is that the aggressive policing of minor offences can have serious unintended consequences or counterproductive effects, including damaging the trust and perceived legitimacy upon which, as procedural justice research demonstrates, effective policing rests (Tyler, 2003). It is often noted that zero-tolerance practices 'tend to be associated with low-level repression, discriminatory use of police powers, and violation of the civil liberties of the poor and minorities' (Garland, 2001, p. 183). Notwithstanding these concerns, as political actors assumed closer control of policing priorities, police effectiveness was tied to community perceptions of their safety. The 'walk and talk' community foot patrols of 1970s America caught the attention of UK policy officials in the 1990s. Used as a means to promote and strengthen the relationship between the community and police (Lurigio & Rosenbaum, 1994), the 'walk and talk' patrols were intended to capture local needs and glean street-level information, thereby embedding local priorities within policing strategy.

The UK government, under New Labour, determined that policing had lost its community focus. Despite falling levels of recorded crime, the government was concerned by the finding that the public *perceived* crime to be on the increase. In an attempt to resolve this paradoxical perception deficit, the government implemented a trial programme: the National Reassurance Policing Programme (NRPP). The NRPP design was predicated upon models of community policing developed elsewhere, notably the Chicago Alternative Policing Strategy (Skogan & Hartnett, 1997), and bound policing to closer public consultation and enhanced street-level visibility (Millie, 2010). This style of community policing constituted two key elements: (i) the presence of visible authority figures, such as police officers or community support police officers (street wardens with significantly curbed enforcement powers who were given an explicitly community-oriented role to reduce low-level crime and anti-social behaviour) and (ii) prioritization of specific sorts of crime set by the local community (Quinton & Tuffin, 2007). The NRPP was rolled out at 16 sites across 8 forces. In their analysis of the trial outcomes, Quinton and Tuffin found evidence to suggest 'the involvement of the public not only in identifying local problems and setting police priorities, but also in the co-production of solutions, can have a positive impact on victimisation (i.e. actual experiences of crime), the perception of ASB [anti-social behaviour] and other public perception measures' (2007, p. 159). The Home Office evaluation reported on nine metrics (Quinton & Tuffin, 2007, p. 155):

Perception of ASB (teenagers hanging around)
Perception of ASB (graffiti on public buildings)
Victimisation
Feelings of safety walking alone after dark
Perception of the crime rate (less crime)
Perception of police foot patrol
Perception of police effort into finding out what people think
Perception of police effectiveness
Trust many or some people in the local area.

The efficacy of the NRPP was measured not only by material decreases in crime levels but also in falls in the public perception of crime and, indeed, falls in the perception of visible crime. Better policing, in this view, was concerned primarily with community perceptions of safety and control in what McLaughlin (2005) described as a 'new localism', which saw police forces perform their duties in 'active cooperation' with local communities. Active community cooperation represents a strong engagement by the police within local communities to elicit local concerns, knowledge, priorities, vulnerable areas or individuals, repeated offending and so on. Such cooperation not only promotes confidence and trust in the police but also provides the police with local or bottom-up intelligence, assisting in resource allocation. This principle is an important one, since it represents how the police engage with the public. Crucially, community engagement became a central plank in the UK government's police performance evaluation model under the Policing and Performance Assessment Framework (PPAF).

Policing and Performance Assessment Framework

New Labour introduced the PPAF in 2004 to monitor the progress of police authorities against measures set out in the *Police Authorities (Best Value) Performance Indicators Order 2002*. This legislative instrument marked the direct codification of public perception of police performance. The *Police Authorities (Best Value) Performance Indicators Order 2002* was revised in 2005 and 2008 and provided the legal mandate for the Home Office to hold police authorities accountable for local policing outcomes, using measures of public perception. The PPAF contained themed sets of statutory performance indicators (SPIs). The SPIs, broadly, were either quantitative descriptions of police performance or qualitative measures of public perception of police performance:

> Measure of public perception: SPI 1a. (2002): 'Percentage of the public satisfied with the time taken to answer a 999 call from a member of the public'.

> Descriptive measure of police function: SPI 2a. (2002): 'Percentage of minority ethnic police officers in the force compared with the percentage of minority ethnic population of working age'.

These legislative developments embedded the 'accounting-ization' ethos of NPM. Under NPM, police authorities, alongside ten other government authorities, were designated a 'best value authority' within the Local Government Act (1999). This placed upon police authorities a legal obligation to 'secure continuous improvement in the way in which its functions are exercised, having regard to a combination of economy, efficiency and effectiveness' (Local Government Act 1999, Part 1). Importantly, the power to determine what targets are set and how they are measured is held by the Home Secretary. With each iteration of the *Police Authorities (Best Value) Performance Indicators Order* (2002, 2005, 2008), the importance of public perception has remained firmly entrenched as a key measure of police performance. Roughly half of all measures pertain to perceptions of public safety and police performance.

The desire to promote an agenda of 'localism' under New Labour engendered a reconfiguration of performance measurement. In the wake of the seeming success of the PPAF, in 2006 and 2007, the PPAF was revived to place greater emphasis on community security. It was renamed the Assessments of Policing and Community Safety (APACS) and then revised again as the Analysis of Policing and Community Safety. APACS uses a basic survey methodology, recording the percentage of respondents that are 'completely', 'fairly' or 'very' satisfied with various aspects of their perception of police performance (Thorpe, 2009).

Issues in survey measurement

This approach to measuring community participation has its limits. The primary objection is that the public's perception of crime is frequently imprecise. In their analysis of the UK Home Office relative measures of police performance, Drake and Simper (2005) found limited evidence to link incidences of crime and the public's fear of crime, yet found clear evidence of the influence of socioeconomic factors on fear of crime: 'The fact that such socioeconomic variables are outside the control of individual police forces, however, serves to reinforce the argument that survey responses, such as fear of crime measures, should not form a domain with respect to police performance measurement' (2005, p. 479). (This does not dispute that styles of policing can counter the effects of socio-economic variables, which is further explored in Chapter 2.) A similar finding pertains in Australia, where a recent study revealed that the majority of Australians surveyed perceived that crime was on the increase, though reported crime statistics indicated an overall downward trend: indeed, only 2.9 per cent of those surveyed correctly identified that crime rates reduced over the period 2005–2007 (Roberts & Indermaur, 2009, p. 9). This divergence between perception and reality is not surprising in light of the fact that most of those surveyed rely on radio broadcasts and tabloid media for knowledge about crime and justice.

In light of this research, it seems hardly fair, or even logical, to gauge performance against public perception. Yet, measures of perception have a long history in many quarters of policing. Indeed, the use of victimization surveys as a measure of police performance confers a number of benefits. Victimization surveys undertake interviews with a representative sample of the public to record individuals' experiences of crime. In particular, these interviews are designed to record and categorize personal and household crime. In addition, the interviews elicit perceptions of crime in their community. Although there is no single methodology to capture all instances of crime, victimization surveys are especially useful for capturing the 'dark figure' of unreported crime. Crimes against the person or household often go unreported for a number of reasons (indifference, mistrust of police or shame, for example), and victimization surveys are designed to tease out these unreported experiences.

Victimization surveys have a particularly crucial role to play in developing countries with a diminished or underdeveloped capacity to collect crime reporting data. Between 1992 and 1994, the International Crime Victimization Survey conducted victimization surveys across a range of developed and developing countries, including, amongst others, Brazil, Costa Rica, Egypt, Tanzania and China. The outputs of these surveys often provide a more reliable picture of criminal activities, notably rape or sexual assault, domestic violence, religious/cultural punishment, corruption and so on, than data on reported crime, where such data are collected at all. Victimization survey data that capture perceptions and experiences of crime and safety and policing can be invaluable to domestic policy officials or NGO/aid agencies in determining the levels of need around the likely direct or indirect effects of crime in developing countries.

The use of victimization surveys has, in particular, been widely employed and well developed by the United States, which employs the National Crime Victimization Survey (NCVS) and by the United Kingdom, where the British Crime Survey (BCS) has been administered annually across the regions since 1982. In its almost 30 years' existence, the BCS has been refashioned and expanded to capture and depict a wider public sample. At present, the sample size stands at around 45,000 (Home Office, 2010). At the outset, the BCS was intended to capture the mood of those most affected by criminal acts and operate as a barometer of police effectiveness. Increasingly, its findings have been used to both measure police performance and determine appropriate policing targets (alongside other measures). As with all victimization surveys, the BCS captures crimes against the person and personal property such as assault, theft and burglary. Yet, there are comparability problems, particularly with the data of the early years of the BCS, whereupon the definitions of crimes have altered and evolved over the years; like-for-like comparisons are thus problematic in longitudinal analyses of crime.

Strengthening police performance measurement

Although the use of victimization surveys to gauge the effectiveness of the police has not been uncontroversial, it is important to note that normative ideas and official measures of what is or is not 'effective policing' remain determined by political leaders. Importantly, victimization surveys are measures of outcomes. This is important, since these surveys represent a methodological alternative to measuring performance, yet they remain reliant on outcomes measured *as a factor of criminal behaviour* as the best gauge of performance. Measures of other factors, not directly concerned with arrests or fear of crime, but with the wider remit of policing activities, might offer (indeed, even 'incentivize') the police a more balanced set of performance measures. We explore this notion further below.

There are numerous competing influences on police officers, on the street and in the command centre, that erode the primacy of the effectiveness principle. Fundamentally, policing involves day-to-day trade-offs between resources, crime prevention, crime detection, community work, high-demand emergencies and so on. Against this backdrop, it seems hardly possible to produce robust, comparable and objective measures of performance. Effective policing cannot always be efficient, nor does it hold that efficient policing is effective policing. Yet, as Grabosky observes, 'No public sector agency should be able to command an increase in resources unless it can demonstrate that its current allocation is being used efficiently, and that its resources are targeted at specific, measurable objectives in a logical manner' (Grabosky, 1988, p. 6).

In an important sense, policing suffers from its historical image as merely being a crime-fighting body. Its role has not changed in regard to its core function of preventing and responding to crime and disorder, yet modern policing is much more than that. For example, the nature of police work necessitates cooperation and collaboration with not only emergency services but also frontline mental health and social (child and adult) services. The assessment of police performance must take account of the wide range of activities that the police undertake. Many such activities are not immediately conducive to statistical measurement, yet are nonetheless core components of policing. Since its inception, the mandate of modern policing has evolved to include a variety of functions that speak directly to the ambitions of securing a more free, fair and democratic society. As a result, police forces in Australia and the United Kingdom have been at the forefront of experimenting with new forms of diversion processes such as restorative justice conferencing (Bronitt & McSherry, 2010, pp. 27–32). With the advent of human rights legislation both in the United Kingdom and Australia in the past decade, police agencies are acknowledging their key roles in the protection of human rights. Indeed, in the United Kingdom, following the 2009 G20 protests, a national review of tactics led to human rights principles set within revised national guidelines on public order (Orde, 2011). Drawing lessons from procedural justice research, police forces in Australia, the United Kingdom and United States are increasingly giving attention to due process and fairness concerns during routine interactions with citizens which have been demonstrated to improve both the level of perceived legitimacy and public confidence in police as well as citizen compliance with the law and with police directions (see Hinds & Murphy, 2007; Tyler & Murphy, 2011). Methodologically, quantitative measures (focusing on numbers of 'services' delivered) are not always suited for an assessment of 'soft outcomes' work such as these. As Fleming and Scott point out, performance measurement tends to neglect the complexity of functions of modern policing, being focused on a narrow range of indicators: 'while it is possible to measure output indicators such as arrest rates and response times, such measurement cannot reflect the professionalism and/or the quality of the performance' (Fleming & Scott, 2008, p. 323). Clearly, more imaginative qualitative methods of measurement are needed to assess the value and impact of policing performance across the board.

As we have seen above, the use of recorded crime (measured by the police) and unreported crime (measured by surveys) as the *de facto* indicator of police performance is problematic for a number of reasons. Indeed, there is a temptation to suppose that the compulsion to measure performance trumps the utility or indeed validity of measurement. As Shilston notes, 'The imperative to find things that can be readily counted rather than things that really matter to the public can lead to goal displacement, the use of meaningless measures and the diversion of resources to meet false targets' (Shilston, 2008, p. 362). In principle, that which 'really matters to the public' should be reflected in the way the public votes for its government. The public assent for policing policy is delegated and entrusted to elected officials; in this view, democratic principles are applied in a top-down manner; that is to say, the police broadly operate according to democratic principles because they are subject to the control of democratically elected public officials. Yet, this is broadly only implicit in policing and far from evident in current measures of police effectiveness.

It is our view that measures of police effectiveness should incorporate outcomes that speak directly to core democratic principles: that is, police performance should be partly read from how often the police themselves undermine, contravene or fail to protect the 'sacred cows' of democratic policing: law and order, fundamental human rights (freedom of expression, peaceful protest, privacy and equality and so on) and probity in office. Below we propose a set of hard and soft indicators of police performance that represent core bottom-up notions of democratic principles and progressive policing. There are three fundamental areas in which such alternative measures might be employed: (1) community participation, (2) confidence in the police and (3) probity of the police. We regard these measures, suggested as complements rather than replacements of existing measures, as being crucial to the evolution of a more balanced performance measurement regime.

1. *Community participation, measured by*

   - receptivity to public input, measured via the police's use of public forums (community meetings and events), digital platforms (such as email or Web portals) and recording of letters, phone calls and oral interactions;
   - solicitation of community input, measured by use of surveys, focus groups and consultation exercises;
   - use of alternative diversionary forms of policing, including use of restorative justice and procedural justice, measured by the number of participants (victim and criminal) engaged in the restorative process (and the related decrease in matters proceeding to court).

2. *Confidence in the police, measured by*

   - the gap between reported and unreported crime, using existing measures;
   - the number of complaints against police by the public, using existing measures;
   - the number of complaints by detainees, using existing measures or via an independent police ombudsman.

3. *Probity of the police, measured by*

   - the number of violations of the human rights of members of the public and detainees, measured by complaints to an independent monitoring body;
   - the levels of knowledge and appropriate application of the law and human rights by police officers, measured respectively via regular individual performance reviews and complaints made against specific officers;
   - disciplinary proceedings against officers for professional misconduct, using existing reporting procedures;
   - deaths/injuries in police custody or resulting from police pursuits, measured by existing reporting procedures.

Measuring these is not a trivial exercise and raises difficult methodological questions. We have included suggested measurement methods with each alternative measure above, yet these are far from conclusive or exhaustive. Measures such as *knowledge and appropriate application of the law and human rights* are particularly problematic since the law in some areas may be applied in an uneven fashion, reflecting the legitimate exercise of police discretion and the circumstances of the case (Bronitt and Stenning, 2011). That said, social scientists have to hand an array of quantitative and qualitative research tools that, adapted appropriately, could provide robust measurement, such as interviews with the public, judges, prosecutors and defence lawyers; quantitative/qualitative surveys with the public, detainees and convicted criminals; and observation of policed events (i.e. sporting events, public rallies and protests). Use of these and innovative methods can directly benefit the use of the alternative measures suggested here as well as police performance measurement more broadly.

Conclusion

It is vital that 'success' in policing is understood and measured in wider terms. There is a clear imperative to measure reductions in crime (including assaults against police) via recorded crime statistics, victimization surveys and increased performance in community satisfaction surveys. However, regard should also be given to measuring unintended, indirect or counterproductive effects of policing. Performance, in this view, should also be concerned with removing any disincentives to protecting the core elements of law and order, such as upholding human rights and the right to peaceful protest.

Although there is not enough space to explore these activities in depth, it has been our aim to point to the shortcomings of the existing assessment practices. Clearly, the evaluation of policing performance is irreducible to single measures. Performance must be addressed holistically (i.e. all activities are taken account of, not simply those that are most easily measured) and should include both qualitative and quantitative measures. Moreover, focus of performance measurement should be directed beyond law-enforcement functions, to include the full range of the functions undertaken by modern police, so that its contribution to the safety and security of society can be better understood, measured and most importantly, improved.

References

Attorney-General's Department. (2008). *Federal criminal justice forum.* Retrieved from http://www.ema.gov.au/www/agd/agd.nsf/Page/Consultations_reforms_and_reviews2008_Federal_Criminal_Justice_Reform_Forum.

Bersten, M. (1990). Police and politics in Australia: The separation of powers and the case for statutory codification. *Criminal Law Journal, 14,* 302–316.

Bronitt, S., & McSherry, B. (2010). *Principles of criminal law* (3rd ed.). Sydney: Thomson Reuters.

Bronitt, S., & Stenning, P. (2011). Understanding discretion in modern policing. *Criminal Law Journal, 35,* 319–323.

Chan, J., & Dixon, D. (2007). The politics of police reform. *Criminology and Criminal Justice, 7*(4), 443–468.

de Bruijn, H. (2002). *Managing performance in the public sector.* London: Routledge.

Drake, L. M., & Simper, R. (2005). The measurement of police force efficiency: An assessment of UK Home Office policy. *Contemporary Economic Policy, 23*(4), 465–482.

Fairclough, N. (2000). *New Labour, new language?* London: Routledge.

Fleming, J. (2009). Performance management. In A. Wakefield & J. Fleming (Eds.), *The SAGE dictionary of policing* (pp. 224–226). London: SAGE.

Fleming, J., & Scott, A. (2008). Performance measurement in Australian police organizations. *Policing, 2*(3), 322–330.

Garland, D. (2001). *The culture of control: Crime and social order in contemporary society.* Chicago: University of Chicago Press.

Grabosky, P. (1988). Efficiency and effectiveness in Australian policing. *Trends & Issues in Crime and Criminal Justice, 16,* 1–6.

Harcourt, B. E. (2001). *Illusion of order: The false promise of broken windows policing.* Harvard: Harvard University Press.

Her Majesty's Inspectorate of Constabulary (HMIC). (2011). *Adapting to austerity: A review of police force and authority preparedness for the 2011/12-14/15 CSR period.* London: HMIC.

Hinds, L., & Murphy, K. (2007). Public satisfaction with police: Using procedural justice to improve police legitimacy. *Australian & New Zealand Journal of Criminology, 40,* 27–42.

Home Office. (2010). *Crime in England and Wales 2009/10.* London: HMSO.

Hood, C. (1995). The 'new public management' in the 1980s: Variations on a theme. *Accounting Organisations and Society, 20,* 93–93.

Kaboolian, L. (1998). The new public management: Challenging the boundaries of the management vs. administration debate. *Public Administration Review, 58*(3), 189–193.

Kelling, G. L., & Wilson, J. Q. (1982). Broken windows. *Atlantic Monthly, 249*(3), 29–38.

Lurigio, A. J., & Rosenbaum, D. P. (1994). The impact of community policing on police personnel: A review of the literature. In D. P. Rosenbaum (Ed.), *The challenge of community policing: Testing the promises* (pp. 147–163). Thousand Oaks, CA: SAGE.

McLaughlin, E. (2005). Forcing the issue: New Labour, new localism and the democratic renewal of police accountability. *The Howard Journal of Criminal Justice, 44*(5), 473–489.

Millie, A. (2010). Whatever happened to reassurance policing? *Policing, 4*(3), 225–232.

Orde, H. (5 May 2011). The British approach to policing protest. *The Guardian*. Retrieved from http://www.guardian.co.uk/commentisfree/2011/may/05/policing-british-protest?INTCMP=SRCH.

Parratt, S. (1938). A scale to measure effectiveness of police functioning. *Journal of Criminal Law and Criminology, 28*(5), 739–756.

Quinton, P., & Tuffin, R. (2007). Neighbourhood change: The impact of the national reassurance policing programme. *Policing, 1*(2), 149–160.

Reiner, R., & Newburn, T. (2007). Policing and the police. In M. Maguire, R. Morgan & R. Reiner (Eds.), *The Oxford handbook of criminology* (pp. 910–952). Oxford: Oxford University Press.

Roberts, L., & Indermaur, D. (2009). *What Australians think about crime and justice: Results from the 2007 survey of social attitudes*. Canberra: Australian Institute of Criminology.

Shilston, T. G. (2008). One, two, three, what are we still counting for? Police performance regimes, public perceptions of service delivery and the failure of quantitative measurement. *Policing, 2*(3), 359–366.

Skogan, W. G., & Frydl, K. (2004). *Fairness and effectiveness in policing: The evidence*. Washington, DC: The National Academies Press.

Skogan, W. G., & Hartnett, S. M. (1997). *Community policing, Chicago style*. New York: Oxford University Press.

Sullivan, R. R. (1998). The politics of British policing in the Thatcher/Major state. *The Howard Journal of Criminal Justice, 37*(3), 306–318.

Thorpe, K. (2009). *Public perceptions of the police and local partners – Results from the BCS year ending September 2008*. London: Home Office Statistical News Release.

Tyler, T. R. (2003). Procedural justice, legitimacy, and the effective rule of law. *Crime & Justice, 30*, 283–357.

Tyler, T., & Allan Lind, E. (2002). Procedural justice. In J. Sanders & V. L. Hamilton (Eds.), *Handbook of justice research in law* (pp. 65–92). New York: Kluwer Academic/Plenum Publishers.

Tyler, T., & Murphy, T. (2011). Procedural justice, police legitimacy and cooperation with the police: A new paradigm for policing. *CEPS Briefing Paper Series*. Retrieved from http://www.ceps.edu.au/?q=CEPS-Briefing-Paper-Series.

Walker, S. (1984). Broken windows and fractured history: The use and misuse of history in recent police patrol analysis. *Justice Quarterly, 1*(1), 75–90.

Weatherburn, D. (2009). Law and order politics. In A. Wakefield and J. Fleming (Eds.), *The SAGE dictionary of policing* (pp. 185–187). London: SAGE.

Winstanley, D., & Stuart-Smith, K. (1996). Policing performance: The ethics of performance management. *Personnel Review, 25*(6), 66–84.

Legislation and reported legal cases

Enever v R (1906) 3 CLR 969.

Gillan and Quinton v. The United Kingdom – 4158/05 (2010) ECHR 28 (12 January 2010).

The Local Government Act 1999 (UK).
The Police Authorities (Best Value) Performance Indicators Order 2002 (UK).
The Police Authorities (Best Value) Performance Indicators Order 2005 (UK).
The Police Authorities (Best Value) Performance Indicators Order 2008 (UK).

2
Legitimacy and Policing

Elise Sargeant, Kristina Murphy, Jacqueline Davis and
Lorraine Mazerolle

Successful policing relies on the ability of police to secure compliance
and cooperation from the public (Tyler, 1990). We all know that police
can, if they choose, use arrest, threat of arrest and graduated forms of
force to obtain compliance. However, given the obvious negative side
effects of arrest and use of force, coupled with their limited resources,
police know that they must employ strategies that do not rely solely
on their unique and legislated powers to maintain order in society
(Mastrofski, Snipes, & Supina, 1996; Tyler, 1990). Indeed, critiques about
the negative consequences of the use of force (e.g. risk of harm to
police and citizens) and concerns about the concomitant result of poor
police–citizen relations point to the growing awareness amongst police,
police scholars and policy makers of the importance of procedurally just
approaches as the primary means of enhancing perceptions of police
legitimacy and thereby generating public compliance and cooperation
(McCluskey, 2003; Sunshine & Tyler, 2003; Tyler, 1990).

Over the past twenty years or so, a wide body of literature has
emerged to explore the ways in which police might obtain citizen
cooperation and compliance. This research suggests that police legitimacy fosters compliance and cooperation with the police, increases the
public's willingness to intervene in community problems and subsequently enhances the capacity of police to control crime and disorder
(e.g. Mastrofski et al., 1996; Murphy, Hinds, & Fleming, 2008; Sunshine & Tyler, 2003; Tyler & Fagan, 2008). Studies find that police
legitimacy comes about not only through 'sanctioning threats' and
'effectively controlling crime', but most importantly through the use
of 'procedural justice' (Sunshine & Tyler, 2003, p. 514; see also Hinds &
Murphy, 2007). Tom Tyler and his colleagues propose that police who
follow the principles of procedural justice can encourage perceptions

of legitimacy (Sunshine & Tyler, 2003; Tyler & Huo, 2002). These principles include 'neutrality' of decision making, treating citizens with 'respect', demonstrating 'trust' to citizens and allowing citizen's participation or 'voice' throughout interactions (Tyler, 2008, p. 30; see also Goodman-Delahunty, 2010; Tyler, 2006; Tyler & Murphy, 2011). Legitimacy and procedural justice are important not only in one-on-one police–citizen encounters but also in the context of police engagement with communities.

This Chapter aims to summarize the large body of literature on police legitimacy and procedural justice, including evaluations of programmes that seek to enhance legitimacy. We start the Chapter by defining police legitimacy and other key concepts including procedural justice. We then outline why police legitimacy is important and examine research to determine how police legitimacy can be improved. We conclude with recommendations for the future of research into, and practice of, legitimate policing.

Defining police legitimacy

Sunshine and Tyler (2003, p. 514) define legitimacy as 'a property of an authority that leads people to feel that that authority or institution is entitled to be deferred to and obeyed'. In other words, when people view an authority as legitimate, they allow that authority to define and regulate norms for behaviour (Kochel, 2011; Sunshine & Tyler, 2003). Legitimacy is considered to be particularly important to compliance and cooperation because it taps into one's own 'internal values about what one ought to do' instead of relying on rewards or sanctions to regulate behaviour (Hinds & Murphy, 2007, p. 30; see also Tyler, 2001; Weber, 1968).

Police legitimacy is traditionally conceptualized as reflecting two judgements (Tyler, 2006). First is the 'obligation to obey' (2006, p. 28). When police are perceived as legitimate, people feel that they ought to defer to their decisions and rules, cooperate with them and follow them voluntarily out of obligation, rather than out of fear of sanctions or anticipation of reward (Tyler, 2006). Second is public 'trust' and 'confidence' in police (2006, p. 28). This is the belief that the police perform their job well, that they are honest and that they can secure public confidence in their ability to perform (Hinds & Murphy, 2007; Tyler, 2006).

Jonathan Jackson and his colleagues (e.g. Jackson & Bradford, 2011; Jackson, Bradford, Hough, & Murray, 2010) have recently expanded on this traditional definition of police legitimacy. In addition to Tyler's conceptualization of legitimacy as the obligation to obey and trust and confidence in police, Jackson et al. (2010, p. 5) suggest 'moral alignment' is a core component of legitimacy. 'Moral alignment' is the belief that the police and the public hold similar beliefs about what constitutes law-abiding behaviour (Jackson et al., 2010, p. 5). Jackson et al. argue that in addition to trust in police and an obligation to obey, legitimacy represents a 'sense of shared purpose' between the police and the public, and that this is important to cooperation and compliance (2010, p. 5). Lastly, Jackson & Bradford (2011, p. 3) suggest that for the police to be viewed as legitimate, they also need to be seen by the public to be acting in an ethical manner and exercising their authority according to established norms – what they call 'legality'. In other words, police need to follow their own rules (Jackson and Bradford, 2011, p. 3).

Having provided a brief definition of police legitimacy, this begs the question: what can police do to build legitimacy? Scholars suggest police legitimacy is shaped by both 'instrumental' and 'normative' factors (Hinds & Murphy, 2007, p. 28; see also Sunshine & Tyler, 2003). According to the instrumental perspective, police can build their legitimacy through tackling crime effectively ('performance'), through being able to deter criminals from offending ('risk') and through ensuring equality of service across different groups in society ('distributive fairness') (Sunshine & Tyler, 2003, p. 514; see also Hinds & Murphy, 2007). In other words, the instrumental perspective of legitimacy suggests that police develop and maintain legitimacy through their effectiveness in controlling, preventing and responding to crime and disorder across people and places.

In contrast, the 'normative' perspective of legitimacy argues that 'procedural justice' is particularly important for police legitimacy (Hinds & Murphy, 2007, p. 28). According to the procedural justice model, 'the legitimacy of police is linked to public judgments about the fairness of the processes through which the police make decisions and exercise authority' (Sunshine & Tyler, 2003, p. 514). Procedural justice, as described in the literature, usually comprises four components. These are 'neutrality', 'respect', 'trust' and 'voice' (Tyler, 2008, p. 30; see also Goodman-Delahunty, 2010; Tyler & Huo, 2002; Tyler & Murphy, 2011). Neutrality involves police making impartial decisions based upon facts, legal rules and principles, as opposed to personal opinions or biases (Goodman-Delahunty, 2010; Tyler, 2008). Perceptions of neutrality can be facilitated by police through transparency or openness about the decision-making process (Goodman-Delahunty, 2010; Tyler, 2008). Respect involves dignified and respectful treatment of citizens during police–citizen encounters (Goodman-Delahunty, 2010; Tyler, 2008; Tyler & Lind, 1992). Trustworthiness involves police demonstrating that they act on behalf of the best interests of the people they deal with (Goodman-Delahunty, 2010; Tyler, 2008; Tyler & Huo, 2002). Finally, voice involves providing citizens with the opportunity to express their own point of view in a conflict, or other interaction with police (Goodman-Delahunty, 2010; Tyler, 2008). For procedural justice to take place police should therefore communicate neutrality and trustworthiness to citizens, treat citizens with dignity and respect and allow citizens a voice when police are making decisions.

Research consistently finds that assessments of police legitimacy are based on people's views about the way police treat them (the normative or procedural justice perspective), independent of their perceptions of police performance (the instrumental perspective). For example, Sunshine and Tyler (2003) found that judgements about the legitimacy of the New York police were influenced more by concerns about procedural justice than by performance and distributive justice. These findings suggest that procedural justice is essential when looking to improve or enhance perceptions of police legitimacy.

Police legitimacy at the individual level of encounters

The importance of improving police legitimacy is emphasized when we contemplate the positive outcomes of police legitimacy. At the level of the individual police–citizen encounter, these benefits include compliance with police during police–citizen encounters, long-term compliance with the law and cooperation with police. Research consistently finds that police are more able to encourage cooperation and compliance with individuals when their authority is perceived to be legitimate and police demonstrate procedural justice (e.g. Sunshine & Tyler, 2003).

Compliance

For police to do their job well they require citizen compliance with both the directives they issue and with the law more generally. Studies show that even though citizens will normally defer to the law, police encounter disobedience with sufficient frequency to justify identifying strategies that encourage compliance (Mastrofski et al., 1996). For example, in their study of 364 police–citizen encounters in Virginia, Mastrofski et al. (1996) found that the overall non-compliance rate was around 22 per cent. Similarly, in Australia, the New South Wales

Ombudsman's report on police use of powers found that approximately 10 per cent of persons given directions by the police did not comply with police requests (Moss, 1999). To address these rates of non-compliance, researchers have employed both observation and survey methods to identify factors that influence compliance with police.

Observational research exploring compliance with police directives provides support for the procedural justice approach to policing. Studies by Mastrofski et al. (1996), McCluskey (2003), and McCluskey, Mastrofski and Parks (1999) showed disrespectful officer behaviour reduced the likelihood of compliance during police–citizen encounters; while demonstrating respect towards citizens promoted greater levels of compliance. Moreover, McCluskey (2003) found that when police react to perceived threats by using force – escalations of conflict, violence and injury can result. Similarly, Mastrofski et al. (1996) found the use of force at the opening of an encounter and the threat of force (i.e. increased number of officers present at the scene) decreased the likelihood of compliance. While force is clearly needed in some situations legitimacy scholars thus argue it should be a last resort. Instead the procedural justice model should be employed.

Studies examining the long-term effects of procedurally fair policing on compliance provide further support for the procedural justice model. For example, Paternoster, Brame, Bachman and Sherman (1997) interviewed offenders who were arrested and charged by police during domestic violence incidents. They found offenders who believed police had treated them with procedural justice during arrest had 40 per cent fewer repeat offences during the six-month period following the interview.

Survey research similarly supports the use of procedural justice to promote perceptions of legitimacy and general compliance with the law. In his survey of 1575 randomly selected Chicago residents, Tyler (1990) found that procedural justice shaped public perceptions of police legitimacy, and that the perceived legitimacy of police affected both short- and long-term self-reported compliance behaviour (i.e. compliance with the law in their everyday lives). Similarly, Tyler and Huo (2002), in their study of 1656 residents from Los Angeles and Oakland, found that people's willingness to accept police decisions was based on whether they viewed decisions to be favourable and fair and on whether the police were seen to be legitimate. The literature thus suggests procedural justice and police legitimacy are fundamental for encouraging compliance with police directives and with the law more generally.

Cooperation

Effective policing also requires the ongoing support and voluntary cooperation of the public. As police are not omnipresent, their ability to detect and deal with social disorder and crime is dependent on citizens' willingness to assist and cooperate with the police by reporting crimes and passing on information. Recent research suggests police legitimacy and procedural justice are particularly important for shaping such voluntary behaviour (Bradford & Jackson, 2010a; Murphy & Gaylor, 2010; Murphy et al., 2008; Sunshine & Tyler, 2003).

Several studies demonstrate an empirical link between procedural justice and willingness to cooperate with the police. For example, through a longitudinal survey of 1600 New Yorkers, Sunshine and Tyler (2003) found that procedural justice shaped individual perceptions of police legitimacy. Perceptions of legitimacy were in turn found to shape compliance with the law and citizen willingness to both cooperate with police and empower police with a wider range of discretion in their duties. Similarly, Murphy et al. (2008) examined the importance of procedural justice for shaping public perceptions of police legitimacy and people's willingness to cooperate with police. Using a random sample of 2611 Australian citizens living in the Australian Capital Territory, Murphy et al. (2008) found procedural justice influenced perceptions of police legitimacy, which, in turn, influenced the willingness to cooperate with police. Murphy and Gaylor (2010) and others (e.g. Hinds, 2009; Reisig & Lloyd, 2009) have also found procedural justice is important in shaping youth perceptions of police legitimacy and their willingness to report crimes to police.

The procedural justice effect also appears to holds across different ethnic groups (for a review see MacCoun, 2005). Research finds some ethnic groups may have different perceptions of the quality of police treatment (e.g. MacCoun, 2005; Tyler & Huo, 2002), yet most studies find 'striking similarities across cultural and ethnic groups in both the antecedents and consequences of procedural justice' (Murphy & Cherney, 2011, p. 238, see also Bradford & Jackson, 2010b; Tyler, Boekmann, Smith, & Huo, 1997; Tyler & Huo, 2002). These studies indicate that procedural justice is more important than instrumental factors for shaping perceptions of police legitimacy, compliance with the law, willingness to cooperate with police, and satisfaction with police encounters, across ethnic groups (although see Murphy & Cherney, 2011; Tankebe, 2009). Most recently, Tyler, Schulhofer and Huq (2010, p. 368) have find that perceived procedural justice is an antecedent of the American-Muslim's perceptions of police legitimacy, and their subsequent 'willingness to report terror-related risks' to the police. This emerging body of research suggests that if police employ the principles of procedural justice in their interactions with all different categories of people, they can build legitimacy and shape the willingness to cooperate with police (Murphy & Cherney, 2011).

Police legitimacy at the community level of engagement

The Section 'Police legitimacy at the individual level of encounters' demonstrated how police legitimacy can have a positive impact at the individual level. Police legitimacy is also anticipated to have a positive impact at the macro level, within neighbourhoods or communities. By macro or community level, we mean studies that examine police legitimacy in the community context and, in some instances, use what Raudenbush and Sampson (1999, p. 2) refer to as 'ecometric' measures to help better understand community variations in different types of outcomes. Specifically, some scholars (Kochel, 2011; Renauer, 2007; Silver & Miller, 2004; Sun, Triplett, & Gainey, 2004) suggest that neighbourhood police legitimacy will influence neighbourhood or community 'collective efficacy' and thus enhance citizen 'willingness to intervene' in local problems (Sampson, Raudenbush, & Earls, 1997, p. 919).

Sampson (2004, p. 108) defines collective efficacy as a sense of 'working trust' and a 'shared willingness' to intervene in neighbourhood or community problems among community residents. In their seminal 'Science' article Sampson et al. (1997) found communities with higher levels of collective efficacy experience lower rates of violent crime. Further research supports this theory, finding that the willingness to intervene in community problems (also known as 'informal social control') and social cohesion and trust among community residents, mediates the relationship between structural characteristics and crime at the community level (e.g. Mazerolle, Wickes, & McBroom, 2010, p. 7; Sampson & Wikstrom, 2008). In light of these significant findings, scholars have sought to identify the factors which encourage informal social control and collective efficacy in the community context (for reviews see Kubrin & Weitzer, 2003; Silver & Miller, 2004). One factor that has been considered is neighbourhood police legitimacy (Kochel, 2011; Sun et al., 2004).

Neighbourhood police legitimacy is anticipated to influence the willingness to intervene in community problems, through both 'direct' and 'indirect' modes of intervention (Warner, 2007, p. 100). Direct intervention involves, for example, community residents chastising neighbourhood children who have engaged in vandalism in the local community, whereas indirect intervention could involve contacting the police or another third party to deal with this problem (Sampson, 2006; Sampson et al., 1997; Warner, 2007). Sampson (2006, p. 154) suggests collective efficacy can refer to the 'shared expectations for social action' by either direct or indirect means, 'ranging from informal intervention to the mobilization of formal controls' (see also Warner, 2007).

Several studies have examined the relationship between police legitimacy and indirect informal social control (i.e. contacting the police about crime problems) at the neighbourhood level of analysis. However, these findings are not as expected. For example, Goudriaan, Wittebrood and Nieuwbeerta (2006) found an ecometric measure of satisfaction with neighbourhood police was not related to crime reporting by victims of crime in the Netherlands. Moreover, Warner (2007, p. 119) found 'faith in the police' was not related to indirect modes of intervention in hypothetical neighbourhood disputes in the United States. These null findings are intriguing considering the positive relationship between trust in police, police legitimacy, procedural justice and the willingness to cooperate with police identified in studies at the individual level of analysis (see Section 'Police legitimacy at the individual level of encounters').

Several studies also examine the relationship between police legitimacy and broader measures of the willingness to intervene (i.e. they do not specify the type of intervention employed). Drawing on the work of Sampson (2002) and LaFree (1998), Kochel (2011) suggests that legitimate police practices may be important to collective efficacy, as police play a role in establishing shared norms and values in a community by enforcing laws and social norms (see Tyler & Fagan, 2008 for a related argument). Kochel (2011, p. 6) explains that when community residents do not believe the police to be legitimate they debase the 'foundation' on which shared expectations for behaviour are built. In turn, a working trust and willingness to intervene are inhibited by the lack of shared norms and values in the community (Kochel, 2011; see also LaFree, 1998; Sun et al., 2004). Kochel (2011) tested this premise in her study of neighbourhoods in Trinidad and Tobago. Interestingly, while she found a null relationship between perceptions of police legitimacy (defined as the obligation to obey police) and collective efficacy at the neighbourhood level, Kochel (2011) did find that perceptions of police misconduct (an extreme measure of procedural justice) and police service quality (also capturing perceptions of fairness) were related to collective efficacy.

Other scholars similarly argue that satisfaction with police, police legitimacy and procedural justice will be important in empowering citizens to intervene in criminal or antisocial activity. For example, Silver and Miller (2004) contend that when community residents view the police as legitimate and effective, community residents are encouraged to intervene when community problems arise. In their study of 343 Chicago neighbourhoods Silver and Miller (2004) found support for this relationship, in that the perceived willingness to intervene in community problems was positively and significantly related to neighbourhood satisfaction with police. Nevertheless still others present null findings. For example, while Renauer (2007, pp. 64–66) suggests that when police are not viewed as procedurally fair, people will be less likely to be 'inspired' to intervene in community problems, he did not find a direct relationship between 'fear of police encounters' (employed as a proxy measure of procedural justice) and informal social control in Oregon neighbourhoods. Similarly, Sun et al. (2004) found no relationship between satisfaction with police and perceptions of fairness, and their measure of collective efficacy.

The conflicting nature of these findings may be due to differences in the way key concepts are measured. For example, Silver and Miller (2004) capture a broad measure of satisfaction with police which may be more representative of the instrumental perspective on legitimacy (i.e. police performance). On the other hand, Kochel's (2011) measure of legitimacy captured the obligation to obey police. However, with so few empirical studies it is difficult to draw any substantive conclusions.

More research is clearly needed to determine the nature of the relationship between police legitimacy and collective efficacy, or the willingness to intervene, at the community level of analysis. There is nevertheless some evidence to suggest that legitimacy is important for community efficacy, and that this may help to explain community variations in crime (Kochel, 2011; Renauer, 2007; Silver & Miller, 2004). Furthermore, research at the individual level confirms police legitimacy is beneficial (see Section 'Police legitimacy at the individual level of encounters'). Considering this, it is important to examine how we can enhance police legitimacy in both the individual and community contexts.

Enhancing police legitimacy in practice

As evidenced above, the overwhelming majority of procedural justice and police legitimacy studies rely on observational, survey or interview methodologies (see also Bennett, Denning, Mazerolle, & Stocks, 2009). Research that seeks to examine how procedural justice can be operationalized into police practice and evaluate the effectiveness of such practice is limited. While only a handful of studies purporting to do this have emerged in the literature, the results appear promising and point to the value of police utilizing procedural justice-based strategies to build their legitimacy at both the individual and community levels.

A focus on police–citizen encounters

One method of increasing perceptions of procedural justice at the individual level is to change the way that police officers interact with citizens. A recent Australian study provides perhaps the most comprehensive example of legitimate policing during one-on-one police–citizen encounters (Mazerolle, Bennett, Antrobus, & Eggins, 2011). In partnership with the Queensland Police Service (QPS) in Brisbane, Australia, researchers sought to adapt police procedure to include procedural justice elements. The study varied police actions during random breath test (RBT) encounters with the public and utilized a randomized field trial design to examine whether procedural justice in such encounters could increase perceptions of police legitimacy.

In the experimental condition police were provided with a scripted procedural justice protocol that emphasized the four procedural justice elements identified in the literature: 'neutrality', 'trust', 'voice' and 'respect' (Tyler, 2008, p. 30; see also Goodman-Delahunty, 2010; Tyler & Huo, 2002; Tyler & Murphy, 2011). To communicate neutrality the officers explained the procedures being followed and that the citizen had been stopped at random. To build trust officers communicated concern for people in the community. To provide voice the officer asked if drivers had any questions or suggestions about crime issues or police conduct in their local area. To demonstrate respect the officer ended the interaction with a courteous gesture to the driver. In the control condition officers conducted RBTs as usual – officers simply instructed drivers to provide a specimen of breath for alcohol analysis.

To assess the effect of the experimental and control conditions, all drivers were invited by police officers to participate in a mail-back survey. The study yielded 1645 surveys from the experimental condition and 1102 surveys from the control condition (Mazerolle et al., 2011).

Table 2.1   Reported citizen perceptions of police in regard to a random breath test encounter

	Experimental mean	Control mean	*p*
Satisfaction	4.43	4.28	<0.0001
Fairness	4.05	3.72	<0.0001
Respect	4.44	4.25	<0.0001
Trust	4.21	4.04	<0.0001
Confidence	4.38	4.30	<0.005
Compliance	4.57	4.52	<0.005

Note: Each construct is measured on a scale from 1 to 5, where a score of 5 represents higher levels of the construct.
Source: Adapted from Mazerolle et al. (2011).

Evidence from the study suggests that, relative to the control condition, the procedural justice approach increased perceptions that police are fair and respectful, and improved satisfaction with police (Mazerolle et al., 2011). Furthermore, the procedural justice approach enhanced the willingness to comply with police directives specifically in regard to the RBT (see Table 2.1) (Mazerolle et al., 2011). While this research shows that procedural justice in one-on-one interactions with police is clearly beneficial, policing strategies are usually implemented over an entire beat or police district (Hohl, Bradford, & Stanko, 2010). Therefore it is also important to investigate strategies for improving procedural justice and legitimacy at these macro levels.

A focus on the community

Research suggests one method of increasing police legitimacy at the community level is through community policing strategies. 'Community policing' as a distinct theory or programme is notoriously difficult to define but generally includes increasing positive police–community interactions and mobilizing or encouraging citizens to 'assume responsibility for their neighbourhoods' (Lombardo, Staton, & Olson, 2010, p. 588; see also Bayley, 1994; Skogan, 2006). Several studies have examined the positive effects of community policing strategies on satisfaction with police and perceptions of police legitimacy.

Murphy et al. (2008) examined the impact of a community policing intervention on perceptions of police legitimacy through a panel study of 102 households in an Australian community. This community was in receipt of a community policing programme, involving local school and community activities run by the police such as barbeques and competitions (Murphy et al., 2008). Residents of the community were surveyed about their perceptions of police legitimacy, procedural justice and cooperation with the police pre and post the community policing intervention. These procedurally just encounters precipitated changes in perceptions of police legitimacy, which, in turn, influenced community members' willingness to cooperate with police (Murphy et al., 2008).

   Hohl et al. (2010) similarly examined the impact of a community policing strategy on perceptions of trust and confidence in the police (i.e. legitimacy) in London communities. In this quasi-experiment, residents in two groups of London electoral wards were surveyed. The experimental group received a newsletter from the police, while the control group did not. Newsletters were designed based upon 'five good practice principles' expected to improve perceptions of legitimacy and trust and confidence in police (Hohl et al., 2010, p. 512). Moreover the newsletter conveyed a sense of police–community engagement and that the police cared about the views of community residents, both of which are key elements of community policing. Residents in both the experimental and control groups were surveyed pre and post the newsletter delivery. In the post test survey residents of the experimental wards reported increased confidence in the police (i.e. legitimacy), whereas, in the control wards, confidence did not improve. These findings indicate that community policing strategies which demonstrate community engagement may increase perceptions of legitimacy in the neighbourhood or community context (Hohl et al., 2010; see also Lombardo et al., 2010).

A focus on police training

While procedural justice based policing strategies show promise in shaping police legitimacy at the individual and community levels, the next step for enhancing legitimacy in policing requires a focus on training. One of the primary opportunities for improved legitimacy is through day-to-day police–citizen interactions. As such, police can implement training interventions to increase the likelihood of positive outcomes during these encounters. Although evaluations of this type of intervention are rare, investigations suggest that internal training to improve legitimacy is carried out by many police departments (Hails & Borum, 2003). For example, in a recent evaluation study, the Chicago Police Department, in collaboration with the University of Illinois, developed a recruit training programme aimed at improving the quality of interpersonal encounters between officers and residents (Schuck & Rosenbaum, 2011). The Quality Interaction Training Program (QIP) incorporated knowledge about procedural justice. The training was evaluated using a randomized design where recruits were matched on demographic characteristics and randomly assigned to either receive QIP training or not. Recruits were surveyed about their views on dealing with the public both before and after receiving training. It was found that the QIP training had a positive impact on a number of police attitudes including the view that remaining calm during an encounter with the public can lessen the possibility of violence (Schuck & Rosenbaum, 2011).

There are a number of mechanisms available for officer training. Many institutions include training on dealing with particular situations and populations in their basic recruit training (see QIP training discussed earlier – Schuck & Rosenbaum, 2011). In-service training for general duties police officers is also used, although the amount and quality of training can vary widely (Hails & Borum, 2003). Another method is the creation of training materials (e.g. pamphlets, CDs or books) by government departments or other organizations that focus on the provision of services to particular societal groups and that are distributed to police officers for their perusal. Organizations may also produce cue cards to aid police in responding to particular situations they may encounter. For example, Mazerolle et al. (2011) employed cue cards to assist officers in delivering procedural justice to drivers undergoing the Random breath test (RBT) in the study described earlier. The use of police training may therefore be a practical way of introducing procedural justice to day-to-day police–citizen interactions.

Conclusion

In this Chapter, we reviewed the legitimacy and procedural justice models of policing and summarized key research studies that have examined the ways in which police can actively work towards fostering greater legitimacy, at both the individual and the neighbourhood or community levels. Here, the Chapter highlights three important areas of research in the field of police legitimacy. First, the Chapter flagged the importance of police legitimacy to successful police practice and identified procedural justice as an important antecedent of legitimacy. Second, the chapter identified the four key elements of procedural justice (recall, these were 'neutrality', 'trust', 'respect' and 'voice') and reviewed how these elements could serve to generate positive outcomes for the police, including increases in police legitimacy and positive outcomes for compliance and cooperation with the police (Tyler, 2008, p. 30). Finally, the chapter highlighted that, perhaps as an outcome of maturation in the field of police legitimacy research, scholars throughout the world are starting to work with police to implement and evaluate police legitimacy and procedural justice training programmes (see Schuck & Rosenbaum, 2011), as well as initiatives that assess the outcome of procedurally just encounters under randomized field trial conditions (see Mazerolle et al., 2011) and programmes that seek to build better police–community relations (see Hohl et al., 2010). These studies, which operationalize the key tenets of procedural justice, serve as a helpful guide to police in their own efforts to improve legitimacy.

References

Bayley, D. H. (1994). *Police for the future*. New York: Oxford University Press.

Bennett, S., Denning, R., Mazerolle, L., & Stocks, B. (2009). *Procedural justice: A systematic literature search and technical report to the National Policing Improvement Agency*. Brisbane, Australia: ARC Centre of Excellence in Policing and Security.

Bradford, B., & Jackson, J. (2010a). *Cooperating with the police: Social control and the reproduction of police legitimacy*. Retrieved from http://ssrn.com/abstract=1640958.

Bradford, B., & Jackson, J. (2010b). *Different things to different people? The meaning and measurement of trust and confidence in policing across diverse social groups in London*. Retrieved from http://ssrn.com/abstract=1628546.

Goodman-Delahunty, J. (2010). Four ingredients: New recipes for procedural justice in Australian policing. *Policing, 4*(4), 403–410.

Goudriaan, H., Wittebrood, K., & Nieuwbeerta, P. (2006). Neighborhood characteristics and reporting crime: Effects of social cohesion, confidence in police effectiveness and socio-economic disadvantage. *British Journal of Criminology, 46*(4), 719–742.

Hails, J., & Borum, R. (2003). Police training and specialized approaches to respond to people with mental illnesses. *Crime and Delinquency, 49*(1), 52–61.

Hinds, L. (2009). Public satisfaction with police: The influence of general attitudes and police-citizen encounters. *International Journal of Police Science & Management, 11*(1), 54–66.

Hinds, L., & Murphy, K. (2007). Public satisfaction with police: Using procedural justice to improve police legitimacy. *The Australian and New Zealand Journal of Criminology, 40*(1), 27–42.

Hohl, K., Bradford, B., & Stanko, E. A. (2010). Influencing trust and confidence in the London metropolitan police. *British Journal of Criminology, 50*(3), 491–513.

Jackson, J., & Bradford, B. (2011). *Police legitimacy*. Retrieved from http://www2.lse.ac.uk/methodologyInstitute/pdf/JonJackson/Wiki%20-%20legitimacy.pdf.

Jackson, J., Bradford, B., Hough, M., & Murray, K. (2010). Compliance with the law and policing by consent: Notes on legal legitimacy and cynicism. Social Science Research Network Working Paper No. 1717812. Forthcoming in

A. Crawford & A. Hucklesby (Eds.), *Legitimacy and compliance in criminal justice*. London: Routledge. Retrieved from http://ssrn.com/abstract=1717812.

Kochel, T. R. (2011). Can police legitimacy promote collective efficacy? *Justice Quarterly*. doi: 10.1080/07418825.2011.561805.

Kubrin, C. E., & Weitzer, R. (2003). New directions in social disorganization theory. *Journal of Research in Crime and Delinquency, 40*(4), 374–402.

LaFree, G. (1998). *Losing legitimacy: Street crime and the decline of social institutions in America*. Boulder, CO: Westview Press.

Lombardo, R. M., Staton, M., & Olson, D. (2010). The Chicago alternative policing strategy: A reassessment of the CAPS program. *Policing, 33*(4), 586–606.

MacCoun, R. J. (2005). Voice, control and belonging: The double-edged sword of procedural fairness. *Annual Review of Law and Social Science, 1*, 171–201.

Mastrofski, S. D., Snipes, J. B., & Supina, A. E. (1996). Compliance on demand: The public's response to specific police requests. *Journal of Research in Crime and Delinquency, 33*(3), 269–305.

Mazerolle, L., Bennett, S., Antrobus, E., & Eggins, E. (2011). Key findings of the Queensland Community Engagement Trial. *CEPS Briefing Paper Series*. Retrieved from http://www.ceps.edu.au/CMS/Uploads/file/FINAL%2520Key%2520Findings%2520of%2520the%2520Queensland%2520Community%2520Engagement%2520Trial.pdf.

Mazerolle, L., Wickes, R. L., & McBroom, J. (2010). Community variations in violence: The role of social ties and collective efficacy in comparative context. *Journal for Research in Crime and Delinquency, 47*(1), 3–30.

McCluskey, J. D. (2003). *Police requests for compliance: Coercive and procedurally just tactics*. New York: LFB Scholarly Publishing.

McCluskey, J. D., Mastrofski, S. D., & Parks, R. B. (1999). To acquiesce or rebel: Predicting citizen compliance with police requests. *Police Quarterly, 2*(4), 389–416.

Moss, I. (1999). Policing public safety. *NSW Ombudsman Report under Section 6 of the Crimes Legislation Amendment (Police and Public Safety) Act*. Sydney: NSW Government Publication.

Murphy, K., & Cherney, A. (2011). Fostering cooperation with the police: How do ethnic minorities in Australia respond to procedural justice-based policing? *The Australian and New Zealand Journal of Criminology, 44*, 235–257.

Murphy, K., & Gaylor, A. (2010). Policing youth: Can procedural justice nurture youth cooperation with police. *Alfred Deakin Research Institute Working Paper No 6*. Geelong, VIC: Deakin University.

Murphy, K., Hinds, L., & Fleming, J. (2008). Encouraging public cooperation and support for police. *Policing and Society, 18*(2), 136–155.

Paternoster, R., Brame, R., Bachman, R., & Sherman, L. W. (1997). Do fair procedures matter? The effect of procedural justice on spouse assault. *Law & Society Review, 31*(1), 163–204.

Raudenbush, S. W., & Sampson, R. J. (1999). Ecometrics: Toward a science of assessing ecological settings, with application to the systemic social observation of neighborhoods. *Sociological Methodology, 29*(1), 1–41.

Reisig, M. D., & Lloyd, C. (2009). Procedural justice, police legitimacy, and helping the police fight crime. *Police Quarterly, 12*(1), 42–62.

Renauer, B. C. (2007). Is neighborhood policing related to informal social control? *Policing: An International Journal of Police Strategies & Management, 30*(1), 61–81.

Sampson, R. J. (2002). Transcending tradition: New directions in community research, Chicago style. *Criminology, 40*(2), 213–230.

Sampson, R. J. (2004). Neighborhood and community: Collective efficacy and community safety. *New Economy, 11*(2), 106–113.

Sampson, R. J. (2006). Collective efficacy theory: Lessons learned and directions for future inquiry. In F. T. Cullen, J. P. Write, & K. R. Blevins (Eds.), *Taking stock: The status of criminological theory* (Vol. 15, pp. 149–168). New Brunswick, NJ: Transaction Publishers.

Sampson, R. J., Raudenbush, S. W., & Earls, F. (1997). Neighborhoods and violent crime: A multilevel study of collective efficacy. *Science, 277*(5328), 918–924.

Sampson, R. J., & Wikstrom, P.-O. H. (2008). The social order of violence in Chicago and Stockholm neighbourhoods: A comparative inquiry. In S. N. Kalyvas, I. Shapiro, & T. Masoud (Eds.), *Order, conflict, and violence* (pp. 97–119). New York: Cambridge University Press.

Schuck, A., & Rosenbaum, D. (2011). *The Chicago Quality Interaction Training Program: A randomized control trial of police innovation.* Washington, DC: National Police Research Platform, National Institute of Justice. Retrieved from http://www.nationalpoliceresearch.org/storage/updated-papers/The%20Chicago%20Quality%20Interaction%20Training%20Program%20a%20Randomized%20%20Control%20Trial%20of%20Police%20Innovation%20FINAL.pdf.

Silver, E., & Miller, L. L. (2004). Sources of informal social control in Chicago neighborhoods. *Criminology, 42*(3), 551–583.

Skogan, W. G. (2006). The promise of community policing. In D. Weisburg & A. A. Braga (Eds.), *Police innovation: Contrasting perspectives* (pp. 27–43). Cambridge: Cambridge University Press.

Sun, I. Y., Triplett, R. A., & Gainey, R. R. (2004). Social organization, legitimacy of local institutions and neighborhood crime: An exploratory study of perceptions of the police and local government. *Journal of Crime and Justice, 27*(1), 33–60.

Sunshine, J., & Tyler, T. R. (2003). The role of procedural justice and legitimacy in shaping public support for policing. *Law & Society Review, 37*(3), 513–548.

Tankebe, J. (2009). Public cooperation with police in Ghana: Does procedural fairness matter? *Criminology, 47*(4), 1265–1293.

Tyler, T. R. (1990). *Why people obey the law.* New Haven, CT: Yale University Press.

Tyler, T. R. (2001). A psychological perspective on the legitimacy of institutions and authorities. In J. Jost, & B. Major (Eds.), *The psychology of legitimacy* (pp. 416–436). Cambridge: Cambridge University Press.

Tyler, T. R. (2006). *Why people obey the law.* Princeton: Princeton University Press.

Tyler, T. R. (2008). Procedural justice and the courts. *Court Review, 44,* 25–31.

Tyler, T. R., Boekmann, R., Smith, H., & Huo, J. (1997). *Social justice in a diverse society.* Boulder, CO: Westview Press.

Tyler, T. R., & Fagan, J. (2008). Legitimacy and cooperation: Why do people help the police fight crime in their communities? *Ohio State Journal of Criminal Law, 6,* 231–276.

Tyler, T. R., & Huo, Y. J. (2002). *Trust in the law.* New York: Russell Sage.

Tyler, T. R., & Lind, E. (1992). A relational model of authority in groups. In M. Zanna (Ed.), *Advances in experimental social psychology* (pp. 115–191). New York: Academic Press.

Tyler, T. R., & Murphy, K. (2011). Procedural justice, police legitimacy and cooperation with the police: A new paradigm for policing. *CEPS Briefing Paper Series.* Retrieved from http://www.ceps.edu.au/?q=CEPS-Briefing-Paper-Series.

Tyler, T. R., Schulhofer, S., & Huq, A. Z. (2010). Legitimacy and deterrence effects in counterterrorism policing: A study of Muslim Americans. *Law & Society Review, 44*(2), 365–402.

Warner, B. D. (2007). Directly intervene or call the authorities? A study of forms of neighborhood social control within a social disorganization framework. *Criminology, 45*(1), 99–129.

Weber, M. (1968). *Economy and society.* New York: Bedminster.

3
The Suppression of Organized Crime: New Approaches and Problems

Julie Ayling and Roderic Broadhurst

Organized crime poses many challenges, not least to the State itself and the very fabric of civic society. Analytically the first challenge is definitional because, as Varese (2010) notes, there is no agreed definition. Nevertheless, a shared understanding of the problem is important because effective strategies against organized crime require an agreed conceptual starting point.

The second challenge is strategic: how best to deal with organized crime in a rapidly changing world? For a long time states have grappled with what to do about organized crime, but increases in its scope, costs and dangers are creating a fresh urgency (UNODC, 2010). Changing economic conditions, such as the global financial crisis, have increased pressures on legitimate businesses and states, amplifying their vulnerabilities. Organized crime has been quick to take advantage of these new opportunities, leading to the emergence of new actors and crime types, the restructuring of criminal groups, sharper rivalries between some groups and active integration between others (Galeotti, 2009), as well as increases in corruption and expansion of so-called 'grey markets' – markets in legal goods sold or distributed illegally (Ruggiero, 2000).

The third challenge is tactical and logistical. What counter-measures are effective against organized crime, and what do they require of police? Once perceived as manageable by domestic law enforcement, organized crime increasingly has a transnational dimension. A single crime may demand responses from producer or host states, transit states and states where illicit product or services are eventually consumed. Innovations in the technologies used by organized crime present issues about jurisdictional responsibility, evidence seizure and retention and law enforcement cooperation and capacities. Moreover the nature of the groups committing organized crimes appears to be moving towards increasingly fluid, flexible, networked and impermanent forms, necessitating 'real-time' intelligence-gathering. Symbiotic relationships between criminal groups, legitimate businesses and officials of the state (including police) call for impartial and independent responses from law enforcement institutions.

This chapter considers how some states have been addressing these challenges, often in creative ways and with some success, and concludes with suggestions for future directions for the policing of organized crime.

Analytical challenges

Paoli (2002, p. 52) describes organized crime as 'an ambiguous conflated concept, produced by a stratification of different meaning which have been attributed to the term...over the years'. Von Lampe (n.d.) lists on his website more than 150 definitions of organized crime by governments, national and international organizations and academics from around the world. Much of the confusion arises over whether 'organized crime' refers to crime groups or to their activities ('structures of association' or 'structures of activity': Cohen, 1977). As a result, there is no universal understanding of organized crime, complicating the discourse over how it should be suppressed. Still, as von Lampe (2011, p. 149) has noted, the term remains 'a "rallying point" for scholarly debates', and therefore perhaps must suffice as the closest thing we have to a unifying concept for 'a diverse and analytically distinct range of actors, activities and harmful consequences' (Edwards & Levi, 2008, p. 364). Organized crime's fluidity and morphology was long ago noted by Thrasher (1927/1963, p. 285):

> Although organized crime must not be visualized as a vast edifice of hard and fast structures, there is a surprising amount of organization of a kind in the criminal community. There is a certain division of labor manifesting itself in the specialized persons and specialized groups performing different but related functions. There are, furthermore, alliances and federations of persons and groups, although no relationship can be fixed and lasting as in the organization of legitimate business.

These observations were largely overlooked when organized crime first became the subject of intense governmental and academic examination, as discussed below.

Organizational forms

Early conceptions of organized crime were drawn from tightly structured 'mafia-style' hierarchical organizations with their specific roles and strong command and control features (see, for example, Cressey, 1969). More recently, however, looser assemblages of criminals have been identified as engaged in organized criminal activities. Descriptive terms for these groups include 'disorganized crime' (Reuter, 1985), 'criminal cooperatives' (Klerks, 2001), 'enterprise crime' (see, for example, Edwards & Gill, 2002; Naylor, 1997) 'criminal networks' (see, for example, Sparrow, 1991; von Lampe, 2009) and 'criminal collectives' (Spapens, 2010). The growing prevalence of fluid and flexible associations of entrepreneurial criminals alongside traditional hierarchical organized crime groups complicates the tasks of understanding these structures and determining the degree of organization necessary to qualify them as 'organized' (Bullock, Clarke, & Tilley, 2010). Although much has been made of the challenges presented by the increasing fluidity of criminal groups, it has not yet been empirically shown whether there is an ongoing structural shift from hierarchy to network or simply a concurrence of the two forms (Levi, 2007). Levi and others point to the absence of empirical research on the natural history of organized crime and the apparent overlap with street and juvenile gangs. Mapping of relationships between participants in criminal groups using techniques of social network analysis has become a popular tool for academics engaged in empirical work (see, for example, Fleisher, 2006; Morselli, 2009; Papachristos, 2006; Xia, 2008) and has been widely employed by practitioners (e.g. Klerks, 2001) using computer-based proprietary programmes and other sociometric techniques (Chantler & Thorne, 2009). These relational maps are contributing to a better understanding of criminal organizational forms, although necessarily constrained by a lack of complete and accurate data.

Activities

All organized criminal activities are primarily aimed at enriching and empowering their perpetrators. That can be done in three basic and often intersecting ways:

1. Organized criminals may obtain a monopoly or near monopoly over the provision of a legal service. This in turn enables them to engage in exploitative practices that Americans call 'racketeering'. In many cases, as Gambetta (1993, p. 2) points out in relation to the Sicilian mafia, the service provided is protection, 'a poor and costly substitute for trust' but one for which many are willing to pay, especially where legitimate authorities are unwilling or unable to provide protection themselves. Others may not be so willing, with the result that protection slips to extortion. Sometimes the service is more tangible, in that criminal groups gain and exploit control over all or most of a legitimate industry, often by violent means. Examples include Cosa Nostra's control over the clothing trade, haulage industry and fresh food markets in New York (Jacobs, with Friel, & Radick, 1999), the control of the waste industry by mafiosi in southern Italy (Massari & Monzini, 2004), the provision of dispute mediation, bankruptcy and debt collection services by yakuza in Japan (Milhaupt & West, 2000) and triad monopoly of loan-sharking and prostitution in Hong Kong and Macau (Broadhurst & Lee, 2009).

2. Profits can also be made by fulfilling a demand for goods or services that may be illegal per se, or legal but rare or expensive (or both). Examples include people smuggling, human trafficking, drug trafficking, cigarette smuggling, wildlife trafficking, toxic waste disposal, intellectual property theft, trafficking in pornographic images and money laundering. Many such crimes are transnational or intra-state cross-border crimes.

3. Criminal groups may enrich themselves by engaging in complex deceptive practices – for example, fraud, identity theft, document forgery, tax evasion, on-line advance fee frauds and so on. These deceptive practices often support the demand for the criminal activities above. However they may also stand alone. For instance, organized crime groups appear to be planning to sell online fake or unauthorized tickets for the London 2012 Olympics (Rossingh, 2011).

The relationship between organizational forms and activities

Cohen (1977) suggests that the attributes of association and activity are interdependent. Research shows, for example, that the form of organized criminal groups often follows their function. Very risky activities, such as drug trafficking, require a high degree of trust between offenders, so the structure of such groups tends to be denser and involve a larger proportion of affective relationships than groups involved in less risky enterprises (Bruinsma & Bernasco, 2004). But function can also be constrained by the group's form (Nohria & Eccles, 1992), especially where criminal activity is only one of several reasons for its existence, as is the case with many juvenile and street gangs (Cohen, 1977). The relative effectiveness of law enforcement also influences the fluidity and structure of criminal networks.

Racketeering, like any business that involves a heavy investment of time and effort into the establishment of relationships and reputation, tends to be the domain of hierarchical organizations that have become institutionalized in particular social contexts, such as the Sicilian mafia. Cross-border crime and deceptive practices, on the other hand, are activities carried out by both institutionalized hierarchies and more fluid groups which can coalesce from the 'criminal macro network' (Spapens, 2010) to take advantage of available opportunities, and then dissipate, disengage or become dormant once the crime (or their part in it) is done. Such networks may incorporate expertise from both criminal and licit sources as needed (Passas, 2002), and be more or less cohesive as the activity demands.

International approach

Despite the diverse set of people and activities covered by the term 'organized crime', a minimalist definition has been established by the international community in the Convention on Transnational Organized Crime (UNTOC), which came into effect in July 2003. One hundred and fifty-eight states and one regional body (the European Union) are now parties to the Convention. It obliges signatories to criminalize serious transnational crime committed by an organized criminal group (Article 3 (1)), defining serious crime broadly and an 'organized criminal group' (Article 2(a)) as:

> a structured group of three or more persons, existing for a period of time and acting in concert with the aim of committing one or more serious crimes or offences established in accordance with the convention, in order to obtain, directly or indirectly, a financial or other material benefit.

A 'structured group' refers to one that is 'not randomly formed for the immediate commission of an offence', although it need not have formally defined roles, continuity of membership or a developed structure (Article 2(c)). This goes some way to recognizing the trend to more fluid criminal groups. However, even states that are parties do not always adopt its definitions. For example, one Australian definition of 'serious and organised crime' requires a minimum of only two offenders (see section 4 of the *Australian Crime Commission Act 2002*). The indeterminacy of the concept of organized crime makes the job of suppressing it more difficult and is complicated by the need for agreement between states about the targets and activities of mutual concern. In addition, national security considerations are relevant in tackling transnational organized crime, while domestic politics often shapes enforcement priorities.

Strategic challenges

Crime groups are complex systems that are more than just a compilation of their parts (their members), and group processes have effects such as increasing crime rates (Klein & Maxson, 2006; Lien, 2005; Thornberry, Krohn, Lizotte, Smith, & Tobin, 2003). Given the group's capacity to amplify harm and the perception of threat, states have often sought ways to combat criminal groups *as* groups (Ayling, 2011a). However, the mechanics of doing this are not simple. It is often easier to prove individual offending on charges such as murder, assault, fraud, extortion, blackmail, bribery, theft, arson or drug trafficking than to embark on the complicated task of proving the existence of collectivities and/or agreements, as is required for offences relating to conspiracy, joint commission and various types of participation in a criminal organization.

It is also important to note the reactive and punitive (deterrence-dependent) nature of most state responses to organized crime. Until recently, little attention has been paid to prevention, but techniques of crime prevention are now beginning to be applied to organized crime, as discussed below.

Countermeasures: Some strategies of suppression

Of course, policing street crime is one thing, policing organized crime, by its very nature hidden and complex, quite another. A reliance on covert techniques of policing characterizes suppression of organized crime. In order to detect, investigate, arrest and prosecute those who have committed serious organized criminal activities, police and other law enforcement agencies have been granted extended powers relating to telecommunications interception, surveillance, search and seizure, undercover work and the use of informants. These techniques are often effective in revealing hidden connections, such as those between the Sicilian mafia, business and politicians such as Giulio Andreotti, three-time president of Italy (Stille, 1995). In addition, some jurisdictions, fearful of the power of organized crime to corrupt, establish special agencies such as judicial commissions and statutory crime commissions that can investigate serious crime through powers to compel testimony or the disclosure of information (e.g. the Australian Crime Commission, the Antimafia Commission of the Italian Parliament and the defunct Quebec Commission d'enquête sur le crime organisé (CECO) established in 1972). These special powers may abrogate the privilege against self-incrimination that usually applies in proceedings against individuals and may sanction, with fines or imprisonment, the refusal to answer questions or provide documents. However, such laws are not always successful – for reasons of loyalty or fear, many witnesses would rather 'do the time' than assist these bodies with their investigations.

Aggressive policing of criminal groups may be coupled with these powers. Certain organized crime groups who advertise their presence through symbols and clothing, such as adult street gangs and outlaw motorcycle gangs (OMCGs), leave themselves open to targeting by police for disorderly conduct. Police in parts of Australia, for example, have successfully used public order laws, laws relating to the licensing of businesses and traffic laws (especially driver licence disqualifications, see Wuth, 2009) to make life (and therefore criminal activities) more difficult for members of these gangs.

Offences have also been tailored to the collective nature of organized crime. These include the following:

- Conspiracy offences making it illegal to agree to commit an illegal act, and requiring proof of an intention on the part of at least two of the parties to the agreement to commit the act and sometimes of an overt act in furtherance of the agreement (but not necessarily by the person being prosecuted);
- Joint commission offences making all members of a group that have agreed to engage in criminal activity jointly responsible for offenses committed as part of, or in the course of, that activity, even where not all members of the group engaged in committing those offenses;
- Proscription, or outlawing, of criminal groups (such as triad societies or those posing as such under the Hong Kong *Societies Ordinance*);
- Offences relating to participation in a criminal group – either simplex (such as is the case in New Zealand under 98A of the *Crimes Act*

1961), or comprised of differing levels of participation with sanctions that are tiered according to the seriousness of the offence (see, e.g., the Canadian *Criminal Code*, R.S.C. 1985, C-46, and the Australian *Crimes Legislation Amendment* (*Serious and Organised Crime*) *Act* (*No. 2*) *2009*);

- Pattern offences, that is, offences requiring proof of a pattern of serious criminal behaviour by individuals linked to the activities of an 'enterprise'. The classic example is the US *Racketeer Influenced and Corrupt Organizations* (RICO) *Act* (Title 18, United States Code, Sections 1961–1968) that has been used successfully against clearly structured and relatively stable criminal organizations in the United States such as the Mafia and outlaw motorcycle gangs (Barker, 2007; Jacobs et al., 1999). RICO makes it possible to bring to a single trial whole criminal groups or families and allows evidence relating to multiple crimes and criminal schemes that would not normally be allowed in a single criminal trial (Jacobs & Dondlinger, 2011);
- Offences that include enhanced sentences for persons who, when they committed the crime, were acting on behalf of a criminal organization or were members of a criminal organization (a strategy used in various jurisdictions in the United States for street gang members: Curry & Mongrain, 2009, and for triad members in Hong Kong);
- Vicarious liability offences, whereby leaders of criminal groups are held responsible for the actions of the group's members (e.g. as occurs in Japan under the *Civil Code*, which has been applied to offences by Yakuza).

When it comes to achieving the disruption and suppression of organized crime groups, each approach has certain advantages and disadvantages, particularly in relation to appropriateness for reaching into the upper ranks and not merely targeting the 'foot soldiers' (Ayling, 2011a). Proving membership or participatory status in such groups, or criminal relationships between participants in these groups, can often present prosecutors with difficulties and overly rely on informants or undercover officers. Furthermore, even when these problems are overcome, the question arises as to whether putting offenders in prison will actually be effective in disbanding the group or stemming its activities. Unless prisons have developed internal control measures, groups may persist and even thrive despite incarceration. Many criminal groups are resilient to police interventions as a result of the environment in which the group exists and/or its inherent characteristics, such as its structure, leadership and operational strategies (Ayling, 2009).

Prevention of organized crime

Strategies for preventing organized crime are currently a focus but have yet to be widely implemented or evaluated. Crime prevention techniques are generally understood as 'non-punitive measures that reduce opportunities to commit crime or address the broader context in which people commit crimes through a range of social and environmental strategies' (McCulloch & Pickering, 2009, p. 629). Recently, though, prevention of suspected criminality, involving punitive measures, has also been adopted as a strategy in some jurisdictions. Greater interest in crime prevention derives from a growing awareness of the harm inflicted on individuals and societies by organized crime groups, including economic, social, physical and psychological damage. Many activities of organized crime are predicated on violence or threats of violence and have adverse effects on public confidence and on victims and witnesses. The social and physical costs of organized crime can be enormous, as the loss of close to 40,000 lives since 2006 in Mexico's drug wars illustrates (L.A.N.D., 2011). Organized crime also impacts on tax revenues, distorting market prices for both licit and illicit good through unfair competition. For example, the Australian Crime Commission (ACC) has recently reported that organized crime costs Australia approximately AUD$15bn each year (Australian Crime Commission, 2011, p. 3).

Prevention strategies have shifted from a focus on offender behaviour to reducing or removing crime's rewards or profits. Thus confiscation of the wealth acquired, enforcement of civil regulations that target criminally controlled enterprises and the use of taxation laws have become accepted means of disrupting organized crime. Next we discuss some prevention, strategies for organized crime, and highlight some problems with them.

Preventing opportunities for crime

There has recently been an interest in whether the theory of situational crime prevention (Clarke, 1995) could be used to combat organized crime. The idea is to focus on the processes by which crimes are committed rather than the offenders who commit them in order to identify 'pinch-points for intervention' (Bullock et al., 2010, p. 2), that is, places along the crime process where an intervention might close off criminal opportunities. Twenty-five techniques of situational crime prevention had been identified for use against crime (POP Center, 2010), grouped under five headings: 'reducing the rewards', 'increasing the effort', 'increasing the difficulty', 'reducing the provocation' and 'removing excuses'. Efforts have recently been made to apply these techniques to the whole range of organized crime activities, including cross-border and deceptive crimes, crimes of facilitation and of racketeering (Bullock et al., 2010). Graycar and Felson (2010), for example, consider organized timber theft and related corruption, suggesting that making timber transportation more traceable and inventory control and accounting more transparent would help curb these crimes. However, using situational crime prevention techniques for organized crime is still relatively new. Indeed, according to von Lampe (2011), before the situational approach will be useful in the organized crime context it needs to shift its focus from volume crime and crime settings to incorporate the societal contexts of crime, such as the availability of resources to offenders and the transparency of state institutions.

One form of situational crime prevention that does appear to have had some success is the use of civil laws and administrative processes to make it more difficult for organized crime groups to conduct their business. In Amsterdam, three inter-related projects established in 2000 involve, among other things, excluding known criminals from tendering for public contracts and receiving licences and subsidies for certain activities, as well as ensuring the integrity of municipal officers involved in granting those contracts and privileges (Nelen & Huisman, 2008). By removing opportunities for organized crime and putting controls on its facilitation, it was hoped that this 'administrative approach' would prevent crimes and disrupt organized crime groups. However in the absence of evaluations, 'it is far from clear that the approach is effective' (Nelen, 2010, p. 107). Similarly, Jacobs et al. (1999) describe the use of civil laws to ensure fair tendering of city contracts, such as rubbish collection, and fair competition in such vital areas as transport services to fresh food markets once dominated by New York mafia families.

In another use of civil laws to prevent crime and its associated harms, the *Wanganui District Council (Prohibition of Gang Insignia) Act 2007* came into force in New Zealand in September 2009, banning the display of gang insignia in specified places designated by Council by-law. Breach attracted a hefty fine. Gang insignia included any representation denoting membership of, affiliation with or support for a gang, including clothing. In mid-2010 the police reported that the by-law had been an effective deterrent to gang activity, with the number of gang members in Wanganui falling by an estimated 15 per cent in 1 year. Thirteen prosecutions for breach of the by-law occurred between September 2009 and May 2010, and prosecutions then declined (New Zealand Police, 2010). There was fierce opposition to the 'patch' law from targeted groups. In March 2011 a challenge by a Hells Angels' member was upheld by the New Zealand High Court on the basis of inconsistency with national laws including the right to freedom of expression. The by-law did not specify in which public places the ban applied – had it done so, the result may have been different. At the time of writing, the Council has resolved to redraft the by-law to limit its geographic coverage and so reduce opportunities for challenge.

In another example, the 'Act on Prevention of Irregularities by Boryokudans' was introduced in Japan in 1991 to disrupt the *yakuza,* as the *boryokudans* (or violent ones) are more commonly known. The Act requires police to work with local Public Safety Commissions that have powers to issue administrative orders based on the Act. Those orders can require yakuza to cease and desist from unjust and violent demands, cease forcible recruitment of juveniles or cease using premises for yakuza offices. 'Prefectural Centres to Promote Movements for Elimination of Boryokudan' have been set up with the local bar association and the police to exchange information on yakuza violence, undertake civil litigation support and help members to leave yakuza groups. Citizens may seek compensation for injuries suffered because of yakuza or request a court order that yakuza vacate certain premises or modify their use. In these cases police often provide protection for citizens. Courts may hold those in charge of yakuza liable. This civil mechanism has had an effect on yakuza activities. For example, after a civil action by residents forced the *Ichiriki-ikka* yakuza in Hamamatsu to stop using a building as an office, it disbanded, due to the damage to its credibility (Hill, 2003).

Preventing profit making

Another preventive strategy is to interfere with the *raison d'être* of an organized criminal group, the pursuit of profit, through the confiscation of assets accumulated from criminal activity, many of which come to light when investigating money laundering. Proceeds of crime laws that institute mechanisms for criminal forfeiture of assets (once there has been a conviction for an offence) and civil forfeiture (whether or not there has been a conviction or ever will be) are increasingly common or under consideration around the world, including in the United States, Canada, the United Kingdom, Australia, South Africa, Hong Kong and Ireland. The aim of such laws is twofold: deterring organized criminality by removing the profit incentive and making further investment in crime difficult. A new form of civil forfeiture, embodied in what are known as 'unexplained wealth' provisions, has also been adopted in some jurisdictions (the United Kingdom, Italy, Hong Kong, some jurisdictions of Australia) over the last decade or so. Unexplained wealth legislation takes civil forfeiture one step further in that the state need not prove that the assets' owner has engaged in serious criminal activity but merely show that the individual's total wealth appears to the state to be greater than the income they can have lawfully acquired. The onus then lies with the individual to establish that the wealth has been obtained legally. Both upper-rank organized criminals and facilitators (those who fund or provide specialist criminal services) who operate mostly outside the gang or criminal network milieu can be targeted using asset forfeiture laws, including public officials who would struggle to hide large amounts of wealth (Broadhurst, 2009). The laws have nevertheless attracted criticisms, such as that they offend fundamental rights (Freiberg & Fox, 2000) and may inflict collateral damage on innocent parties (Naylor, 2001).

Preventing the formation and operation of criminal networks

Approaches to prevention based on analysis of structures of criminal networks have been advocated, on the basis that network analysis can bring to light vulnerabilities in the connections between participants. This then allows law enforcement to exploit them (Williams, 2001). For example, brokers (intermediaries between different sub-groups in a network) are considered to be pivotal to the operation of organized crime networks because they control access to needed resources and thus 'bring flexibility, integration and creativity to the ensemble of an organization' (Morselli, 2009, p. 16). Taking action against brokers could be a way to disable such networks and prevent further crime.

More recently, rare empirical work by Morselli (2009) has brought together network analysis, which focuses on participants in organized crime, and the crime scripts approach first suggested by Cornish (1994), which, as a situational crime approach, focuses on the sequence of activities needed to complete a crime. Any one of these steps or scripts in a sequence may be vulnerable to detection or intervention. Using data from Canadian investigations into two 'ringing scripts' (sequences of steps involved in the resale of stolen vehicles), Morselli showed that a reduction in script permutations (different ways the steps in the script might be executed) would have resulted from removal of participants in the criminal networks during the crime, with a consequential impact on the networks' effectiveness.

While network and crime scripts approaches are beginning to be used by law enforcement agencies, they require sophistication in analysis and the use of detailed offender and modus operandi databases to uncover the steps and sequences within a crime. Such databases are not readily available, and so these approaches have had patchy impact on the ground (Hancock & Laycock, 2010). Some crimes may require fewer and less complicated steps than others – for example, protection compared to credit card fraud.

Another popular structural approach, despite little empirical research, is one that seeks to curb the rights of participants in criminal organizations to associate with each other, on the basis that 'the criminals' ability to associate in order to build networks, groups and syndicates is the problem, while the commission of crime is the symptom' (Powell, 2009, p. 20). The argument, in other words, is that preventing criminals from getting together prevents crime.

Unlawful associations or consorting laws have had a long history in common law jurisdictions such as the United Kingdom and Australia. The notion of criminalizing 'association' has formed the basis for counter-terrorism laws in Australia and the United Kingdom and has recently been extended into the domain of organized crime. For example, since 2008 legislation has been passed in South Australia, New South Wales, the Northern Territory and Queensland that aims to prevent members of criminal organizations from planning and engaging in criminal activities by empowering the state to control their communications and associations. This is achieved through court-issued declarations relating to the organizations and control orders relating to individual members. The breach of a control order by an individual can attract severe criminal penalties, including imprisonment for up to five years. The purpose for which the order is breached is irrelevant. Although broadly drafted, the primary targets of these laws are OMCGs. Quite apart from identified problems with the laws relating to constitutionality, legality and human rights (*South Australia v Totani* [2010] HCA 39; *Wainohu v New South Wales* [2011] HCA 24; Cowdery, 2009; Loughnan, 2009), their likely effectiveness is debatable, given that research has indicated that the social structures of criminal networks and the economic structures for conducting criminal business are often different (Ayling, 2011b). Unintended consequences of these laws, such as the potential for them to push these overt groups underground, are also of concern since their current visibility is an aid to intelligence-gathering (McLaren, Barlow, & staff, 2009). It is as yet too early for judgements about the laws' efficacy, and it will be important to keep a watching brief on the ways OMCGs react and adapt to them.

Tactical and logistical challenges

Many policing agencies have set up specific taskforces and special units to deal with aspects of organized crime such as drug trafficking and vice, or particular groups such as outlaw motorcycle gangs, Asian, Russian and other ethnic-specific crime groups and street gangs. Such specialized units channel resources towards particular problems and have met with a degree of success. However, their narrow focus can mean that recognition of the links between the group or crime of interest and other groups and crimes is missed.

Barriers to the sharing of criminal intelligence between agencies and even within agencies have long been recognized as a problem. Managing information flows without compromising the integrity and security of crucial intelligence about criminal activities and personalities has been an abiding issue in effective responses to organized crime. States sometimes set up institutions explicitly to facilitate sharing; for example, the first function of the Australian Crime Commission is 'to collect, correlate, analyse and disseminate criminal information and intelligence and to maintain a national database of that information and intelligence', a task that requires coordination across nine jurisdictions and several federal agencies. Another recent institutional response is the creation of Criminal Fusion Centres that bring together law enforcement, public safety and private partners to work on common security problems. The United States has established a national network of fusion centres (Department of Homeland Security, 2011) designed to make more permanent the ad hoc cross-agency task forces created to tackle especially complex criminal activity. This idea has been criticized with respect to effectiveness, mission creep and the infringement of civil liberties (Monahan & Palmer, 2009).

The increasingly transnational nature of organized crime has also forced states to think about sharing intelligence with other states and to find common grounds for cooperation. A growing number of international agencies attempt to monitor and co-ordinate responses; these include long-established groups such as the UNODC that, *inter alia*, assists states in the control of illicit drugs, although its mandate has broadened considerably to include other transnational crime threats such as cybercrime, arms smuggling and so on (see generally http://www.unodc.org/). Interpol, one of the oldest international policing agencies (188 countries are members) provides expertise on transnational organized crime and acts as a clearinghouse for information relating to organized crime. Interpol has focused attention recently on Eurasian and Asian criminal organizations (Interpol, 2011). It also co-ordinates international investigations but has no arrest powers itself, which reside with domestic agencies alone.

Another initiative is the Financial Action Task Force (FATF), an inter-governmental body created in 1989 under the auspices of the OECD to develop and promote policies against money laundering and terrorist financing. The FATF recommends that countries criminalize money laundering and require financial institutions to undertake customer due diligence measures, reporting of suspicious transactions and development of programmes against money laundering. So far, 34 countries, including China and Russia, and two regional organizations (the European Commission and the Gulf Co-operation Council) have become members of the FATF (see http://www.fatf-gafi.org/). The FATF itself has no enforcement powers and relies on education, mutual evaluations and 'naming and shaming' to encourage improvements in the detection of money laundering. The absence of the involvement of emerging states such as Brazil and Vietnam and a reliance on persuasion limits the usefulness of the FATF.

The existence of an international agreement, moreover, is no guarantee of implementation. The 2005 United Nations Convention against Corruption (UNCAC) has 151 parties, but corruption is hardly a diminishing problem. As long as states differ in their laws, sanctions and political sensitivities, the exchange of intelligence over organized crime will continue to face hurdles. But the above initiatives exhibit an awareness of the need for multilateral responses to non-traditional security threats that suggests that steady progress is being made.

Future directions

There is little doubt that organized crime will continue to evolve to become more transnational, more flexible, more networked, more technologically savvy and more costly to the community, or that policing agencies face analytical, strategic and logistical challenges in attempting to combat it. Our observations indicate that law enforcement agencies, spurred by a growing state interest in crime as a national security issue, are becoming more adventurous in exploring innovative ideas for combating organized crime, including preventive strategies and the use of partnerships with other public agencies, private businesses and individuals.

Not every experiment, of course, will be successful. Many of the newer approaches as yet lack empirical support. Nelen (2010, p. 108), for example, notes with respect to 'administrative' approaches to controlling organized crime that '...little is known empirically about patterns of displacement, diffusion of benefits, and the preventative effects' of such measures. It is, after all, very difficult to measure organized crime in the first place. It is even harder to measure an apparent absence of it following a law enforcement intervention. Evaluation of law enforcement responses is therefore essential. In our view, academics can play a key role in this area by undertaking evidence-based evaluations of the effectiveness of counter-measures and by engaging with police, legislators and victims in ethical and effective research about the prevalence, nature and harms of organized crime.

References

Australian Crime Commission. (2011). *Organised crime in Australia 2011.* Canberra: Commonwealth of Australia.

Ayling, J. (2009). Criminal organizations and resilience. *International Journal of Law, Crime and Justice, 37*(4), 182–196.

Ayling, J. (2011a). Criminalizing organizations: Towards deliberative lawmaking. *Law and Policy, 33*(2), 149–178.

Ayling, J. (2011b). Pre-emptive strike: How Australia is tackling outlaw motorcycle gangs. *American Journal of Criminal Justice*, Online First 4 May 2011. doi 10.1007/s12103-011-9105-7.

Barker, T. (2007). *Biker gangs and organized crime.* Newark, NJ: LexisNexis.

Broadhurst, R. (2009). Submission 12, *Inquiry into the Crimes Legislation Amendment (Serious and Organised Crime) Bill 2009.* Canberra: Senate Standing Committee on Legal and Constitutional Affairs, Commonwealth Parliament.

Broadhurst, R., & Lee, K. W. (2009). The transformation of triad 'dark societies' in Hong Kong: The impact of law enforcement, socio-economic and political change. *Security Challenges, 5*(4), 1–38.

Bruinsma, G., & Bernasco, W. (2004). Criminal groups and transnational illegal markets. *Crime, Law and Social Change, 41*, 79–94.

Bullock, K., Clarke, R. V., & Tilley, N. (2010). Introduction. In K. Bullock, R. V. Clarke, & N. Tilley (Eds.), *Situational prevention of organised crime* (pp. 1–16). Cullompton, Devon: Willan Publishing.

Chantler, N., & Thorne, C. (2009). Intelligence-led policing. In R. Broadhurst & S. E. Davies (Eds.), *Policing in context: An introduction to police work in Australia* (pp. 123–143). Melbourne: Oxford University Press.

Clarke, R. (1995). Situational crime prevention. In M. Tonry & D. Farrington (Eds.), *Building a safer society: Strategic approaches to crime prevention* (pp. 91–150). Chicago: The University of Chicago Press.

Cohen, A. K. (1977). The concept of criminal organization. *British Journal of Criminology, 17*, 97–111.

Cornish, D. B. (1994). The procedural analysis of offending and its relevance for situational prevention. In R. Clarke (Ed.), *Crime prevention studies* (pp. 151–196). Monsey, NY: Criminal Justice Press.

Cowdery, N. (2009). Comments on organisation/association legislation – 'bikie gangs', May (updated November). Retrieved from http://www.odpp.nsw.gov.au/speeches/speeches.html.

Cressey, D. (1969). *Theft of the nation: The structure and operations of organized crime in America*. New York: Harper and Row.

Curry, P. A., & Mongrain, S. (2009). What is a criminal organization and why does the law care? *Global Crime, 10*(1), 6–23.

Department of Homeland Security. (2011). *State and major urban area fusion centers*. Retrieved from http://www.dhs.gov/files/programs/gc_1156877184684.shtm.

Edwards, A., & Gill, P. (2002). Crime as enterprise? The case of 'transnational organised crime'. *Crime, Law and Social Change, 37*, 203–223.

Edwards, A., & Levi, M. (2008). Researching the organization of serious crimes. *Criminology and Criminal Justice, 8*(4), 363–388.

Fleisher, M. S. (2006). Degree centrality and youth gangs as an ecological adaptation. In J. Short & L. Hughes (Eds.), *Studying youth gangs* (pp. 85–98). Walnut Creek, CA: AltaMira Press.

Freiberg, A., & Fox, R. (2000). Evaluating the effectiveness of Australia's confiscation laws. *Australian and New Zealand Journal of Criminology, 33*(3), 239–265.

Galeotti, M. (2009). Hard times – Organised crime and the financial crisis. *Jane's Intelligence Review*, 24 July.

Gambetta, D. (1993). *The Sicilian Mafia: The business of private protection*. Cambridge, MA: Harvard University Press.

Graycar, A., & Felson, M. (2010). Situational prevention of organised timber theft and related corruption. In K. Bullock, R. V. Clarke, & N. Tilley (Eds.), *Situational prevention of organised crime* (pp. 81–92). Cullompton, Devon: Willan Publishing.

Hancock, G., & Laycock, G. (2010). Organised crime and crime scripts: Prospects for disruption. In K. Bullock, R. V. Clarke, & N. Tilley (Eds.), *Situational prevention of organised crime* (pp. 172–192). Cullompton, Devon: Willan Publishing.

Hill, P. B. E. (2003). *The Japanese mafia: Yakuza, law and the state*. Oxford: Oxford University Press.

Interpol. (2011). Criminal organizations. Retrieved from http://www.interpol.int/Public/OrganisedCrime/default.asp.

Jacobs, J. B., & Dondlinger, E. A. (2012). Organized crime control in the United States of America. In L. Paoli (Ed.), *Oxford handbook of organized crime*. New York: Oxford University Press. Forthcoming.

Jacobs, J. B., with Friel, C., & Radick, R. (1999). *Gotham unbound: How New York City was liberated from the grip of organized crime*. New York: New York University Press.

Klein, M. W., & Maxson, C. L. (2006). *Street gang patterns and policies*. New York: Oxford University Press.

Klerks, P. (2001). The network paradigm applied to criminal organisations: Theoretical nitpicking or a relevant doctrine for investigators? Recent development in the Netherlands. *Connections, 24*(3), 53–65.

L.A.N.D. (2011). Mexico debates drug war death toll figure amid government silence. *Latin America News Dispatch*, 3 June. Retrieved from http://latindispatch.com/2011/06/03/mexico-debates-drug-war-death-toll-figure-amid-government-silence/.

Levi, M. (2007). Organized crime and terrorism. In M. Maguire, R. Morgan, & R. Reiner (Eds.), *The Oxford handbook of criminology* (4th ed.). Oxford: Oxford University Press.

Lien, I-L. (2005). The role of crime acts in constituting the gang's mentality. In S. H. Decker & F. M. Weerman (Eds.), *European street gangs and troublesome youth groups* (pp. 105–125). Lanham, MD: AltaMira Press.

Loughnan, A. (2009). The legislation we had to have? The Crimes (Criminal Organisations Control) Act 2009 (NSW). *Current Issues in Criminal Justice, 20*(3): 457–465.

Massari, M., & Monzini, P. (2004). Dirty businesses in Italy: A case-study of illegal trafficking in hazardous waste. *Global Crime, 6*(3), 285–304.

McCulloch, J., & Pickering, S. (2009). Pre-crime and counter-terrorism. *British Journal of Criminology, 49*, 628–645.

McLaren, O., Barlow, K., & staff (2009). 'Useless' bikie bans drive clubs underground. *ABC News*, 31 March 2009. Retrieved from http://www.abc.net.au/news/stories/2009/03/31/2531499.htm.

Milhaupt, C. J., & West, M. D. (2000). The dark side of private ordering: An institutional and empirical analysis of organized crime. *University of Chicago Law Review, 67*, 41–98.

Monahan, T., & Palmer, N. A. (2009). The emerging politics of DHS fusion centers. *Security Dialogue, 40*, 617–636.

Morselli, C. (2009). *Inside criminal networks*. New York: Springer.

Naylor, R. T. (1997). Mafias, myths and markets: On the theory and practice of enterprise crime. *Transnational Organized Crime, 3*(3), 1–45.

Naylor, R. T. (2001). License to loot? A critique of follow-the-money methods in crime control policy. *Social Justice, 28*(3), 121–152.

Nelen, H. (2010). Situational organised crime prevention in Amsterdam: The administrative approach. In K. Bullock, R. V. Clarke, & N. Tilley (Eds.), *Situational prevention of organised crime*. Cullompton, Devon: Willan Publishing.

Nelen, H., & Huisman, W. (2008). Breaking the power of organized crime? The administrative approach in Amsterdam. In D. Siegal & H. Nelen (Eds.), *Organized crime: culture, markets and policies* (pp. 207–218). New York: Springer.

New Zealand Police. (2010). Wanganui District Council (Prohibition of Gang Insignia) Act 2009. *Policing Fact Sheet*, July. Retrieved from http://www.police.govt.nz/wanganui-district-council-prohibition-gang-insignia-act-2009.

Nohria, N., & Eccles, R. G. (Eds.). (1992). *Networks and organizations: Structure, form, and action*. Boston, MA: Harvard Business School Press.

Paoli, L. (2002). The paradoxes of organized crime. *Crime, Law and Social Change, 37*, 51–97.

Papachristos, A. V. (2006). Social network analysis and gang research: Theory and methods. In J. Short & L. Hughes (Eds.), *Studying youth gangs* (pp. 85–98). Walnut Creek, CA: AltaMira Press.

Passas, N. (2002). Cross-border crime and the interface between legal and illegal actors. In P. C. van Duyne, K. von Lampe, & N. Passas (Eds.), *Upperworld and underworld in cross-border crime* (pp. 61–84). Nijmegen, The Netherlands: Wolf Legal Publishers.

POP Center. (2010). Twenty-five techniques of situational prevention. Center for Problem-Oriented Policing. Retrieved from http://www.popcenter.org/25techniques/.

Powell, D. (2009). Serious and organized crime in South Australia. *RCMP Gazette*, *70*(4), 20–21.

Reuter, P. (1985). *Disorganized crime: Illegal markets and the mafia*. Cambridge, MA: MIT Press.

Rossingh, D. (2011). Organized crime groups are targeting London 2012 ticket sales, police say. *Bloomberg News*, 7 February, Retrieved from http://www.flarenetwork.org/learn/europe/article/organised_crime_groups_are_targeting_london_2012_ticket_sales.htm.

Ruggiero, V. (2000). *Crime and markets: Essays in anti-criminology*. Oxford: Oxford University Press.

Spapens, T. (2010). Macro networks, collectives, and business processes: An in integrated approach to organized crime. *European Journal of Crime, Criminal Law and Criminal Justice*, *18*, 185–215.

Sparrow, M. K. (1991). The application of network analysis to criminal intelligence: An assessment of the prospects. *Social Networks*, *13*(3), 251–274.

Stille, A. (1995). All the Prime Minister's men. *The Independent*, 24 September. Retrieved from http://www.independent.co.uk/arts-entertainment/all-the-prime-ministers-men-1602608.html.

Thornberry, T. P., Krohn, M. D., Lizotte, A. J., Smith, C., & Tobin, K. (2003). *Gangs and delinquency in developmental perspective*. Cambridge: Cambridge University Press.

Thrasher, F. M. (1927/1963). *The gang: A study of 1,313 gangs in Chicago*. Abridged with a new introduction by J. F. Short Jr. Chicago: University of Chicago Press.

UNODC. (2010). The globalization of crime: A transnational organized crime threat assessment. *United Nations publication*, Sales No. E.10.IV.6. New York: United Nations.

Varese, F. (2010). Introduction. In F. Varese (Ed.), *Organized crime* (Vol. 1). London: Routledge.

von Lampe, K. (n.d.). Definitions of organized crime. Retrieved from www.organized-crime.de/OCDEF1.htm.

von Lampe, K. (2009). Human capital and social capital in criminal networks: Introduction to the special issue on the 7th Blankensee Colloquium. *Trends in Organized Crime*, *12*, 93–100.

von Lampe, K. (2011). The application of the framework of situational crime prevention to 'organized crime'. *Criminology and Criminal Justice*, *11*, 145–163.

Williams, P. (2001). Transnational criminal networks. In J. Arquilla & D. Ronfeldt (Eds.), *Networks and Netwars: The future of terror, crime and militancy*. Santa Monica, CA: RAND.

Wuth, R. (2009). Hydra hits Coast bikies hard. Retrieved from http://www.goldcoast.com.au/article/2009/08/13/107675_gold-coast-top-story.html.

Xia, M. (2008). Organisational formations of organized crime in China: Perspectives from the state, markets, and networks. *Journal of Contemporary China*, *17*(54), 1–23.

4
Policing Contemporary Protests

David Baker

Public order policing, in particular the policing of protest, is increasingly complex, ambivalent and unpredictable. Contemporary large-scale protests, often an amalgam of diverse and diffuse affinity groups and agendas, represent considerable challenges for police. As regulatory agents, police encounter the perennial dilemma of how to reconcile the rights of protesters to express their grievance while maintaining order, safety and security. *Adapting to Protest,* the report of Chief Inspector Denis O'Connor of Her Majesty's Inspectorate of Constabulary (HMIC, 2009, p. 5) into the G20 London protests on 1 April 2009, highlights this public order paradox: 'Balancing the rights of protesters and other citizens with the duty to protect people and property from the threat of harm or injury defines the policing dilemma in relation to public protest.' William Blair, Toronto Police Service Chief, after the 18–24 June 2010 G20 summit, asserted that 'the policing challenges of facilitating these very large, lawful, peaceful protests, while at the same time, arresting those who chose violence and destruction were immense' (Toronto Police Service, 2011, p. 3).

The policing challenge is even more pressing in the 'age of terrorism'. After S11 in America, Western nations have increased police powers of surveillance and detention. When police plan contingencies for large-scale protests, police focus on potential terrorist infiltration and threats. Since 9/11, the Bali bombings, the British underground rail system attack, the Madrid train bombings and numerous suicide bombings in Pakistan, India and the Middle East, the pendulum has swung back towards a harsher climate of policing dissent. Due to intelligence of potential terrorist activity, some summits have been moved and conducted beyond the access of protesters; for instance, the 2002

G8 summit was moved from Ottawa to Kananaskis, Canada (Redekop & Pare, 2010).

Tactically, should police remove perceived ringleaders and trouble-makers prior to or during a protest? Will such action incite or calm a crowd? Should police treat all protest groups in the same manner or differentiate between causes and individuals? Do police tactics facilitate the majority of protesters to cooperate with police, or do they alienate the majority towards more radical and extremist elements? Should police enforce summary offences relating to obstruction or allow street protest to proceed?

The police mandate to preserve law and order and protect life and property is tested by street protest if it is perceived as an affront to police and societal authority. Policing by its nature is conservative and concerned with maintaining the status quo; police prefer order and tranquillity on the streets and winning all public disorder confrontations. A large protest presents an affront to the orderly street mentality; it represents an undisciplined situation, a potential problem for 'street cleaning'. Police, with a highly visible street presence, are expected to maintain social control; unruly and riotous behaviour raises questions about police legitimacy and capability. Police employ discretionary judgements about the use of force, riot squads and weaponry. They determine the parameters of acceptable and unacceptable protest behaviour on the street, the boundaries of freedom of dissent. Police in the Western world pragmatically claim to facilitate protest, but their coercive powers remain latent to halt the escalation of conflict. The nexus between police and protesters is contentious and unpredictable: no matter how much liaison and dialogue may take place, both sides usually remain somewhat suspicious and distrustful of the motives of the other.

When compared to the police's traditional crime fighting role of pursuit of criminals, the police's order maintenance role is less clear, less supported and legally and morally ambiguous. Police utilize varied responses to protest events and to the perceived situational threats posed by protesters (Earl & Soule, 2006). The task facing police is demanding as HIMC (2011, p. 4) elicits: 'Crowded public order events cannot be easily managed or orchestrated smoothly when violent individuals or groups are present and are determined to attack people, property or leave their mark.'

This chapter explores the paradoxes facing policing in handling demonstrations; the significance of public protest to democracy; and the problems of poor practice in traditional violent police–protester confrontations. The academic literature documents some improved forms of police–protester dialogue and interaction, but such developments have been curtailed at major demonstrations in the twenty-first century. The case study of the 'mixed' policing of the 2007 Sydney Asia Pacific Economic Corporation (APEC) summit is evaluated in the context of contemporary policing trends.

Protest relevance

Protest has been a dynamic and vibrant force behind much fundamental democratic change in the Western world. Labour movement, suffragette, land rights, human rights, independence movements, anti-apartheid, anti-war, environmental and numerous diverse protests have achieved remarkable advances, often against considerable opposing forces. Many protest movements have been curtailed by authorities acting under the mantra of security and order, but many others have achieved political and social change. The power of protest cannot be denied: the 2011 mass protests in Egypt, Libya, Syria and across the Middle East are driving revolutionary change.

Police have been present at many defining moments in history; the dynamics of police interaction with protesters can be significant in determining the legitimacy of protest behaviour. Even certain protest tactics such as marches, camps and the blocking of traffic have evolved to be seen as semi-legitimate means of gaining attention and affecting change (Lovell, 2009, p. 6). It must be remembered that most protests in Western democracies do not incite police confrontation: Redekop and Pare (2010) claim that 'there is now consistency around the figure of 90 per cent of protest crowds that take place without incident.' Reicher (2011, p. 13) argues that violence 'is rather rare' in crowds.

Although protest has achieved much, some have threatened life and property and either been led or been subverted by extremist elements with unlawful or criminal intent. Melbourne's G20 protests in November 2006 were generally non-violent, but those that were aggressive captured the headlines. Violent-prone protesters mostly belonged to a series of splintered and uncoordinated groups, including extreme factions of Mutiny and the Arterial Bloc who spurned negotiation with police. These militants, clad in hooded overalls and bandanas covering faces, controlled part of Melbourne's central business district (CBD): buildings were invaded; police cowered behind a police van; other police were taunted and pelted with missiles; and extensive damage was done to city property (Human Rights Observer Team Final Report, 2007, p. 8).

Historical context

The Western world has a chequered history of police handling of large-scale protest. In the latter half of the nineteenth century, police quickly learnt that superior numbers were essential to deal with political and industrial protest. For much of twentieth century, the police approach involved large police presence to act decisively with force to disperse crowds of protesters (Lovell, 2009, p. 109). Often protest activity encountered aggressive and at times violent police responses. Brecher (1997, p. 1) chronicles an extremely pessimistic account of repeated and bloody repression of American worker dissent 'by company-sponsored violence, local police, State militias and the U.S. Army and National guard'.

A few examples of violent suppression of protest or civil disobedience from the 1960s onwards follow:

- After a day of anti-pass law demonstrations by blacks, 300 besieged South African Police on 21 March 1960 fired on a crowd of about 25,000 outside the Sharpeville police station and killed 69 people (70 per cent shot in the back as they ran from the police attack) with more than 180 injured in what became known as the 'Sharpeville massacre'. Heavily armed, inexperienced and inadequately trained police officers had panicked and shot more than one thousand rounds spontaneously and indiscriminately (Frankel, 2001). The following weeks witnessed further demonstrations, strikes and riots, culminating in the government declaring a state of emergency and detaining 18,000 activists.
- The American urban racial riots of the 1960s revealed bloody confrontations between black people and the police. The Watts (35 dead), Newark (23 dead) and Detroit (43 dead) riots stemmed from street and ghetto protest where destruction, looting and disorder occurred. David Waddington (1992, p. 63) argues that American police policies and practices reflected the non-concessional, hard-line preferences of prominent local politicians, especially mayors.
- The era of the Vietnam War protests heralded clashes between police and student activists in many countries. On Monday, 4 May, at Kent State University, Ohio, some National Guard members fired 67 rounds indiscriminately amongst students, killing four and wounding seven.
- A student-staff anti-Vietnam war march from La Trobe University (Melbourne) on 16 September 1970 was 'ambushed' by the local

police in waiting who attacked and beat the marchers with batons in a 'sickening use of force by the police' (*Age*, 22 September 1970, p. 9). The response of the officer-in-charge, Inspector Plattfuss, revealed police contempt of student protesters at that time: 'They got some baton today and they'll get a lot more in the future' (*Sunday Observer*, 20 September 1970, p. 4).

- The catalyst for the Brixton race riots of April 1981 was 'Swamp 81', an intensive police operation of indiscriminate stop and search to counteract street crime and burglary. Police attention was focused on young black males; 943 individuals were stopped and searched and 118 arrested on suspicion (Alderson, 1998, p. 24) The Brixton riots were caused by a cocktail of factors: social disadvantage and disorganization, poverty, poor housing, high unemployment, racial discrimination and deprivation and mistrust of the police (Waddington, 2007). Although police were not responsible for the socio-economic depression and hopelessness, Lord Scarman, in accord with the sentiments of the 1967 Kerner Commission for American race riots, reported that rectification lay with police adjusting 'their policies and operations so as to handle these difficulties with imagination as well as firmness' (Alderson, 1998, p. 127).

Traditionally, when police actively intervened to suppress protest (and on many occasions they merely observed or monitored proceedings), they usually did so in an aggressive and belligerent manner. Police attitude and tactics often provoked considerably more criticism than the actual monitoring of protest behaviour (Baker, 2005). If police authority was challenged, police responses were usually quick, forceful and even brutal. The traits of bad practice in such violent and punitive situations were manifest:

- The police attitude was one of 'us vs. them'; the protesters were perceived as the enemy.
- Superior numbers (police saturation) were not necessarily the appropriate means of defusing the situation.
- Armed police could be a recipe for disaster as police, especially the inexperienced and ill-trained who could become panic-stricken when confronted by a milling and angry crowd.
- As police public order training and planning was often non-existent, a resort to force became the default strategy.
- No dialogue took place between police leaders and protest organizers.
- Police were distant, even hostile, to local communities.

- Many protesters perceived police as being too closely and willingly aligned with government structures.

Superior numbers historically were the key to police victory, but today information gathering, intelligence, covert surveillance and ultimately riot technology are the weapons of police dominance of protest disorder. Almost invariably confrontations are weighted in favour of police with their modern armoury of guns, rubber bullets, tear gas, chemical sprays, riot shields and helmets, horses, dogs, water cannon and armoured personnel carriers.

Divergent contemporary trends

Violent clashes between police and students in the late 1960s and early 1970s have been the subject of much review (Skolnick, 1971). Much public order policing in Britain has been a response to industrial disputation (1926 general strike, 1972 Saltley, 1977 Grunwick, 1984–1985 miners' strike, 1987 Wapping dispute), soccer hooliganism and perceived threats to energy infrastructure (Waddington, 2007). Transformation from the 'escalated force' approach stemmed from several government-sponsored commissions in the United States that reviewed the bad practice prevalent during the urban unrest of the 1960s and the anti-war protests of the late 1960s and early 1970s. The Scarman Inquiry (1981) was instrumental in changing British policing practices.

According to Kratcoski, Verma and Das (2001), policing of protest had become less violent over the last quarter of the twentieth century. della Porta and Reiter (1998, p. 2) contend that in Western democratic countries, many of which historically were noted for militarized and armed policing, there was a widespread trend towards 'softer', more tolerant, accommodating, flexible, preventive, selective and less coercive styles of policing protest. As harsh lessons were learnt from past confrontations, policing protest in the 1990s was characterized by under-enforcement of the law, the complex procedures of negotiation and the large-scale collection and sharing of prevention-oriented information and intelligence (Waddington, 2001). Despite negotiations, police remained dominant because the 'soft' response of police is based on the compliance of demonstrators following certain procedures such as applications for protest marches and rallies. Hall and de Lint (2004, p. 360) depict how police in negotiations adroitly communicate the law and lessons of self-regulation to protest organizers as 'the substance of communication is to shift the onus of security onto the parties themselves'. Police inform protest organizers of their legal liabilities and responsibilities, which can be a daunting revelation for them.

There is agreement in the public order literature that 'negotiated management' has significantly decreased the number and intensity of street clashes between police and demonstrators (Gillham & Noakes, 2007, p. 42). In the Western world, many policing agencies publicly advocate the importance of dialogue with protest organizers (Baker, 2008; Hall & de Lint, 2004). The six state police forces in Australia, although determined to maintain control and authority, conduct some form of 'negotiated management' approach through communication and other violence minimization strategies. They are generally less inclined to arrest for minor infringements than their American counterparts who often feel compelled to justify their intervention by making numerous arrests (Lovell, 2009, p. 104). Through 'negotiated management' strategies, the New South Wales (NSW) Police Force seek compromise, 'a zone of potential agreement... working together is so much easier, come to a general understanding' about march routes and media access so 'that a lot of people are more willing to work with police to achieve their goals' (Cullen, 2011).

Post-9/11, police have received increased powers; riot technology has become more sophisticated and available; and paramilitary response squads are resourced and prevalent. Research in many countries indicates the proliferation and the increasing use of police paramilitary units and special weapons and tactical teams. When economic and trade interests are at stake, policing has tended to be openly coercive. Special riot units have been deployed at protest counter-summits and police have discouraged protests (della Porta, Peterson, & Reiter, 2006, pp. 7–10, 179). Despite considerable militaristic capabilities, it is pertinent to note that in some countries such as Australia riot personnel and technology have only been deployed on a limited basis to date. Less-than-lethal weapons (bean bag rounds, rubber bullets, sprays, water cannon) exist, and protest leaders and organizers are well aware of their availability (Baker, 2008).

The academic literature has focused on the heavy-handed, confrontational and militaristic police responses at contemporary anti-globalization protests when dealing with diffuse, disorganized and potentially violence-prone activists. della Porta et al. (2006) present a compelling case that in the new millennium there has been a reversion to tougher policing of large-scale protest in Europe, based on the control and command ethos. Police generally have shown an inclination to use force, construct no-go areas, discourage presence at protests by tactics of warnings and threats of violence, utilize riot technology and accumulate extensive intelligence. However, covert surveillance and intelligence gathering rest uneasily with the trust required between police and protesters to maintain negotiated arrangements.

Anti-globalization protests at the turning of the millennium (Davos, Seattle, Melbourne, Gothenburg, Genoa, Washington, Prague, Ottawa, Quebec City) have highlighted the problems of maintaining public order in a shrinking world. The 1999 Seattle battle from 28 November to 3 December, when an estimated 50,000 protesters massed to successfully impede the World Trade Organization (WTO)'s negotiations, is often cited as either a turning point or a reversion to confrontational policing of protest (Lovell, 2009, pp. 28–29). Noakes and Gillham (2007, p. 335) depict Seattle as 'not merely a place but also a time, a series of historic events, and a moment of significant social change'. Police were unprepared for the number and intent of certain protesters, especially anarchical affinity groups who adopted destructive Black Bloc tactics. A common sight at anti-globalization summits, these tactics involve individuals donning black clothing and wearing balaclavas or ski-masks to conceal identity while committing criminal activities. They return to 'street clothing' and mingle with peaceful demonstrators (Toronto Police Service, 2011, p. 11).

Many protesters, using lockdown formations, controlled major Seattle intersections which prevented delegates from access to the summit and which divided police resources. Protesters stopped some WTO ministerial meetings, received international attention and portrayed themselves as police victims (Gillham & Marx, 2000, p. 214). Police fired pepper spray and tear gas canisters to disperse protesters, and subsequently stun grenades and rubber bullets, but this escalated the protest hostility and aggression (Waddington, 2007, p. 111). As police eventually were overwhelmed, the commercial activity of downtown Seattle came to a halt. The mayor, criticized for being unprepared for the demonstrators' tactics, imposed a curfew and a 50-block 'No-Protest Zone' which inhibited protesters from communicating with their targeted audience. Seattle Police blamed their failure on inadequate preparation and resources, a well-coordinated adversary, and a city ordinance that prohibited police from gaining information about suspect political groupings (Gillham & Marx, 2000, pp. 222, 226).

Post-Seattle, street confrontations at anti-globalization summits have become more common involving in some cases increasingly more repressive police tactics (della Porta et al., 2006). The proliferation of transgressive protesters into diffuse and non-hierarchical affinity groups test police capacity to negotiate arrangements, monitor protest preparations and predict actions (Noakes & Gillham, 2006).

The location of certain summits in remote or tourist areas with limited access and egress have intensified the problems of security and control. Preparations for the 27th Group of Eight summit meeting in the medieval city of Genoa from 18 to 22 July 2001 were a logistical nightmare; the location resembled the fortification of a walled city in anticipation of an enemy siege. Rubber bullets, stun grenades and water cannon were utilized to stem the bloody protest. Hundreds of demonstrators and police were injured. After the death of a young demonstrator in Genoa, 150,000 protesters occupied the streets the next day. Activists accused police of brutality and impeding the progress of passive dissent. The G8 meeting proceeded in an off-limits 'Red Zone' which was surrounded by a barricade that prevented protesters from being seen and heard.

During the 2001 anti-globalization protest in Gothenburg, violent clashes between police and protesters occurred in the city's main street, and parts of the CBD were ransacked and stores looted. Police who shot three protesters in Gothenburg were under investigation but argued that the shootings took place amid life-threatening circumstances. The 2001 Gothenburg and Genoa police shootings raise the spectre of extremist agitators becoming more marginalized and militant and special tactical response units becoming the flagship of police operations at such economic summits. If violence is to be avoided, much of the challenge lies in the dialogue, precautions and planning arrangements prior to the actual event.

A series of diverse and confrontational anti-globalization protests has questioned policing capacity both to maintain order and to facilitate mass protest. After the violent Seattle, Genoa and Gothenburg summit battles, Gillham and Noakes (2007, p. 343) coined the phrase 'strategic incapacitation' to depict policing characterized by extensive no-protest zones, availability of less-lethal weapons, strategic use of arrests and heavy surveillance (della Porta et al., 2006, pp. 7–10, 179). Noakes and Gillham (2006) depict a repressive American policing of protest based on the principles of neoconservative new penology. This harder edge to policing protest, especially against anti-globalization groups that are perceived as threats to the political elites and governments, has re-ignited confrontation between police and protesters. Fernandez (2008, p. 4) describes increased fear of violence and police unwillingness to allow protest as a consequence of 9/11. Some disruptive protests are seen as politically illegitimate and hence repressed by police (Vitale, 2007, p. 404). Mass arrests and lengthy detentions incapacitated and successfully contained protesters in New York during the 2004 Republican National Convention. Authorities, led by the police, plan for the 'worst-case scenario' in order to suppress diverse, discordant, fragmented and unstructured protest (Waddington, 2001, pp. 3–14). A widespread show of force by police is interpreted as a tactic of intimidation against would-be protesters.

Case study of policing the 2007 Sydney APEC summit

NSW Police Commander, Stephen Cullen (personal communication, 31 January 2011) detailed how the Force had reacted vigorously both to the August 2005 Forbes CEO Global Conference protest outside the Sydney Opera House when 'protesters in some respects were holding our city to ransom' and to the violent 2005 Cronulla racial riots. The Public Order and Riot Squad (PORS), under Cullen, was formed and resourced. NSW Police, conscious that only a small minority engages in unlawful behaviour, developed an early interventionist strategy involving quick, surgical, professional and lawful removal of identified potential trouble-makers in order to show police 'zero tolerance' of certain behaviours and to prevent the excesses of Melbourne's 2006 G20 experience when militants ran amuck and trashed part of the city (S. Cullen, personal communication, 31 January 2011). Policing tradition and philosophy demands that police contain situations and take control of events, especially unannounced protest events 'that do not allow time for planning' (NSW Police, 2008, pp. 476–477).

The advent of anti-globalization protests in the Western world has ushered in a new phase, arguably a reversion to the confrontational approach of previous decades. Australian police agencies remain committed to negotiation in planning for controlling public protest, but there are signs of adjustments to the handling of mass dissent and a harsher edge to the policing of major protest events. During Sydney's APEC preparations, terrorism fears meshed with plans to control protests directed at foreign dignitaries. The *APEC Meeting (Police Powers) Act 2007* provided police with extraordinary powers to detain persons entering a restricted area without special justification. Police were given extensive powers to establish road blocks, search people and vehicles and seize prohibited items (Hutchinson & Creenaune, 2010, p. 33).

'Show' – display of force and message of danger – was central to police APEC preparations which were designed to deter unruly crowd behaviour. Prior to APEC, NSW Police displayed their state-of-the-art riot technology: PORs had purchased its fleet of ten black Hummers specially equipped with LA-style sidewalks; newly acquired $700,000 water cannon vehicle; special broad horizon cameras; disorientating high-beam torches, high-speed boats, dirt bikes and modified helicopters. Whether such weaponry as the intimidating water cannon acts as a catalyst for protester – police violence or whether it acts as a deterrent to confrontation is a moot point (Waddington, 2007, pp. 111, 116). It was not used, but it was available and, more importantly, known to be ready for deployment. The NSW Police Association in an arrangement with the NSW Government had declared that its members would not use the newly acquired water cannon, at union pickets and protests, although other demonstrators such as those at APEC might not be so fortunate (*Sydney Morning Herald*, 21 August 2007). Unionists, who are led, organized, disciplined and follow a specific agenda, were categorized as 'good' demonstrators, but anti-globalization ones were labelled as potentially 'bad'.

The 2–9 September 2007 APEC summit in Sydney constituted arguably the largest security event in Australia's history: 3500 of the 15,000 NSW officers were assigned to the forum duty; 450 AFP, 1500 defence personnel and various commonwealth agencies including ASIO deployed. Police-military exercises, including a fortnight-long operation codenamed Blue Luminary Two, were staged as a display of strength to discourage dissent. One commentator termed the police rhetoric as 'physiological warfare of sorts against a population repeatedly reminded that anyone who ventured into central Sydney to shop, let alone protest, would be doing so while there were [police] snipers on the rooftops' (Wynhausen, 2007). Surveillance was intensified and concentrated; special powers allowed police to detain anyone 'suspicious'; 35 activists were banned from the declared APEC zone; police leaked photos of the 'blacklisted' to the devouring media (Creenaune, 2007, pp. 29–30). The week involved a $170 million security operation; 500 jail cells awaited dissidents; officers donned full riot garb; and snipers were positioned in the CBD. A 5-kilometre 2.8-metre high steel and concrete fence was erected around the northern part of the CBD (*Australian*, 3 September 2007). In hindsight, were the preparations – especially the high-tech precautions – 'overkill', or were they necessary for fear of unknown and unpredictable hostile acts?

APEC presented NSW Police Force with unique challenges of balancing the lawful right for peaceful protest with the public safety and security of 21 world leaders. Some inconvenience was inevitable by staging the meeting in the CBD. The NSW Police Force negotiated over some months with the Stop Bush Coalition activists about the protest march route, but both sides appeared suspicious of the other. Protesters believed that they were being duped while police alleged that the Mutiny activists distributed a detailed manual of how to incite public mayhem (*Weekend Australian,* 1–2 September 2007). Police, arguably in the interests of public safety, closed off an intersection in the CBD with barriers where control measures would be applied by police. The PORS Commander addressed the NSW Supreme Court, advocating a ban against the 'Stop Bush Coalition' marching in the city: 'Police lines will come under attack and a full-scale riot is probable.... I have absolutely no doubt that minority groups will engage in a level of violence not previously experienced in Sydney' (Cullen, 2007). Justice Michael Adams (2007, paragraph 33) supported the Police Commissioner's proposed alternative route, still in the centre of the CBD, as 'reasonable' to move the assembly 'a few blocks' to prevent possible injury to person and property. Justice Adams also endorsed the right of free expression: 'a certain amount of disruption and public inconvenience is the price that we must pay as a free society to enable fundamental rights to be exercised' (2007, paragraph 28).

NSW Police Force feared, like other anti-globalization protests, 'that violent minority groups will infiltrate the march' and generate 'a mob mentality whereby normally peaceful people are influenced to engage in violent behaviour' as part of a progressive crowd panic (Cullen, affidavit, 2007, p. 5). PORS Commander Cullen's belief that 'by and large, people generally act at a protest like sheep', expresses a common police adherence to Gustave Le Bon's theory of crowd behaviour as a process of contagion with a void of individual control and rationality (King & Brearley, 1996, p. 19). Observational research (Adang & Brown, 2008; McPhail, 1991), which explores crowd behaviour complexity and dynamics, has questioned the concept of the irrational, degenerate, mindless and aggressive crowd. Even if trouble occurs during a protest, the assumption that all protesters are troublemakers is false and dangerous for police responses. If police assume that all protest behaviour is 'suspect' and suppress protest actions, they may violate protester rights and ignite violent reactions (Reicher, 2011, pp. 9, 16)

The policing of APEC 2007 is an example of police utilization of exclusionary tactics in a less violent setting than many of the European and American counter summit confrontations (Baker, 2008). However, in the style of European and American policing tactics post 9/11, APEC 2007 saw senior police and other security officials, empowered with unprecedented powers, instigating extensive exclusionary zones. Sydney's CBD was a sight of empty streets with concrete barriers, riot squad sharpshooters and helicopters. In accordance with some European public order strategies 'tending to exclusion instead of inclusion' (della Porta & Reiter, 2006, p. 37), the objective was to prevent violence and confrontation by keeping potential protesters away from the proximity of APEC delegates whose security was paramount. Critics of the restrictions claimed that the policing intelligence was flawed and aimed at discouraging protest activism (Ferguson, 2007). P. A. J. Waddington (2007, pp. 130–131) argues that there is a fine line between intelligence, 'spying' and other forms of disruption and if abused, the intelligence can undermine perfectly legitimate protest action.

Despite police predictions of 20,000 people, the largest protest rally attendance was estimated at 5000 on the Saturday morning. Heavy rain, police preparations and warnings, the psychological intimidation and media prophecies of violent clashes were credited with the small attendance. Although there were only 17 arrests, some protesters felt 'bullied', intimated, but none were physically touched. Police had used force, not in the overt physical sense, but rather by subtle tactics to restrict movement and thereby limit the possibilities of mass gatherings encountering and confronting police (Creenaune, 2007, p. 29). The Chaser comedy team in a notorious stunt easily breached the APEC restricted zone in a fake Canadian motorcade, but otherwise security was maintained and violence prevented.

Criticism of police actions originated from civil rights lawyers and the Greens political party who unsuccessfully called for an independent inquiry into police behaviour. Peace activist Dale Mills (personal communication, 1 February 2011) expressed the protesters' perspective that the policing of APEC represented 'massive overkill' and veered 'overboard' but that the event was 'very educational' because it raised the question of the validity of protest. As the predicted violent confrontation failed to eventuate, journalists focused on police behaviour, particularly failure to wear identification badges.

The NSW Police Force made concerted, sustained and successful efforts before and during APEC to avoid violence, but at what cost to civil liberties and the right to protest? Although NSW Police prevented violence at APEC, the exclusionary strategy should not unquestionably become the appropriate model for the policing of mass protest.

'Best practice' recommendations

Police confront the challenge of how to make negotiation and other violence minimization strategies effective when dealing with diffuse, disorganized and potentially violence-prone twenty-first century protesters. Best practice for the policing of protest requires a positive mindset and strategy. British police have recently been subjected to much criticism over the handling of large-scale protests. Chief Inspector Denis O'Connor's report into the G20 London protests on 1 April 2009, *Adapting to Protest*, concluded that police planned too much on confronting violence instead of facilitating peaceful protest. O'Connor instructed police that the initial planning should 'not be defining protest as lawful or unlawful', but 'the presumption should be in favour of facilitating peaceful protest, unless levels of disruption require the police to place legitimate restrictions upon them' (HMIC, 2009, p. 9). Reicher (2011, p. 20) argues that the 'facilitation rather than repression should be the default option' until evidence exists that 'relevant individuals are pursuing a course of disruption'. The O'Connor report advocated 'a certain degree of tolerance towards peaceful gatherings where demonstrators do not engage in acts of violence, even if these protests cause a level of obstruction or disruption' (HMIC, 2009, pp. 4, 9). The O'Connor review has had considerable impact around policing in the Western world because it was not the views of an outsider criticizing police tactics but rather a distinguished member of the policing establishment, a former Metropolitan Police Service (MET) commander (Waddington, 2009). The HMIC report challenges the perceived police mindset of making protest experience unpleasant in order to discourage further protest activity (as it was for many at London's G20, Seattle, Genoa, Gothenburg).

Best practice approaches are dependent on variables, some of which are within police control and others not so. A key dynamic of any large-scale demonstration is the interaction between police, protesters, bystanders, media and potential protest targets. Police responses to a protest event can either inflame or diffuse a potentially violent situation. My suggestions include the following:

- Best practice requires clear communication and liaison between police leadership and protest organizers whenever possible, with 'no surprises'. Protesters and the public should be made aware of likely police action in order to make informed decisions (HMIC, 2011, p. 39). Although not a panacea, 'negotiated management' encourages and facilitates peaceful protest. It needs to develop pre-event, be communicated to all protesters during the event, be on-going and be complemented by open post-event briefings of police and protest organizers. The latter is often ignored, but it is significant for developing an on-going liaison for future protest events.

- Police need intelligence and understanding of the identities and intentions within protest groups in order to liaise, predict eventualities, maintain safety and security and facilitate legitimate protest activities (Reicher, 2011, p. 17). Labelling all protesters as having one intent can be hazardous and counter-productive.
- Police need to develop procedures and processes to identify and extract individuals from a demonstration who pose a threat to public safety, without alienating the rest of the assembly (Toronto Police Service, 2011, p. 63).
- Effective policing of protest has often occurred when the protest group has successfully 'self-policed' with police monitoring at a distance.
- Situational factors in potentially volatile situations, especially the positioning of global summits, demand planned strategic locations because close physical interaction is likely to occur between police, security and protesters.
- Police tactics need to be flexible and whenever expedient, also transparent. Police need to display and use weaponry (tanks, riot shields, batons, canisters) only when absolutely necessary and appropriate. If coercion is required in a particular situation, such force should be appropriate and the minimum necessary.
- Appropriate training of police personnel of all levels is identified as a key ingredient of successful monitoring and control of protest (HMIC, 2009; Toronto Police Service, 2011, p. 63).
- Operational policing decisions need to be independent and devoid of both direct political interference and any subservience to the concept of 'police knowledge', an accumulated awareness and wisdom of how the authorities expect police to act regarding protesters (della Porta & Reiter, 1998, p. 22).
- Accountability of both police and protest actions must be thorough, appropriate and balanced.

Conclusion

della Porta et al. (2006, p. 12) argue that protest rights have receded into the background in the twenty-first century and that police 'control and command' dominate strategy. The use of brutal police force at transnational demonstrations across parts of America and Europe 'has not been perceived as a successful strategy' because the widespread show of force by police is interpreted as a tactic of intimidation against would-be protesters (della Porta & Reiter, 2006, p. 183). Although police conduct dialogue with leaders of planned protests, they also aggressively prepare for worst-case scenarios, especially when there are perceived threats to dignitaries and vital infrastructure. Despite the fact that police in Australia have experienced some successes with the 'negotiated management' approach (most notably during the 1998 national waterfront dispute; see Baker, 2005), there are signs that policing of anti-globalization protests is following a two-edged approach of both negotiations and extensive paramilitary preparations.

The process of long-term, attitudinal change and trust is challenging for protesters and police alike: protesters need to view police as a conduit keeping peace and safety, not as the enemy to confront; police need to accept the legitimacy of peaceful protest. If exclusionary, 'no-go' areas – anathema to protesters determined to be heard and seen – are to become standard features of the policing of contemporary large-scale protests, demonstrators need the opportunity to be peacefully seen and heard. Area denial strategies and the threat of force run the risk of excluded activists adopting more extreme and innovative methods of agitation. Best practice of policing mass protests hinges upon a delicate and fragile balance between the maintenance of security and the facilitation of the rights of peaceful protesters.

References

Adams, Justice. Statement: New South Wales Commissioner of Police v Bainbridge. [2007]. NSWSC 1015 175 A Crim R, 226–233.

Adang, O., & Brown, E. (2008). *Policing football in Europe: Experiences from peer review evaluation teams*. The Netherlands: Politieacademie Apeldoorn.

Alderson, J. (1998). *Principled policing*. Winchester: Waterside Press.

Baker, D. (2005). *Batons and blockades: Policing industrial disputes in Australasia*. Melbourne: Circa.

Baker, D. (2008). Paradoxes of policing and protest. *Policing, Intelligence and Counter Terrorism, 3*(2), 8–22.

Brecher, J. (1997). *Strike!* Cambridge, MA: South End Press.

Creenaune, H. (2007, Summer). Turning back the terrorism tag: Organising against APEC. *Chain Reaction*, 28–31.

Cullen, S. (2007). Affidavit: NSW commissioner of police v Bainbridge. NSWSC 1015.

Cullen, S. (2011). Commander of NSW Public Order Riot Squad, recorded interview, 31 January.

della Porta, D., & Reiter, H. (1998). *Policing protest: The control of mass demonstrations in western democracies*. Minneapolis: University of Minnesota Press.

della Porta, D., & Reiter, H. (2006). The policing of transnational protest: A conclusion. In D. della Porta, A. Peterson & H. Reiter (Eds.), *The policing of transnational protest* (pp. 175–189). Aldershot: Ashgate.

della Porta, D., Peterson, A., & Reiter, H. (2006). Policing transnational protest: An introduction. In D. della Porta, A. Peterson & H. Reiter (Eds.), *The policing of transnational protest* (pp. 1–12). Aldershot: Ashgate.

Earl, J., & Soule, S. (2006). Seeing blue: A police-centered explanation of protest policing. *Mobilization: An International Journal, 11*(2), 145–164.

Ferguson, J. (11 September 2007). Now good cop turns bad cop. *Herald-Sun*, 20.

Fernandez, L. (2008). *Policing dissent: Social control and the anti-globalization movement.* New Brunswick: Rutgers University Press.

Frankel, P. (2001). *An ordinary atrocity: Sharpeville and its massacre.* New Haven: Yale University Press.

Gillham, P., & Marx, G. (2000). Complexity and irony in policing and protesting: The World Trade Organization in Seattle. *Social Justice, 27*(2), 212–236.

Gillham, P., & Noakes, J. (2007). More than a March in a circle: Transgressive protests and the limits of negotiated management. *Mobilization: An International Quarterly, 12*(4), 341–357.

Hall, A., & de Lint, W. (2004). Making the pickets responsible: Policing labour at a distance in Windsor, Ontario. In S. N. Nancoo (Ed.), *Contemporary issues in Canadian policing* (pp. 337–375). Mississauga: Canadian Educators Press.

Her Majesty's Inspectorate of Constabulary (HMIC). (2009). *Adapting to protest: Review of the policing of public protest.* London: HMIC.

Her Majesty's Inspectorate of Constabulary (HMIC). (2011). *Policing public order.* London: HMIC.

Human Rights Observer Team Final Report. (2007). *G20 protests November 17–19, 2006.* Carlton South: Federation of Community Legal Centres.

Hutchinson, Z., & Creenaune, H. (2010). A stifling climate: Targeting social movements and policing protests. *Dissent, Autumn/Winter*, 33–38.

King, M., & Brearley, N. (1996). *Public order policing.* Leicester: Perpetuity Press.

Kratcoski, P., Verma, A., & Das, D. (2001). Policing of public order: A world perspective. *Police Practice and Research: An International Journal, 2*(1–2), 109–143.

Lovell, J. (2009). *Crimes of dissent: Civil disobedience, criminal justice and the politics of conscience.* New York: New York University Press.

McPhail, C. (1991). *The myth of the madding crowd.* New York: Aldine de Gruyter.

New South Wales Police Force Handbook. (11 December 2008). Sydney: NSW Police Force. Released under FOI legislation.

Noakes, J., & Gillham, P. (2006). Aspects of the 'new penology' in the police response to major political protests in the United States, 1999–2000. In D. della Porta, A. Peterson, & H. Reiter (Eds.), *The policing of transnational protest* (pp. 97–116). Aldershot: Ashgate.

Redekop, V., & Pare, S. (2010). *Beyond control: A mutual respect approach to protest crowd–police relations.* London: Bloomsbury Academic.

Reicher, S. (2011). From crisis to opportunity: New crowd psychology and public order policing principles. In T. Madensen & J. Knutsson (Eds.), *Preventing crowd violence* (pp. 7–23). London: Lynne Rienner.

Skolnick, J. (1971). *The politics of protest.* New York: Ballantine.

Toronto Police Service. (June 2011). *After-action review: G20 summit Toronto, Ontario, June 2010.* Retrieved from http://www.documentcloud.org/documents/207475-g20-toronto-police-service-self-assessment.

Vitale, A. (2007). The command and control and Miami models at the 2004 republican national convention: New forms of policing protests. *Mobilization: An International Quarterly, 12*(4), 403–415.

Waddington, D. (1992). *Contemporary issues in public disorder.* London: Routledge.

Waddington, D. (2007). *Policing public disorder: Theory and practice.* Devon: Willan.

Waddington, P. A. J. (2001). Negotiating and defining 'public order'. *Police Practice and Research: An International Journal, 2*(1–2), 3–14.

Waddington, P. A. J. (2007). Public order: Then and now. In A. Henry & D. Smith (Eds.), *Transformations of policing* (pp. 113–140). Aldershot: Ashgate.

Waddington, P. A. J. (2009). Proud report could come before fall. *Police Review, 27* November, 14–15.

Wynhausen, E. (15–16 September 2007). The aura of a police state. *Weekend Australian,* 29.

5
Integrating Intelligence into Policing Practice

Janet Evans and Mark Kebbell

An 'intelligence-led' approach to policing is now well established as a key element of modern accountable police work. Broadly, intelligence-led policing involves a process for enhancing law enforcement effectiveness and has been defined by Ratcliffe (2008) as:

> a business model and managerial philosophy where data analysis and crime intelligence are pivotal to an objective, decision-making framework that facilitates crime and problem reduction, disruption and prevention through strategic management and effective enforcement strategies that target prolific and serious offenders.
>
> (p. 89)

Within the current financial climate, including cut-backs and tighter management of public sector resources, it is essential that law enforcement is able to effectively prioritize resources and demonstrate value for money. It is therefore a prudent time to focus on the use of intelligence as part of a 'business model'. The business model treats policing as a business where tasks (e.g. responding to different crimes, reassuring the public, etc.) are prioritized to deliver optimal dividends. Strategic decisions are made as would also occur in a conventional business. Intelligence has a central role in guiding the business of policing. In this chapter we discuss some of the key issues in the small but growing administrative and academic literature in the field of intelligence. Specifically, the chapter addresses the following topics:

1. Definitions and examples of intelligence;
2. The National Intelligence Model (NIM), adopted in the United Kingdom and elsewhere, including an outline of a model organizational

philosophy about intelligence and appropriate structuring of intelligence units and processes within police organizations;

3. Factors that impede the implementation of effective intelligence-led policing; and

4. An illustrative case study of problems and issues in the implementation of an intelligence-led policing model in the Australian intelligence community.

The chapter concludes by emphasizing the value of the UK model and the need to systematically implement the model into police organizational structures and practices.

Background: Criminal intelligence in police work

The British Association of Chief Police Officers (ACPO, 2005) defines 'intelligence' as 'information that has been subject to a defined evaluation and risk assessment process in order to assist with police decision making ... requirements for a professional intelligence capability are timely recording, evaluation, dissemination and management of information', p. 13). This intelligence is used to identify who is committing crimes, how they are committing them, where they are committing them, when they are committing them and the reasons for committing such crimes. This can then be used to disrupt criminals from their activity through arrests or other methods such as making items more difficult to steal (c.f. Scott, 2000).

Intelligence has had a long history, for instance, Sun Tzu wrote extensively on the importance of intelligence in relation to military objectives circa 490 BC (Grieve, 2008). More contemporary paper-based police systems developed in the last century included information such as crime reports from witnesses and informants, surveillance reports, files on habitual criminals, information on criminals' modus operandi (MO) and even media reports. More recently, the capacity of intelligence organizations has increased dramatically with the use of modern computer systems. These systems include access to DNA databases, police records of criminal convictions and sophisticated mapping software. One downside of these systems is that they create new challenges with regard to making sense of massive volumes of information.

Two following examples illustrate how modern intelligence can work successfully in solving crime or disrupting criminal enterprises and recovering proceeds of crime. The first concerns a UK case involving the rape and murder of three young women in South Wales in 1973.

DNA found on their bodies could not be directly linked with anyone on the DNA database. Ten thousand vehicles matched the description of one seen near one of the crime scenes including one owned by a man called Joe Kappen. A relative of Kappen was subsequently included in the DNA database for an unrelated offence, and his DNA was identified as being similar, but not identical to that found on the victims. This intelligence led the police to target Kappen for investigation. In the meantime Kappen had died. However, his body was exhumed nearly 30 years after the murders, and his DNA was found to match semen found on the murdered women (British Broadcasting Corporation, 2001). The second, more recent, example concerns a man in London originally stopped by local police officers while driving a car. A stash of Euros, which were unusually in large denominations, was found wrapped in envelopes in his glove box and in his pockets. This intelligence was used to mount an investigation that recovered over €380,000, a large quantity of drugs and revealed the man was part of a larger organized criminal network involved in the supply of drugs in London (Metropolitan Police Authority, 2010).

The UK National Intelligence Model

A growing number of police agencies are developing practices which are termed 'intelligence models' to define, describe and demonstrate that they are intelligence-led. A detailed and robust model was developed by the National Criminal Intelligence Service in Britain. The NIM and intelligence-led policing are now formally embodied in British policing (Newburn, 2007). This is arguably the pre-eminent intelligence model internationally, and it has been adopted in a number of countries, including some Australian police departments and in New Zealand (Jones & Newburn, 2007; Newburn, 2002).

The NIM supports a whole of agency approach to implementing the practice of being intelligence-led, by providing a business model within which to operate (ACPO, 2005). This means that intelligence is drawn into the business practice of policing, and the model clearly describes how there is a need for skilled intelligence people who use computer systems that do away with multiple platforms that limit information sharing and that have adequate integration with analytical software (systems assets) (Maguire & John, 2004). The model also provides a framework for assigning and managing policing priorities through Tasking and Coordination Group (T&CG) meetings that are detailed to the level of who should attend, what intelligence products need to be generated and intelligence requirements that are sought to inform police decision making.

The NIM also usefully describes four types of intelligence products that suit different levels of operations within a police organization and which suit associated meeting cycles:

1. 'Strategic assessments' provide decision-makers with an accurate picture of law enforcement business, including an understanding of what is happening on the ground, the nature and extent of problems, influential trends and main threats to the business. With this product, business planners have the necessary information to make accurate judgements which are necessary to set priorities and commit resources.
2. 'Tactical assessments' inform operational day-to-day planning. Tactical assessments identify emerging patterns and trends that could require further analysis or action. They also track progress in investigations or preventative initiatives and provide the opportunity for immediate changes to be made in resourcing or tactical options.
3. 'Target profiles' are person-specific and contain sufficient detail to initiate a target operation or to support an ongoing operation against an individual or networked group.
4. 'Problem profiles' identify established and emerging issues (e.g. crime series, hotspots) and present potential preventive options to assist decision-makers in choosing a course of action.

The four intelligence products are intended to take account of policing priorities and are designed to enable efficient tasking and co-ordination to occur.

A further value of the NIM is that it moves intelligence-led policing from a support role to a key facilitator of decision making. It does this by placing the intelligence product as a central document for consideration when coordinating resources and tasking individuals or units. Intelligence products provide well-researched options for action that can be evaluated and decided upon by the tasking and coordination group or chair of the meeting. The NIM is a means of organizing knowledge and information to facilitate the best possible decisions (John & Maguire, 2004).

Additionally, the NIM facilitates collaborative work within and between agencies. Each agency has the same or similar meeting cycles and products or sanitized versions of products that can be shared between agencies. A strategic example is where multiple agencies work together in a policing capacity. Decision-makers from all involved agencies can attend the strategic T&CG: bringing their respective strategic assessments and indicating their evaluated priorities, and joint decisions can be made or well-researched rationales for proposed action can be offered. There is also the possibility of having aggregated products to concretize decisions and action priorities. Having a standard model shared by organizations reduces barriers to effectiveness by producing standardized processes and language. These decisions can then be fed into the tactical-level meetings for each agency.

Lastly, the NIM works well with existing approaches to policing, such as problem-oriented policing. Kirby and McPherson (2004) explore how problem-oriented approaches fit in the NIM. For example, the problem-oriented policing 'Scan, Analyse, Respond, Assess' (SARA) process links directly into the intelligence products and T&CG of the NIM. They comment that both approaches endorse enforcement and prevention techniques. As mentioned in the point above, both foster working in partnership with agencies who use an NIM structure as well as with agencies who could partner police on discreet interventions or projects.

Challenges for police intelligence

The following sub-sections discuss some of the difficulties encountered when implementing model systems that require organizational integration of intelligence and propose strategies for advancing implementation.

Moving from theory to practice

In their study of intelligence, Harfield and Harfield (2008) explore definitions generated by academics, practitioners and official sources. They note that there is a general consensus about the process of intelligence as the collection of raw information, which is then processed and used to inform decision making. However, academic analyses frequently fail to address the question of how theoretical definitions can be fully implemented into the existing working structures of policing. This is the most important aspect of the NIM, as it articulates intelligence-led policing in an actionable format.

While there are many documented reasons why the NIM is an appropriate model for implementing intelligence-led policing, the term '*intelligence* model' is problematic. The model is a policing business model rather than a model exclusively for intelligence practitioners. Flood and Gaspar (2009), two of the architects of the NIM, acknowledge this as a risk area, and they note it was likely that the model would not be well accepted coming from one intelligence agency (National Criminal Intelligence Service) and that it was unlikely to alter the existing policing paradigm. Certainly this was the case with the initial implementation of the model in the United Kingdom, and appears to also be the case in New Zealand and Australia (see below). It would be more accurate to call it a policing business model, and for policing agencies to engage with it as such, recognizing that the model provides specific direction to intelligence practitioners and decision-makers who use intelligence product. It may be most useful to think about the model in two parts: Firstly, as a business model that would underpin an organizational philosophy and, secondly, that it would standardize the handling of information and intelligence which would professionalize the work of intelligence-led policing. This identifies two pervasive challenges for the integration of an intelligence model such as the NIM into policing: the need for an organizational philosophy that holds intelligence as essential and the valuing of intelligence units and the staff who occupy intelligence roles.

Philosophy

Becoming an intelligence-led organization involves more than accepting an NIM-styled model. NIM is only one part of intelligence-led policing (Harfield & Harfield, 2008). Being an intelligence-led organization involves having an organization for which intelligence is part of the way they think, is inherent in their values and is a way of doing business (e.g. incorporating NIM into the elemental structure of the organization). In short, this means an organization needs to have senior managers and executives who understand what intelligence-led means in the organization and who can demonstrate intelligence success. That is to say, they can show examples where intelligence has been critical. Having an approach integrated into the philosophy of the organization is demonstrated when there is executive commitment to education on the topic, defining it, teaching it and celebrating its success.

A good example of success in integrating intelligence into the philosophy of policing comes from Lancashire Constabulary in the United Kingdom. Lancashire Constabulary initially implemented problem-oriented policing with a high level of vigour in the 1990s (e.g. Lancashire Constabulary, 1998). Staff were trained in POP, refresher courses were offered, senior managers (including superintendents) provided coaching to staff and the executive were committed. When executives asked how crime problems were tackled in performance meetings, they expected a response that included the use of the POP-based SARA system (see above) (see Leigh, Read, & Tilley, 1996). The organizational philosophy of Lancashire Constabulary included POP as their problem-solving strategy, and this provided a foundation for the later introduction of the NIM process (Maguire & John, 2006).

However, examples can be found where intelligence is not well articulated within organizations, and where senior and executive commitment can at best be said to be lip service (Harfield & Harfield, 2008). For example, theoretically the NIM should ensure that intelligence about crime problems is used to guide investigation and prevention strategies. However, performance indicators can be used to reverse this process, so that crime statistics and the outcomes of investigations are retrospectively represented as the results of an intelligence process. Intelligence products and intelligence staff are used to explain decisions after the fact (Cope, 2004; Harfield & Harfield, 2008).

Leadership in intelligence-led policing is therefore highly problematic. Successful implementation and sustainability of intelligence-led policing obviously requires strong leadership commitment (Ratcliffe, 2008). Leaders determine the goals and direction of an organization; and if intelligence is not part of their philosophy, then it is not part of the organizational philosophy. Leaders begin by setting the organizational direction and future vision, aligning people to the vision by creating coalitions that understand the vision and are committed to it, and then the leaders need to motivate and inspire their people towards that vision despite obstacles to change (Kotter, 1990). But, in relation to the situation in the United Kingdom, Harfield and Harfield have observed that, 'A decade into the era of intelligence-led policing, there is enough evidence in various forms to suggest that the police service has not yet fully embraced the intelligence profession' (Harfield & Harfield, 2008). Organizational leaders and senior police need to be able to demonstrate consistency between their words and their deeds (Kotter, 1990). For intelligence to be successful there needs to be support for an intelligence-led approach. This links directly to the beliefs policing organizations have about intelligence units and the people who staff them.

Intelligence units

Hawley (2008) describes 'tribal rivalries' between intelligence and other areas in policing. The origins of these tribal rivalries involve misunderstandings about what intelligence is, competition for resources and fear of the unknown. In many organizations where intelligence staff are viewed as playing a supporting role – not part of 'real' police work – there is a tendency to view intelligence staff as less than competent. Intelligence units, like most work units, can have a mix of staff – some very competent, some lacking skills and some who are not at all suitable for the role. A number of reasons for this can be proposed, some of which include insufficiently trained staff to fill positions, inadequate remuneration to attract the right staff, poor working conditions and a lack of management support. Trained intelligence officers and analysts (most commonly civilian police staff) who work well in intelligence units are sought by agencies other than police and are frequently attracted by higher salaries and career structures. Macvean and Harfield (2008) explain how analysts are often lost because their roles tend to be 'demand-driven' and not 'purpose-driven', resulting in less than optimal working conditions for analysts. For sworn officers, working in intelligence may mean losing a shift allowance, although some sworn officers are attracted to intelligence because of the more typically desk-based nine-to-five role.

If negative factors are present, a 'vicious' intelligence cycle can occur – as opposed to a more desirable 'virtuous' cycle. Figure 5.1 depicts how a vicious cycle becomes mutually reinforcing at each stage of the intelligence process. If the wrong staff or poorly trained staff are in the intelligence unit, they will produce weak intelligence products at best because they lack the knowledge, experience or initiative required to collect, analyse and disseminate a product that is accurate and includes actionable recommendations. The bottom box in Figure 5.1 delineates how decision-makers' needs are not met when they receive a product that is not well synthesized and has no key findings or recommendations on

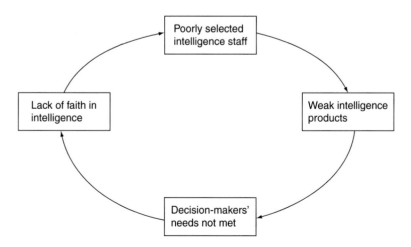

Figure 5.1   The 'vicious' intelligence cycle

which they can confidently base a decision. This in turn means there is a generalized lack of faith in intelligence. Intelligence moves down the list of units that can positively contribute to policing outcomes. There is then reduced scope for positive recruitment. When vacancies arise, it may seem appropriate to fill them with applicants willing to work in the unit regardless of their skills. If positions are not filled by applicants, they can easily be filled with staff in need of 'development'. This is a difficult cycle to break and indicates the importance of a business model, such as the NIM, which requires skilled and trained individuals (referred to in the NIM as 'people assets') in order to provide the best possible service and intelligence products. Figure 5.2 depicts the ideal 'virtuous' cycle where capable and well-trained staff produce high-quality intelligence which meets decision-makers' needs and there is a generalized faith in intelligence.

If the intelligence collective is not trusted or valued, the whole unit can become marginalized. In this scenario the intelligence unit operates outside operational policing – an effect which contradicts the business model of the NIM. This silo effect is often identified as a major contributing factor to intelligence failures: more specifically organizational failures to predict, pre-empt or resolve policing problems (Ratcliffe, 2003). To truly integrate intelligence-led policing into the business model of policing, there needs to be a recognition that well-trained, specially selected, intelligence officers and analysts are required, as stipulated in the minimum requirements of the NIM (ACPO, 2005).

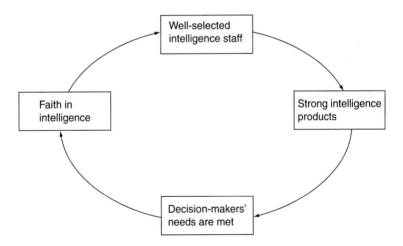

Figure 5.2 The 'virtuous' intelligence cycle

Promoting the professionalism of intelligence work involves more than the use of the NIM business process however. It involves recognizing the skills required to collect and analyse intelligence and then investing in those skills (Evans & Kebbell, in press). 'Products are only outputs. Capacity and capability create outcomes, which is the purpose of intelligence' (Harfield & Harfield, 2008, p. 96). Many policing agencies, for example in Australia, New Zealand and the United Kingdom, have accepted intelligence-led policing in principle, and many of those have put intelligence-led policing or a NIM business process in place. However, few (with a notable exception being New Zealand Police) have sought to tackle the problem of having the 'wrong' people in intelligence units and so policy without resources becomes mere rhetorical (Harfield & Harfield, 2008).

Workplace culture

Policing organizations in the majority have as their mission to reduce crime, solve crime and increase public safety while decreasing fear of crime, as can be read in police strategic plans and mission statements. This is done primarily by addressing calls for service, attending the scenes of crimes, putting investigative power to work to resolve offences, and by being visible to the community. All of this good work is for the most part done on a case-by-case basis, which forms the basis of one aspect of the organizational culture for the police: responsive or reactive policing. 'Organisational culture refers to the belief and assumptions which organisational members share about their organisation' – its mission or purpose, its core values, major strategies and so on (Schein, 1985). Put simply, culture reflects what makes the organization tick, why it exists and what it is endeavouring to accomplish (see, for example, Kalliath, Brough, O'Driscoll, Mamimala, & Siu, 2009).

Traditional policing is characterized by a pervasive concern with individual crimes, and single-event needs (Ratcliffe, 2008). Policing in the main operates on a case-by-case basis and this is deeply embedded in policing culture. This remains so even in the face of increases in the volume, complexity and transnational nature of offending, and despite a clear articulation by policing agencies that they are moving to a more proactive model of policing. Case-by-case policing has been functional when the volume of crimes was sufficiently low that each call for service could be responded to in a timely fashion and every crime scene could be visited and investigated individually. Working in this fashion and viewing each offence or call for service as an individual entity, whilst sometimes essential, contributed to the perpetuation of the existing structures in policing. In this context, Hawley (2008) considers overcoming what is ostensibly an intelligence-operations divide as the single most important issue facing the effectiveness of current law enforcement.

The importance of intelligence-led policing is that it typically moves policing from considering the individual crime to considering the impact and threats of multiple crimes. This does not mean that the individual offence is no longer important, but it does mean that examining more than one offence at a time is productive. Newburn (2007) points out that traditional 'reactive' response styles continue to restrict proactive policing models, like the NIM. An intelligence-led philosophy is proactive in that it seeks to predict criminal activity and pre-empt its development. It provides actionable options on which managers can base their decisions at all levels of policing.

Intelligence by its nature is proactive and works towards the possibility of hypothesized future events and ways of disrupting or preventing future crime(s). But its impacts are inherently difficult to measure and thus difficult to hold up as performance measures. Two issues interplay here. Firstly, as mentioned, there is an existing culture of reactivity that has served policing well in the past, and hence there is a reluctance to accept the more proactive stance of intelligence-led policing. Secondly, policing has become performance-oriented to enhance management of resources, and measuring the reactive element of policing is substantially easier than measuring success gained through proactive policing endeavours. A compounding factor is there is often little time made for evaluation, and police agencies frequently lack the skills for effective evaluation and fear that what they have done may not withstand scrutiny. Evans and Kebbell (in press) contend that evidence of effectiveness is still to be demonstrated and there is a paucity of research in this domain.

A case study in Australian intelligence

This section summarizes a recent study of the characteristics of intelligence systems in Australia (Evans, Walsh, Herrington, & Kebbell, 2010). Interviews were conducted with Directors of Intelligence from 19 government agencies in Australia, including police, Federal bodies (e.g. national bodies with a crime reduction role) and regulatory agencies (e.g. anti-corruption agencies). Questions were asked about organizational structure, the role and function of intelligence, staff employed in intelligence and what each agency considered to be important issues in the future of intelligence. The findings illustrate how substantial progress has been made at the level of official acceptance of NIM-style principles, but also how significant problems remain in the areas of full implementation and demonstration of impacts.

Policy and practice

All interviewees were asked which intelligence products their agencies' intelligence section produced, with reference to the four categories described earlier. Seventy-four per cent produced strategic assessments, 89 per cent produced tactical assessments, 84 per cent produced target profiles and 79 per cent produced problem profiles. The Directors of Intelligence were then asked if their agency had a definition for intelligence and if their agency had an explicit intelligence-led approach to its activities. Almost a third (63.2%) of respondents said their agency had no definition of intelligence. Similarly, approximately one-third could not show an explicit intelligence-led approach that would demonstrate to employees what 'intelligence-led' means, how it operates within a policing environment, what the expectations of general members are and what should be expected of those working in intelligence.

Directors of Intelligence were also asked to comment on how their agency used intelligence to achieve a number of activities: to drive all agency activity, to support investigations, to inform decision making, to monitor the development of known threats and to monitor the development of unknown threats. They were asked to describe how this use of intelligence was designed to work in theory and then to explain how it eventuated in practice. The majority of Directors claimed that intelligence drove activity in theory but less so in practice. The greatest alignment between what agencies said in theory and what happened in practice occurred when intelligence was required to support investigations and to monitor known threats. The weakest alignment between theory and practice was when intelligence was used for driving activity, decision making or monitoring unknown threats.

Investment in intelligence section

Sixteen of the nineteen Directors were able to provide staffing details for the intelligence section. It is apparent that there was a large range in the number of intelligence staff employed by the different agencies with the lowest number being five intelligence employees and the highest being 475 intelligence employees, with a mean number of 109.3 people employed in the intelligence area. To establish a relational measure of the number of employees employed in intelligence, the participants were asked what proportion of their staff were employed in this area. Here the range was less and ranged from less than 1 per cent to 35 per cent of the organization, with a mean of 6.8 per cent of employees being employed in intelligence function.

To gain an understanding of how intelligence staff were viewed by others, the Directors were asked the extent to which intelligence staff were supported by the organization, regarded as professional by non-intelligence staff and regarded as competent by non-intelligence staff. The findings indicated that 53 per cent of the 19 Directors thought that their organization supported intelligence staff 'quite a lot' or 'very much'. Directors thought, on average, that intelligence staff were regarded as 'professional to some extent' (47%). The Directors had more varied opinions on whether or not intelligence staff were regarded as competent. Five said 'not very much', six said 'to some extent' and five said 'quite a lot'.

Critique

One should, of course, be cautious about bias in self-reporting by senior managers. However, some of the less positive findings suggest the Directors of Intelligence interviewed for this project were honest about intelligence policies and practices in their organizations. The findings confirm those of an earlier study by Ratcliffe (2003), which reported that the rhetoric of intelligence-led policing has spread to every State and Territory in Australia. The present study also found that many agencies have products that are in line with the intelligence products nominated in the ideal UK NIM. A number of the Australian agencies, specifically police agencies, have adopted part or all on the UK NIM with modifications specific to their jurisdiction. In this study, the most accessible indicator of the implementation of the UK NIM was the intelligence product output. The fact that Australian products appeared to be in line with the UK NIM suggests there has been a successful integration of the NIM into Australian intelligence practice. However, it was not clear how well-embedded the model is in relation to tasking and coordination, systems assets and knowledge assets. Additionally, few Australian agencies have definitions of intelligence or an explicit intelligence-led model that impacts on the whole of the agency. This lack of definition implies an absence of investment by the most senior management and executive of the agency – perhaps because of a lack of philosophical buy-in. This is further supported by the clear discrepancy between what Directors say the organization's theoretical position is on intelligence and what is reported to happen in practice.

Furthermore, these interviews uncovered some contradictions. According to the UK NIM, intelligence products should feed into the decision-making process, but it appears from this research that intelligence products are not routinely used to guide decision making or further intelligence requirements. Ninety five per cent of Directors thought that intelligence fed into decision making. They also thought that the product was being targeted to the appropriate client who was the decision-maker. And the respondents reported that the clients were either satisfied or very satisfied with the intelligence products. However, there could still be a discrepancy between what these agencies do in theory, and what happens in practice in relation to *using* intelligence products for decision making. Future research could be targeted at uncovering some of the reasons for this, although a number of reasons could be postulated. These possible reasons include the following:

- The product didn't fully meet clients' needs (a poor method of seeking feedback is being used or the reason clients didn't respond to the satisfaction section was because they weren't satisfied).
- The product was not fit for purpose and therefore didn't assist with decision making.
- The product was discounted because intelligence wasn't understood within the organization (e.g. you are not expected to use it; it is what they do 'over there' in intelligence and isn't directly relevant to you).
- The wrong people were getting the product or the right people were getting the product but didn't know what to do with it (e.g. lack of training or knowledge).

Examining the reasons for the discrepancy between theory and practice in criminal intelligence is critical. As Innes, Fielding and Cope (2005) point out, perhaps in somewhat extreme terms, 'The product of intelligence work are objectifications whose status is dependent upon how they are understood and reacted to in police organisations rather than any quality intrinsically inherent in them' (p. 54).

Conclusion

There can be little debate over the view that modern policing should be 'intelligence-led'. However, available evidence suggests that best-practice models – such as the UK NIM – have been adopted more at the level of rhetoric and policy than in the structure and everyday practices of police organizations. Australian intelligence agencies, including police, are a case in point. While it is apparent in the Australian context that there is high compliance to the generation of intelligence product, the product appears to not be routinely used for its designed purpose of assisting decision making. It has been argued that some of the reasons for this stem from a lack of organizational acceptance and philosophy of intelligence and the pervasive 'reactive' culture of police work. Effective use of intelligence products can be further stymied because the intelligence community and law enforcement agencies have not developed a tradition of evaluation to demonstrate the success and utility of intelligence. To ensure effective intelligence, a vicious cycle of marginalization and failure must not be allowed to take hold. A virtuous cycle of intelligence must include an organization-wide commitment, integration into decision-making processes and evidence of success in the police mission to reduce and solve crime.

Acknowledgements

We would like to thank Tim Prenzler, Eleanor Groat and Lauren Vogel for their helpful comments on this chapter.

References

ACPO. (2005). *Guidance on the National Intelligence Model*. Wyboston, UK: National Centre of Policing Excellence.

British Broadcasting Corporation. (2001). *Dead murders suspect is named*. Retrieved from http://news.bbc.co.uk/2/hi/uk_news/wales/1719984.stm.

Cope, N. (2004). Integrating volume crime analysis into policing. *The British Journal of Criminology, 44*, 188–203.

Evans, J. M., & Kebbell, M. R. (in press). The effective analyst: A study of what makes an effective crime and intelligence analyst. *Policing and Society*.

Evans, J. M., Walsh, P., Herrington, V., & Kebbell, M. R. (2010). *Where the heck are we? Intelligence in Australia*. Brisbane: Australian Research Council Centre of Excellence in Policing and Security, Griffith University.

Flood, B., & Gaspar, R. (2009). Strategic aspects of the UK National Intelligence Model. In J. H. Ratcliffe (Ed.), *Strategic thinking in criminal intelligence*. Sydney: Federation Press.

Grieve, J. (2008). Lawfully audacious: A reflective journey. In C. Harfield, A. MacVean, P. Grieve, & D. Phillips (Eds.), *The handbook of intelligent policing* (pp. 13–24). Oxford: Oxford University Press.

Harfield, C., & Harfield, K. (2008). *Intelligence: Investigation, community and partnership*. Oxford: Oxford University Press.

Hawley, M. (2008). Consilience, crime control and community safety. In C. Harfield, A. MacVean, P. Grieve, & D. Phillips (Eds.), *The handbook of intelligent policing* (pp. 211–227). Oxford: Oxford University Press.

Innes, M., Fielding, N., & Cope, N. (2005). The appliance of science? The theory and practice of crime intelligence analysis. *The British Journal of Criminology, 45*, 39–57.

John, T., & Maguire, M. (2004). The National Intelligence Model: Early implementation experience in three police force areas. *Paper No. 50, Working Paper Series, School of Social Sciences.* Cardiff: Cardiff University.

Jones, T., & Newburn, T. (2007). *Policy transfer and criminal justice.* Maidenhead: Open University Press.

Kalliath, T., Brough, P., O'Driscoll, M., Manimala, M., & Siu, O. L. (2009). *Organisational behaviour: An organisational psychology perspective.* Melbourne: McGraw-Hill.

Kirby, S., & McPherson, I. (2004). Integrating the National Intelligence Model with a 'problem solving' approach. *Community Safety Journal, 3*, 36–46.

Kotter, J. P. (1990). *What leaders really do.* Boston: Harvard Business School Press.

Lancashire Constabulary. (1998). *Operation exodus.* Lancaster: Lancashire Constabulary.

Leigh, A., Read, T., & Tilley, N. (1996). Problem-oriented policing: Brit Pop. *Police Research Group: Crime Detection and Prevention Series, Paper 75.* London: Home Office.

MacVean, A., & Harfield, C. (2008). Science or sophistry: Issues in managing analysts and their products. In C. Harfield, A. MacVean, P. Grieve, & D. Phillips (Eds.), *The handbook of intelligent policing* (pp. 93–104). Oxford: Oxford University Press.

Maguire, M., & John, T. (2006). Intelligence-led policing, managerialism and community engagement: Competing priorities and the role of the National Intelligence Model in the UK. *Policing and Society, 16*, 67–85.

Metropolitan Police Authority. (2010). *Specialist crime directorate: December quarterly report.* London: Metropolitan Police Authority.

Newburn, T. (2002). Atlantic crossings: 'Policy transfer' and crime control in the USA and Britain. *Punishment and society, 4*, 165–194.

Newburn, T. (2007). The future of policing in Britain. In A. Henry & D. Smith (Eds.), *Transformations of policing* (pp. 225–248). Aldershot: Ashgate.

Ratcliffe, J. H. (2003). Intelligence-led policing. *Trends and Issues in Crime and Criminal Justice, 248*, 6.

Ratcliffe, J. H. (2008). *Intelligence-led policing.* Cullompton: Willan Publishing.

Schein, E. H. (1985). *Organizational culture and leadership.* San Francisco, CA: Jossey-Bass.

Scott, M. S. (2000). *Problem-orientated policing: Reflections of the first 20 years.* Washington D.C.: U.S. Department of Justice, Office of Community-Oriented Policing Services.

6

The Effectiveness of Traffic Policing in Reducing Traffic Crashes

Lyndel Bates, David Soole and Barry Watson

Many governments throughout the world rely heavily on traffic law enforcement programmes to modify driver behaviour and enhance road safety. There are two related functions of traffic law enforcement, apprehension and deterrence, and these are achieved through three processes: (1) the establishment of traffic laws, (2) the policing of those laws and (3) the application of penalties and sanctions to offenders. Traffic policing programmes can vary by visibility (overt or covert) and deployment methods (scheduled and non-scheduled), while sanctions can serve to constrain, deter or reform offending behaviour. This chapter will review the effectiveness of traffic law enforcement strategies from the perspective of a range of high-risk, illegal driving behaviours, including drink/drug driving, speeding, seat belt use and red-light running. Additionally, this chapter discusses how traffic police are increasingly using technology to enforce traffic laws and thus reduce crashes.

The chapter concludes that effective traffic policing involves a range of both overt and covert operations and includes a mix of automatic and more traditional manual enforcement methods. It is important to increase both the perceived and actual risk of detection by ensuring that traffic law enforcement operations are sufficiently intensive, unpredictable in nature and conducted as widely as possible across the road network. A key means of maintaining the unpredictability of operations is through the random deployment of enforcement and/or the random checking of drivers. The impact of traffic enforcement is also heightened when it is supported by public education campaigns. In the future, technological improvements will allow the use of more innovative enforcement strategies. Finally, further research is needed to continue the development of traffic policing approaches and address emerging road safety issues.

Traffic crashes and road trauma

Trauma resulting from traffic crashes is a significant global concern with more than a million people killed, and an additional 50 million seriously injured, on roads throughout the world each year (Peden et al., 2004; Richter, Berman, Friedman, & Ben-David, 2006). Consequently, road trauma is associated with substantial economic and social costs, with traffic crashes estimated to cost nations throughout the world approximately $518 billion per annum. Road crashes have enormous social and economic impacts on individuals, families, communities and nations with many injured individuals still having a functional disability 6–12 months after a road crash (Peden et al., 2008). Family and friends of victims can experience adverse social, physical and psychological outcomes, such as poverty, depression and suicide in both the short- and long-term (Sharma, 2008). For instance, when children are injured in road crashes, adults may have to leave their jobs leading to poverty.

Table 6.1 describes the impact of traffic-related deaths in selected countries throughout the world. While the table is far from exhaustive,

Table 6.1 Road traffic fatalities in International Road Traffic and Accident Database (IRTAD) member countries

Country	Fatalities[a]					
	2009 data			Average annual change (%)		
	Total number	Per 100,000 population	Per billion vehicle kms	2000–2009[b]	1990–1999	1980–1989
Argentina[c]	7,364	18.4	N/A	N/A	N/A	N/A
Australia	1,492	6.8	6.7	−2.2	−3.0	−1.7
Austria	633	7.6	9.0[d]	−4.7	−4.0	−2.7
Belgium[e]	955	8.9[d]	9.6[d]	−4.7	−3.8	−2.0
Cambodia[c]	1,717	12.6	N/A	17.5	N/A	N/A
Canada[e]	2,130	6.3	6.3	−3.4	−3.1	−2.8
Czech Republic	901	8.6	19.4[d]	−5.4	1.3	−1.7
Denmark	303	5.5	8.2[d]	−5.4	−2.3	−0.3
Finland	279	5.2	5.2	−3.8	−4.4	3.2
France	4,273	6.8	7.8	−6.9	−0.7	−1.8
Germany	4,152	5.1	6.0	−6.4	−3.8	−4.7

Table 6.1 (Continued)

Country	Total number	Per 100,000 population	Per billion vehicle kms	2000– 2009[b]	1990– 1999	1980– 1989
		2009 data			Average annual change (%)	
Greece	1,456	12.9	N/A	−3.7	0.4	−3.7
Hungary	82	8.2	N/A	−4.1	−6.7	3.2
Iceland	17	5.3	5.5	−6.8	−1.5	1.3
Ireland	238	5.3	4.9	−6.0	−1.6	−2.2
Israel	314	4.2	6.4	−4.0	1.2	1.0
Italy	4,237	7.1	N/A	−5.5	−0.7	−3.1
Japan	5,772	4.5	7.7	−6.3	−3.7	2.7
Korea	5,838	12.0	20.0	−6.0	−3.0	9.4
Lithunia[c]	370	11.0	N/A	−5.9	−3.2	2.9
Luxembourg	48	9.7	N/A	−5.0	−2.2	−4.1
Malaysia[c]	6,745	23.8	17.7	1.2	N/A	N/A
Netherlands	644	3.9	5.6	−5.6	−2.6	−3.4
New Zealand	384	8.9	9.6	−2.0	−3.9	2.7
Norway	212	4.4	5.4	−5.1	−1.0	0.6
Poland	4,572	12.0	9.1[d]	−3.5	−0.9	1.3
Portugal	840	7.9	N/A	−8.5	−3.1	0.5
Slovenia	171	8.4	9.6	−6.5	−4.7	−0.1
Spain	2,714	5.9	N/A	−8.0	−4.9	4.1
Sweden	358	3.9	4.4	−5.4	−3.1	0.7
Switzerland	349	4.5	5.7	−5.7	−5.0	−3.3
United Kingdom	2,337	3.8	4.6	−4.6	−4.5	−1.2
United States	33,808	11.1	7.1	−2.4	−0.7	−1.3

Note: [a]Police-recorded fatalities. Death within 30 days. Lithuania: death within 7 days for 1990.
[b]2004–2009 for Argentina.
[c]Accession countries. Data are under review.
[d]Provisional data for 2008.
[e]Provisional data for 2009.
Source: OECD (2011) from original source *IRTAD*, see www.irtad.net.

the differential impact of road trauma in developing (e.g. Malaysia, Cambodia) and developed countries (e.g. United Kingdom, European nations, Australia) is evident. Indeed, the contribution of traffic crashes to mortality and morbidity has been cited as a particularly pertinent issue in developing countries, which are experiencing rapid motorization (Naci, Chisholm, & Baker, 2009).

Causes of traffic crashes

Human factors, such as driver error, are a leading contributing factor in traffic crashes, with estimates suggesting road user error is a contributing factor in up to 90 per cent of traffic crashes (Peden et al., 2004). Moreover, a number of high-risk behaviours have found to be associated with an increased risk of crash involvement and increased severity of crash consequences including driving while impaired by alcohol and/or drugs, speeding, fatigue and monotony, inattention and failing to wear a restraint (Peden et al., 2004; Petridou & Moustaki, 2000). The specific contribution of a number of these behaviours to the overall incidence and prevalence of traffic crashes is explained in the following section, 'The need to enforce: The incidence and prevalence of high-risk driving behaviours'.

Recidivist offenders are particularly problematic from a road safety perspective. Research has shown that repeat offenders are typically less likely to be deterred by enforcement operations and sanctions, largely as a function of experiences of punishment avoidance (Stafford & Warr, 1993). Moreover, consistent evidence has highlighted the association between recidivism and increased traffic crash involvement (Masten & Peck, 2004), identifying the need for targeted interventions and appropriate penalties for recalcitrant offenders.

The need to enforce: The incidence and prevalence of high-risk driving behaviours

The decision to enforce particular driving behaviours is largely a function of the degree to which they contribute to the risk and severity of traffic crashes. In motorized countries throughout the world, numerous behaviours are consistently evidenced as key contributing factors in the prevalence of traffic crashes, including drink and drug driving (Griggs et al., 2007); speeding (Aarts & van Schagen, 2006); red-light running (Retting, Ulmer, & Williams, 1999); and failure to use a seat belt (Cummings, Wells, & Rivara, 2003).

While the prevalence of drink-driving has declined in recent decades, in many highly motorized countries these reductions appear to be plateauing (Sweedler, 2007). In a comprehensive review with international scope, it was reported that as many as 52 per cent of fatalities and up to 80 per cent of injury crashes are alcohol-related, while best estimates suggest between 5 per cent and 25 per cent of crash-involved drivers are impaired by illicit drugs (Kelly, Darke, & Ross, 2004). Overall, drink-driving has been reported as more common than drug driving, however the prevalence of drug driving is reported to be increasing relative to drink-driving (Davey & Freeman, 2007). Common illicit substances detected among crash-involved drivers include cannabis, benzodiazepines, cocaine, amphetamines and opioids, with polydrug use and prescription drugs also problematic (Kelly et al., 2004).

The positive and exponential relationship between vehicle speed and crash risk and severity is well established (Aarts & van Schagen, 2006; Kloeden, McLean, & Glonek, 2002; Lynam & Hummel, 2002). Indeed, even small changes in vehicles' speed have been found to produce significant increases in crash risk and severity (Kloeden et al., 2002). Nonetheless, there arguably remains a general 'social acceptance' of speeding behaviour in many countries, particularly at relatively low levels over the speed limit (Fleiter, Lennon, & Watson, 2010; Forward, 2006), evidenced in part by the continuing pervasive and relatively ubiquitous nature of the behaviour.

Violations at signalized intersections are also a common contributing factor to crashes, particularly side or angle collisions (Erke, 2009). In the United States, it has been reported that 44 per cent of fatalities at signalized intersections are attributable to red-light offences (Smith, McFadden, & Passetti, 2000) and that such crashes account for approximately 3 per cent of all fatalities and a substantial number of injuries (Retting et al., 1999; Wahl et al., 2010). Violation of red signals have been described as relatively common among drivers, with punishment avoidance also common and perceptions regarding the risk of detection perceived to be low (Porter & Berry, 2001; Retting et al., 1999).

Unlike the aforementioned behaviours, the non-use of safety restraints in motor vehicles does not increase the likelihood of traffic crash involvement, but rather increases the severity of injuries sustained (e.g. likelihood of fatality) in the event of a crash. Indeed, prior research estimates that the use of seat belts by vehicle occupants can reduce the likelihood of injury by up to 65 per cent (Cummings, McKnight, Rivara, & Grossman, 2002; Cummings et al., 2003). The prevalence of non-use of vehicle restraints depends heavily on the legislation enacted in a particular country, including laws associated with the fitting and use of seat belts, as well as the enforcement of such laws. Not surprisingly then, rates of non-use are typically greatest in low-income countries without such legislation, however non-compliance also continues to be a substantial road safety issue in highly motorized countries with appropriate legislation or levels of enforcement (Peden et al., 2004).

The role and purpose of traffic law enforcement in road safety

Traditionally, the reduction of traffic crashes has been achieved through three predominate approaches: engineering, education and enforcement (OECD, 1997; Zaal, 1994). Engineering approaches range from environmental countermeasures (e.g. road design) to the revision of speed limits and improvement of road surfaces. Education approaches range from public awareness through media campaigns to offender rehabilitation programmes. However, arguably the most relied-upon approach to reducing the prevalence and incidence of traffic crashes is law enforcement initiatives aimed at modifying driver behaviour.

From the perspective of law enforcement, deterrence of traffic offences and the apprehension of offenders are typically achieved through three integrated processes: (1) the establishment of traffic legislation, (2) the policing of those laws and (3) the application of penalties and sanctions to offenders (Watson et al., 1996). Legislation dictates specific prohibited road user actions and identifies subsequent penalties and sanctions for offending. These laws are enforced primarily through police operations with penalties generally associated with detected offences. Sanctions may include monetary fines, loss of demerit points, licence suspension or disqualification, rehabilitation and education programmes and even incarceration. Penalty structures are typically graduated so that more serious or recidivist offending is associated with more severe sanctions.

Enforcement of any kind serves a number of integrated functions, including retribution, incapacitation, rehabilitation and deterrence (Ross, 1982). While it has been argued that the fundamental principle of traffic enforcement programmes should be to deter proscribed driving behaviours, rather than identifying the most effective way to apprehend and punish offending drivers (Zaal, 1994), the importance of apprehension and punishment cannot be ignored. Indeed, in the interest of public safety, recidivist offenders who show a persistent disregard for traffic laws – even in the face of countermeasures developed to deter such behaviours – need to be apprehended and discouraged from further offending, whether that is achieved through deterrence, rehabilitation or incapacitation.

Jurisdictions differ in respect to who is tasked with the responsibility of traffic policing. While in many countries, traffic enforcement is subsumed under the umbrella of general policing agencies, other countries have designated specific traffic policing departments whose primary responsibility is the policing of traffic laws.

The theoretical underpinnings of traffic law enforcement

Numerous theories have been utilized to provide an explanatory framework for understanding road user behaviours, and in particular driver reactions to enforcement activities. These have included psychological models, such as 'social learning theory' (Bandura, 1977), the 'theory of reasoned action' (Fishbein & Ajzen, 1975) and the 'theory of planned behaviour' (Ajzen, 1985). However, arguably the most common theoretical approach utilized in traffic psychology is 'deterrence theory', a criminological perspective that focuses on the effect of enforcement activities and legal sanctions on behaviour (Homel, 1988; Vingilis, 1990). Indeed, many enforcement programmes throughout the world have been developed on the theoretical principles of deterrence theory.

Deterrence theory proposes that the ability for enforcement practices to deter proscribed behaviours is a function of the perceived risk of detection, as well as the perceived certainty, severity and swiftness of punishment (Homel, 1988; Ross, 1982; Vingilis, 1990). Specifically, deterrence theory suggests that enforcement activities achieve optimal effectiveness when the driving public perceive that they are likely to be caught and punished, that punishment is severe and that it is administered in a timely fashion (Akers & Sellers, 2009; Homel, 1988; Ross, 1982). However, research has suggested that there may be a critical threshold at which point further increases in punishment severity produce diminished returns and may be counterproductive (Elliott, 2003; Legge & Park, 1994).

The classical approach to deterrence theory has more recently been expanded to include the concepts of 'punishment avoidance' and 'vicarious learning' (Stafford & Warr, 1993). Specifically, it is suggested that the absence of negative consequences (e.g. fine, loss of demerit points) associated with the commission of an offence can have a strong reinforcing influence on continued behaviour and that indirect experiences of punishment or punishment avoidance can also influence behaviour (Stafford & Warr, 1993).

Deterrence can be achieved via two processes: 'general deterrence' and 'specific deterrence' (Akers & Sellers, 2009; Homel, 1988; Ross, 1982). Through the process of general deterrence, the driving population is discouraged from committing traffic offences by increasing the perceived threat of apprehension and legal consequence. In contrast, specific deterrence is the process whereby actual offenders are deterred from reoffending due to experiencing the consequences of detection and punishment. General and specific deterrence, however, are not mutually exclusive and may more accurately reflect 'the same mechanism applied to different populations' (Elliott, 2003; p. 5).

The road safety literature has highlighted the positive relationship between deterrence theory constructs and a number of risky driving behaviours. These include drink-driving (Freeman & Watson, 2006; Piquero & Pogarsky, 2002), drug driving (Watling, Palk, Freeman, & Davey, 2010), speeding (Fleiter, 2010), unlicensed driving (Watson, 2004) and hooning behaviour (Leal, Watson, Armstrong, & King, 2009). Indeed, the traffic enforcement policies and practices of many jurisdictions around the world are formulated on the theoretical underpinnings of deterrence theory.

Evidence of the effectiveness of traffic law enforcement

Drink and drug driving

The most common countermeasure for deterring drink and drug driving involves the roadside testing of drivers using devices developed to measure the concentration of specific substances in the human body, most commonly through an examination of breath or saliva. Depending on the jurisdiction, such testing programmes are either conducted in a compulsory (e.g. random breath testing (RBT) programmes) or selective manner (e.g. selective breath testing (SBT) of only those drivers suspected to be substance impaired). In addition, random drug testing (RDT) is a relatively recent addition to the enforcement practices of a number of countries.

Such interventions can also be conducted in a mobile (e.g. as part of routine traffic patrol duties) or static (e.g. roadside checkpoint) manner. While neither approach is wholly deterrence or detection-oriented, the former are typically associated with higher detection rates and predominantly serve a specific deterrent function, while the latter, which are predominantly conducted in a highly overt fashion, typically serve more of a general deterrent function (Harrison, Newman, Baldock, & McLean, 2003).

Numerous evaluations conducted in various countries, including Australia, the United States and throughout Europe, have highlighted the effectiveness of RBT and SBT to reduce traffic crash rates. In a comprehensive review of both RBT and SBT, a reduction of up to 36 per cent in fatal crashes, up to 20 per cent in fatal and serious injury crashes, up to 22 per cent in overall crashes and a 24 per cent reduction in drivers with a BAC above .08 per cent, associated with RBT, was reported (Shults et al., 2001). Conversely, SBT was reported to be associated with a reduction of up to 26 per cent in fatal crashes, up to 23 per cent in fatal and serious injury crashes and up to 27 per cent in overall crashes. Similarly, Elvik (2001), in a meta-analysis of 39 studies, reported significant reductions of 9 per cent for fatal crashes, 7 per cent for injury crashes and 4 per cent for property damage crashes. Finally, in a review of 14 studies evaluating RBT only, Peek-Asa (1999) revealed that all studies reported reductions in alcohol-related crash fatalities and injuries, ranging from 8 per cent to 71 per cent.

There is considerably less evidence highlighting the effectiveness of RDT, particularly regarding its impact on drug-related crashes. While a number of studies have revealed evidence of reductions in offending (Verstraete & Raes, 2006), the majority of research has focused on the potential benefits of RDT by examining self-reported intentions to drive under the influence of illicit substances (Degenhardt, Dillon, Duff, & Ross, 2004; Jones, Donnelly, Swift, & Weatherburn, 2005; Terry & Wright, 2005) or consultations and interviews with police organizations (Mallick, Johnston, Goren, & Kennedy, 2007). Similarly, a number of studies have highlighted intentions to continue offending in instances where perceived risk of detection is low, penalties are perceived as not being severe and punishment avoidance is perceived to be common (Davey, Davey, & Orbst, 2005; Donald, Pointer, & Weekley, 2006; Watling et al., 2010).

Best practice principles for drink and drug driving enforcement

A number of reviews have identified best practice principles for the operation of random and compulsory testing countermeasures, operated using both mobile and static methods (Harrison et al., 2003; Wundersitz & Woolley, 2008). Indeed, there is general consensus among road safety practitioners of the effectiveness of compulsory testing procedures, compared with selective approaches (Watson, Fraine, & Mitchell, 1994; Wundersitz & Woolley, 2008; Zaal, 1994). While less literature is currently available outlining best practice for the detection of drug-impaired drivers, many of the principles outlined below, in relation to detecting and deterring drink-drivers, should be generalizable.

Arguably the most common feature of successful programmes is high, sustained levels of enforcement conducted with the aim of increasing the perceived risk of detection (Homel, 1988; Watson et al., 1994). As a result, there exists a critical need to identify the optimal mix of mobile and static, overt and covert, and targeted and random approaches, which will invariably differ by context (Harrison et al., 2003).

Static operations (e.g. RBT) operated in an overt manner – and augmented with concentrated and highly intensive activities conducted periodically – are regularly cited as the most effective approaches to achieving the goal of general deterrence (Harrison et al., 2003). Conversely, mobile operations conducted either overtly or covertly, are argued to be most effective for the detection of offenders during non-peak periods and as a means of detecting those offenders engaging in punishment avoidance strategies (Harrison et al., 2003).

In addition, a mix of targeted and randomized approaches is required, with each facilitating separate deterrent functions. While it has typically been argued that operations should predominantly target peak times and locations, the importance of random operations at non-peak times and locations has also been identified as essential to facilitating the unpredictability of enforcement efforts (Wundersitz & Woolley, 2008). The development of effective programmes can also be optimized by adopting intelligence-led enforcement strategies (Wundersitz & Woolley, 2008), although this should not result in enforcement operations that are predictable.

Finally, a number of evaluations have suggested additional effectiveness of countermeasures conducted in association with mass media and public education campaigns (Elder et al., 2004). Such optimized effects are likely a function of the increased public awareness of police activities and the additional general deterrent impact of such campaigns.

Speeding

As a consequence of the well-established relationship between vehicle speed and crash risk and severity, an increasing range of speed enforcement countermeasures, and in particular automated technologies, have experienced widespread global use as in recent decades. Such approaches include both fixed and mobile speed cameras, hand-held and moving mode (e.g. vehicle-attached) lasers and radars and routine traffic patrols. To date, the empirical literature evaluating police speed enforcement approaches has typically supported the hypothesis that such countermeasures produce reductions in vehicles speeds and traffic crashes. While these findings must be considered in light of a number of methodological caveats, the consistently positive results reported across the literature are promising (Wilson, Willis, Hendrikz, Le Brocque, & Bellamy, 2010).

In a Cochrane Collaboration review of 35 studies, the effectiveness of speed enforcement detection devices on speed and crash outcomes was assessed (Wilson et al., 2010). The review revealed a number of road safety benefits for areas employing speed cameras and other automated speed-detection devices, compared to control areas. Specifically, average vehicle speeds were reduced by up to 15 per cent, with the proportion of speeding vehicles reduced by up to 65 per cent. Moreover, all studies with crash outcomes reported reductions in the vicinity of enforcement locations, with fatal and serious injury crashes reduced by up to 44 per cent, injury crashes by up to 50 per cent and overall crashes by up to 49 per cent. A diffusion of benefits across the entire road network was noted in a number of studies, as well long-term maintenance of outcome effects.

More recently, an innovative approach to speed enforcement involving point-to-point (P2P) camera systems has attracted considerable attention. The approach is most commonly used in the United Kingdom and Europe and has more recently been implemented in Australia. Early evidence regarding the effectiveness of the approach suggests high rates of compliance, reductions in vehicle speeds, reductions in crashes and numerous other ancillary benefits associated with the technology, such as improved traffic congestion and reduced traffic noise and emissions (Soole & Watson, 2009). While promising, these findings must be considered in light of the methodological quality of the literature.

Best practice principles for speed enforcement

A number of reviews have highlighted recommendations for best practice in speed enforcement. Similar to impaired driving, the fundamental need to increase the actual and perceived risk of detection has been highlighted. In addition, there is a critical requirement to identify the optimal mix of automated and manually operated approaches, as well as overt and covert operations. Overall, the available evidence suggests that automated methods tend to have more localized, site-specific effects on speeding behaviour and crash rates (Champness, Sheehan, & Folkman, 2005), while manually operated approaches are typically associated with more network-wide impacts on behaviour (Shinar & Stiebel, 1986). In addition, there is growing evidence to suggest optimal effects associated with a mixture of both overt and covert approaches (Elliott & Broughton, 2005).

Automated and overt operations are more likely to serve a general deterrent function given their ability to detect a higher proportion of offending drivers; however deployment must be carefully conducted to ensure activities are not predictable and thus prone to punishment avoidance strategies (Harrison, 2001). Conversely, manually operated approaches are more likely to have a greater specific deterrent effect, particularly when conducted covertly, as a function of the focus on more serious offences, direct interaction with authorities, greater perceived preparedness to apprehend and swifter application of punishments (Tay, 2009).

In addition, the random deployment of speed enforcement activities across the road network has been argued to increase the efficacy of operations (Elliott & Broughton, 2005; Leggett, 1997). Such an approach serves to increase the general deterrent impact of speed enforcement, by increasing the perceived uncertainty of enforcement locations and times. Moreover, evidence also suggests greater effectiveness of enforcement operations of greater intensity (Harrison, 2001); however the impact on road safety outcomes will eventually plateau as the level of enforcement intensity reaches a point of saturation (Oei, 1996).

Red-light running

The enforcement of red-light offences using traditional, manual methods can produce additional dangers both for drivers and police officers conducting the activities and is an extremely resource-intensive enterprise for limited net benefit (Aeron-Thomas & Hess, 2005). As a result, the majority of enforcement conducted at signalized intersections involves automated methods, specifically red-light cameras that have the capacity to operate at all times, irrespective of weather and traffic conditions.

Overall, evidence confirming the effectiveness of red-light cameras to reduce traffic crashes and red-light offences is inconclusive, reflecting a lack of rigorously designed and controlled studies (Retting, Ferguson, & Hakkert, 2003). Of particular concern is the claim that installation of red-light cameras, while reducing angle and side impact crashes, produce increases in rear-end collisions and spill-over effects to nearby intersection that may offset net benefits associated with the countermeasure (Retting et al., 2003). Furthermore, numerous methodological shortcomings of the available literature have been highlighted (Decina, Thomas, Svrinivasan, & Staplin, 2007). Such uncertainty regarding the effectiveness of red-light cameras has resulted in a less widespread implementation of such efforts, relative to other forms of automated enforcement.

More recently, a meta-analytic review of 21 studies found an increase in total crashes of 15 per cent, with rear-end crashes increased by approximately 40 per cent and right-angle crashes reduced by approximately 10 per cent (Erke, 2009). However, none of the findings reached statistical significance. More promising results were reported by less rigorous studies controlling for fewer extraneous factors, highlighting the need for controlled designs. For instance, an earlier meta-analysis conducted by Flannery and Macubbin (2002) identified only two studies meeting selection criteria, with results suggesting a significant reduction of approximately 26 per cent in right-angle and rear-end crashes at controlled intersections. However, less rigorous studies that were not included in the meta-analysis suggested before–after reductions in red-light offences between 15 per cent and 62 per cent.

At present it appears difficult to make conclusions regarding best practice in relation to enforcement of signalized intersections, due to the inconclusive evidence associated with automated enforcement such as red-light cameras. Given the inconclusive evidence regarding red-light cameras, the use of engineering approaches, such as increased signal timing and providing dedicated turning phases and active warning signs (e.g. flashing lights warning of approaching intersection or red phase), deserve more investigation (Retting, Williams, & Greene, 1998).

Seat belt use

Unlike enforcement associated with the aforementioned behaviours, operations associated with the enforcement of seat belt legislation are not designed to reduce the likelihood of crash involvement. Instead, such countermeasures represent an attempt to reduce the severity of crashes, such that crashes that might have otherwise been fatal are survivable given the wearing of an appropriate restraint. Indeed, numerous studies have highlighted reductions in the number of fatal and serious injury crashes associated with the enforcement of vehicle restraint use (Cummings et al., 2003).

Perhaps more so than with aforementioned offences, the enforcement of seat belt use is fundamentally affected by the specific legislation enacted in a jurisdiction. At the broadest level legislation must first mandate the fixture of appropriate restraints. In addition, the legislation must also mandate that such restraints be worn by vehicle occupants.

Two forms of seat belt legislation exist, which significantly impact upon the degree to which such laws can be monitored (Dinh-Zarr et al., 2001). One the one hand primary legislation allows police officers to intercept a driver exclusively on the basis of a seat belt infringement. On the other hand, secondary legislation requires officers to have some other manner of business for stopping a driver before such seat belt laws can be enforced.

There is a general consensus among road safety practitioners favouring primary legislation for optimal enforcement of seat belt laws and improved public safety outcomes, even when controlling for baseline use rates (Shults, Nichols, Dinh-Zarr, Sleet, & Elder, 2004).

Indeed, in a systematic review of 33 evaluations of seat belt enforcement programmes, strong evidence for the effectiveness of primary restraint laws to reduce fatal and injury crashes, relative to secondary laws, was revealed (Dinh-Zarr et al., 2001). Specifically, fatal crashes were reduced by between 2 per cent to 18 per cent, while results for non-fatal injury crashes ranged from a 15 per cent reduction to an 11 per cent increase. Overall however, total crashes were reduced in the range of 3–20 per cent. In addition, increases in observed seat belt use 20–36 per cent were reported. Finally, enhanced enforcement programmes for seat belt laws were also reported to be effective in reducing traffic crashes and increasing compliance.

However, seat belt infringements are by their very nature inconspicuous and difficult to overtly detect, creating barriers to effective enforcement (Hunter, Stewart, Stutts, & Marchetti, 1993). As a result, enforcement typically involves mobile operations, such as routine traffic patrols in police vehicles, particularly on motorcycles. Nonetheless, the opportunity to conduct checks for seat belt compliance in association with other automatically detected offences, such as speeding and red-light offences, has also been identified as a method that would increase the perceived risk of detection without placing a substantial additional burden on police resources (Zaal, 1994).

Conclusions

An examination of the prevalence of traffic crashes attributable to high-risk driving behaviours demonstrates the need for continued focus on enforcement of such behaviours and the development of innovative approaches to facilitate improved road safety. From the available research a number of characteristics of best practice for traffic policing are evident. Most notably, enforcement operations need to be tailored to the specific context and driving environment, such that a 'one-size-fits-all' approach is unlikely to be effective. Thus, a range of operations varying in visibility and automaticity are required, and differing approaches are likely to serve differing deterrent functions. To reduce the likelihood of punishment avoidance, enforcement activities need to be optimized through random scheduling of activities, in regards to time and location, which serves to increase the unpredictability of enforcement and foster general deterrence. Enforcement should also be intensive enough to increase the perceived and actual risk of detection, and media and public education campaigns can also aid in the achievement of this goal.

There is also the need for enforcement to adapt and address emerging issues. For example, the use of mobile phones and other forms of technology while driving, and the subsequent impacts on attention, have become an increasingly important road safety issue as society adapts to rapid technological advancement (Young, Regan, & Hammer, 2003). The use of mobile phones, whether hand-held or hands-free, has been evidenced to detract from driver attention (Collet, Guillot, & Petit, 2010) and increase the risk of crash involvement (Laberge-Nadeau et al., 2003). As a result, a number of countries throughout the world have introduced legislation prohibiting mobile phone use and have increased enforcement activities associated with the behaviour. While most have prohibited hand-held use of phones, others have also enacted legislation to prohibit use of hands-free use of phones and use of other technologies such as navigation systems.

Moreover, technological advances will also allow for innovative approaches to policing, such as the introduction of point-to-point speed enforcement, which involves a series of linked cameras installed at multiple locations along a section of road enabling the calculation of average vehicle speed using Automatic Number Plate Recognition and GPS technologies. In addition, future innovative approaches may facilitate automated policing of other risky driving behaviours, such as tailgating. Finally, while much of the evidence evaluating traffic policing is positive and suggests effectiveness in the reduction of offence rates and traffic crashes, such evidence must be considered in light of common methodological limitations that plague social research. Indeed, the need for more scientifically rigorous research to better understand the precise impact of various enforcement operations, and allow for greater application and generalization of results, remains a priority.

References

Aarts, L., & van Schagen, I. (2006). Driving speed and the risk of road crashes: A review. *Accident Analysis & Prevention, 38*(2), 215–224.

Aeron-Thomas, A. S., & Hess, S. (2005). Red-light cameras for the prevention of road traffic crashes. *The Cochrane Database of Systematic Reviews, 18*(2), CD003862.

Ajzen, I. (1985). From intentions to actions: A theory of planned behavior. In J. Kuhl & J. Beckmann (Eds.), *Action control: From cognition to behavior*. New York: Springer-Verlag.

Akers, R. L., & Sellers, C. S. (2009). *Criminological theories: Introduction, evaluation, and application*. New York, Oxford University Press.

Bandura, A. (1977). *Social learning theory*. New York: General Learning Press.

Champness, P., Sheehan, M., & Folkman, L. M. (2005). *Time and distance halo effects of an overtly deployed mobile speed camera*. Paper presented at the Australasian Road Safety Research, Policing and Education Conference, Wellington, New Zealand.

Collet, C., Guillot, A., & Petit, C. (2010). Phoning while driving I: A review of epidemiological, psychological, behavioural and physiological studies. *Ergonomics, 53*(5), 589–601.

Cummings, P., McKnight, B., Rivara, F. P., & Grossman, D. C. (2002). Association of driver air bags with driver fatality: A matched cohort study. *British Medical Journal, 324*, 1119–1122.

Cummings, P., Wells, J. D., & Rivara, F. P. (2003). Estimating seat belt effectiveness using matched-pair cohort methods. *Accident Analysis & Prevention, 35*(1), 143–149.

Davey, J. D., Davey, T. M., & Obst, P. L. (2005). Drug and drink driving by university students: An exploration of the influence of attitudes. *Traffic Injury Prevention, 6*(1), 44–52.

Davey, J. D., & Freeman, J. E. (2007). *Screening for drugs in oral fluid: Illicit drug use and drug driving in a sample of Queensland motorists*. Paper presented at the International Conference on Alcohol Drugs and Traffic Safety, Seattle, USA.

Decina, L. E., Thomas, L., Srinivasan, R., & Staplin, L. (2007). *Automated enforcement: A compendium of worldwide evaluations of results*. Washington DC: National Highway Traffic Safety Administration.

Degenhardt, L., Dillon, P., Duff, C., & Ross, J. (2004). *Driving and clubbing in Victoria: A study of drug use and risk among nightclub attendees* (NDARC Technical Report No. 209). Sydney: National Drug and Alcohol Research Centre, University of New South Wales.

Dinh-Zarr, T. B., Sleet, D. A., Shults, R. A., Zaza, S., Elder, R. W., Nichols, J. L., et al. (2001). Reviews of evidence regarding interventions to increase the use of safety belts. *American Journal of Preventative Medicine, 21*(4 Suppl.), 48–65.

Donald, A., Pointer, S., & Weekley, J. (2006). *Risk perception and drug driving among illicit drug users in Adelaide*. Adelaide: Drug & Alcohol Services South Australia, Australian Institute of Health and Welfare.

Elder, R. W., Shults, R. A., Sleet, D. A., Nichols, J. L., Thompson, R. S., & Rajab, W. (2004). Effectiveness of mass media campaigns for reducing drinking and driving and alcohol-involved crashes: A systematic review. *American Journal of Preventive Medicine, 27*(1), 57–65.

Elliott, B. (2003). *Deterrence theory revisited.* Paper presented at the Australasian Road Safety Research, Policing and Education Conference, Sydney.

Elliott, M., & Broughton, J. (2005). *How methods and levels of policing affect road casualty rates* (TRL Report TRL637). London: TRL.

Elvik, R. (2001). *Cost-benefit analysis of police enforcement,* Working Paper 1, ESCAPE Project. Helsinki: Technical Research Centre of Finland (VTT).

Erke, A. (2009). Red light for red-light cameras? A meta-analysis of the effects of red-light cameras on crashes. *Accident Analysis & Prevention, 41*(5), 897–905.

Fishbein, M., & Ajzen, I. (1975). *Belief, attitude, intention, and behavior: An introduction to theory and research.* Reading, MA: Addison-Wesley.

Flannery, A., & Macubbin, R. (2002). *Using meta-analysis techniques to assess the safety effect of red light running camera.* TRB 2003 Annual Meeting. Washington, D.C.: Transportation Research Board.

Fleiter, J. (2010). *Examining psychosocial influences on speeding in Australian and Chinese contexts: A social learning approach.* Brisbane: Queensland University of Technology.

Fleiter, J., Lennon, A., & Watson, B. (2010). How do other people influence your driving speed? Exploring the 'who' and the 'how' of social influences on speeding from a qualitative perspective. *Transportation Research Part F: Traffic Psychology and Behaviour, 13*, 49–62.

Forward, S. E. (2006). The intention to commit driving violations – A qualitative study. *Transportation Research Part F: Traffic Psychology and Behaviour, 9*(6), 412–426.

Freeman, J. E., & Watson, B. (2006). An application of Stafford and Warr's reconceptualization of deterrence to a group of recidivist drink drivers. *Accident Analysis & Prevention, 38*(3), 462–471.

Griggs, W., Caldicott, D., Pfeiffer, J., Edwards, N., Pearce, A., & Davey, M. (2007). *The impact of drugs on road crashes, assaults and other trauma – A prospective trauma toxicology study monograph series no. 20.* Payneham, South Australia: National Drug Law Enforcement Research Fund.

Harrison, W. (2001). *What works in speed enforcement?* Paper presented at the NRMA Insurance National Speed and Road Safety Conference, Adelaide, Australia.

Harrison, W., Newman, S., Baldock, M. R. J., & McLean, A. J. (2003). *Drink driving enforcement: Issues in developing best practice.* Sydney: Austroads.

Homel, R. (1988). *Policing and punishing the drinking driver: A study of general and specific deterrence.* New York: Springer-Verlag.

Hunter, W. W., Stewart, R., Stutts, J. C., & Marchetti, L. M. (1993). Nonsanction seat belt law enforcement: A modern tale of two cities. *Accident Analysis & Prevention, 25*(5), 511–520.

Jones, C., Donnelly, N., Swift, W., & Weatherburn, D. (2005). *Driving under the influence of Cannabis: The problem and potential countermeasures contemporary issues in crime and justice: Number 87.* Sydney: NSW Bureau of Crime Statistics and Research and the National Drug and Alcohol Research Centre.

Kelly, E., Darke, S., & Ross, J. (2004). A review of drug use and driving: Epidemiology, impairment, risk factors and risk perceptions. *Drug and Alcohol Review, 23*, 319–344.

Kloeden, C. N., McLean, A. J., & Glonek, G. (2002). *Reanalysis of travelling speed and the risk of crash involvement in Adelaide, South Australia.* Canberra: Department of Transport and Regional Services, Australian Transport Safety Bureau.

Laberge-Nadeau, C., Maag, U., Bellavance, F., Lapierre, S. D., Desjardins, D., Messier, S., et al. (2003). Wireless telephones and the risk of road crashes. *Accident, Analysis and Prevention, 35,* 649–660.

Leal, N., Watson, B., Armstrong, K., & King, M. (2009). 'There's no way in hell I would pull up': Deterrent and other effects of vehicle impoundment laws for hooning. Paper presented at the Australasian Road Safety Research, Policing and Education Conference and the 2009 Intelligence Speed Adaptation (ISA) Conference, Sydney.

Legge, J. S., & Park, J. (1994). Policies to reduce alcohol-impaired driving: Evaluating elements of deterrence. *Social Science Quarterly, 75*(3), 594–606.

Leggett, L. M. W. (1997). Using police enforcement to prevent road crashes: The randomised scheduled mangement system. In R. Homel (Ed.), *Policing for prevention: Reducing crime, public intoxication and injury* (Vol. *Crime prevention studies, Volume 7*). Monsey, New York: Criminal Justice Press.

Lynam, D., & Hummel, T. (2002). *The effect of speed on road deaths and injuries: Literature review.* Prepared for the Swedish National Road Administration, Sweden.

Mallick, J., Johnston, J., Goren, N., & Kennedy, V. (2007). *Drugs and driving in Australia: A survey of community attitudes, experience and understanding.* Melbourne: Australian Drug Foundation.

Masten, S. C., & Peck, R. C. (2004). Problem driver remediation: A meta-analysis of the driver improvement literature. *Journal of Safety Research, 35,* 403–425.

Naci, H., Chisholm, D., & Baker, T. D. (2009). Distribution of road traffic deaths by road user group: A global comparison. *Injury Prevention, 15,* 55–59.

OECD. (1997). *Road safety principles and models: Review of descriptive, predictive, risk and accident consequence models.* Paris: Organisation for Economic Co-operation and Development.

OECD. (2011). *IRTAD road safety annual report 2010.* Paris: OECD Publishing.

Oei, H. (1996). Automatic speed management in the Netherlands. *Transportation Research Record, 1560,* 57–64.

Peden, M., Oyegbite, K., Ozanne-Smith, J., Hyder, A., Branche, C., Rahman, A., et al. (2008). *World report on child injury prevention.* Geneva: World Health Organization.

Peden, M., Scurfield, R., Sleet, D., Mohan, D., Hyder, A. A., Jarawan, E., et al. (2004). *World report on road traffic injury prevention.* Geneva: World Health Organization.

Peek-Asa, C. (1999). The effect of random alcohol screening in reducing motor vehicle crash injuries. *American Journal of Preventive Medicine, 16*(1 Suppl.), 57–67.

Petridou, E., & Moustaki, M. (2000). Human factors in the causation of road traffic crashes. *European Journal of Epidemiology, 16,* 819–826.

Piquero, A. R., & Pogarsky, G. (2002). Beyond Stafford and Warr's reconceptualization of deterrence: Personal and vicarious experiences, impulsivity, and offending behaviours. *Journal of Research in Crime and Delinquency, 39*(2), 153–186.

Porter, B. E., & Berry, T. D. (2001). A nationwide survey of self-reported red light running: Measuring prevalence, predictors, and perceived consequences. *Accident Analysis & Prevention, 33*(6), 735–741.

Retting, R. A., Ferguson, S. A., & Hakkert, A. S. (2003). Effects of red light cameras on violations and crashes: A review of the international literature. *Traffic Injury Prevention, 4*(1), 17–23.

Retting, R. A., Ulmer, R. G., & Williams, A. F. (1999). Prevalence and characteristics of red light running crashes in the United States. *Accident Analysis & Prevention, 31*(6), 687–694.

Retting, R. A., Williams, A. F., & Greene, M. A. (1998). Red-light running and sensible countermeasures: Summary of research findings. *Transportation Research Record, 1640*, 23–26.

Richter, E. D., Berman, T., Friedman, L., & Ben-David, G. (2006). Speed, road injury and public health. *Annual Review of Public Health, 27*, 125–152.

Ross, H. L. (1982). *Deterring the drinking driver.* Lexington, MA: Lexington Books.

Sharma, B. (2008). Road traffic injuries: A major global public health crisis. *Public Health, 122*, 1399–1406.

Shinar, D., & Stiebel, J. (1986). The effectiveness of stationary versus moving police vehicles on compliance with the speed limit. *Human Factors, 28*(3), 365–371.

Shults, R. A., Elder, R. W., Sleet, D. A., Nichols, J. L., Alao, M. O., Carande-Kulis, V. G., et al. (2001). Reviews of evidence regarding interventions to reduce alcohol-impaired driving. *American Journal of Preventive Medicine, 21*, 66–88.

Shults, R. A., Nichols, J. L., Dinh-Zarr, T. B., Sleet, D. A., & Elder, R. W. (2004). Effectiveness of primary enforcement safety belt laws and enhanced enforcement of safety belt laws: A summary of the Guide to Community Preventive Services systematic reviews. *Journal of Safety Research, 35*(2), 189–196.

Smith, D. A., McFadden, J., & Passetti, K. A. (2000). Automated enforcement of red light running technology and programs: A review. *Transportation Research Record, 1723*, 29–37.

Soole, D. W., & Watson, B. (2009). *Point-to-point speed enforcement: A review of the literature.* Unpublished report prepared for Main Roads Queensland.

Stafford, M. C., & Warr, M. (1993). A reconceptualization of general and specific deterrence. *Journal of Research in Crime & Delinquency, 30*(2), 123–135.

Sweedler, B. M. (2007). *Worldwide trends in alcohol and drug impaired driving.* Paper presented at the Joint Meeting of The International Association of Forensic Toxicologists (TIAFT) and International Council on Alcohol, Drugs and Traffic Safety (ICADTS) and featuring the 8th Ignition Interlock Symposium (IIS).

Tay, R. (2009). The effectiveness of automated and manned traffic enforcement. *International Journal of Sustainable Transportation, 3*(3), 178–186.

Terry, P., & Wright, K. (2005). Self-reported driving behaviour and attitudes towards driving under the influence of cannabis among three different user groups in England. *Addictive Behaviors, 30*(3), 619–626.

Verstraete, A., & Raes, E. (2006). *Rosita-2 project: Final report.* Gent, Belgium: Ghent University, Department of Clinical Biology.

Vingilis, E. R. (1990). A new look at Deterrence. In R. J. Wilson & R. E. Mann (Eds.), *Drinking and driving: Advances in research and prevention.* New York: Guilford Press.

Wahl, G. M., Islam, T., Gardner, B., Marr, A. B., Hunt, J. P., McSwain, N. E., et al. (2010). Red light cameras: Do they change driver behavior and reduce accidents? *Journal of Trauma-Injury Infection & Critical Care, 68*(3), 515–518.

Watling, C. N., Palk, G. P., Freeman, J. E., & Davey, J. D. (2010). Applying Stafford and Warr's reconceptualization of deterrence theory to drug driving: Can it predict those likely to offend? *Accident Analysis & Prevention, 42*(2), 452–458.

Watson, B. (2004). *How effective is deterrence theory in explaining driver behaviour: A case study of unlicensed driving.* Paper presented at the Australasian Road Safety Research, Policing and Education Conference, Perth, Western Australia.

Watson, B., Fresta, J., Whan, H., McDonald, J., Dray, R., Bauermann, C., et al. (1996). *Enhancing driver management in Queensland.* Brisbane: Land Transport & Safety Division, Queensland Transport.

Watson, B. C., Fraine, G., & Mitchell, L. (1994). *Enhancing the effectiveness of RBT in Queensland. Prevention of alcohol-related road crashes.* Paper presented at the Social and Legal Approaches Conference, Brisbane.

Wilson, C., Willis, C., Hendrikz, J. K., Le Brocque, R., & Bellamy, N. (2010). Speed cameras for the prevention of road traffic injuries and deaths. *Cochrane Database of Systematic Reviews, 11,* CD004607.

Wundersitz, L. N., & Woolley, J. E. (2008). *Best practice review of drink driving enforcement in South Australia.* Adelaide: Centre for Automotive Safety Research.

Young, K. L., Regan, M. A., & Hammer, M. (2003). *Driver distraction: A review of the literature* (Report No. 206). Clayton, Victoria: Monash University Accident Research Centre.

Zaal, D. (1994). *Traffic law enforcement: A review of the literature* (Report No. 53). Melbourne: MUARC.

7
Approaches to Improving Organizational Effectiveness: The Impact of Attraction, Selection and Leadership Practices in Policing

Jacqueline M. Drew

The performance of police has come under increasing scrutiny in the previous few decades. The expectations placed on police organizations and their employees, driven by the goals pursuing optimal effectiveness and efficiency, have shifted along with demands for significant programmatic, technological, administrative and strategic innovation (Braga & Weisburd, 2006; Moore, Sparrow, & Spelman, 1997). Analogous with changes in police practice, modern police organizations must embrace contemporary standards of organizational functioning, leadership and performance management. In essence, police organizations need to operate according to accountability and governance frameworks, similar to other complex organizations (Casey & Mitchell, 2007):

> The extent to which police executives and operational police officers create beneficial changes within their organizations to accommodate the evolving demands will not only determine the ultimate success and failure of policing as an institution, but will say a great deal about the quality and determination of police leadership. . . .
>
> (Henry, 2003, p. 151)

Organizational police performance is inextricably linked to those who work within and lead increasingly complex police organizations (Dobby, Anscombe, & Tuffin, 2004; Krimmel & Lindenmuth, 2001; Schafer, 2010a). Therefore, it is somewhat surprising that police leadership remains an understudied area (Schafer, 2010a).

This chapter presents a qualitative review and analysis of the police leadership literature, identifying a number of factors that underpin highly effective police organizations. A number of best practice principles are developed for the purpose of guiding police organizations in disentangling the complexity of leadership factors that influence performance and organizational outcomes. It is recommended that police organizations commit to increasing the educational standards of police officers and provide professional development opportunities that are relevant to fostering effective leaders. This involves establishing leadership programmes, employing curriculum designed to develop effective characteristics, particularly transformational leadership characteristics, and ensuring that officers at all ranks are encouraged to engage in leadership development programmes. Police organizations should commit to increasing the representation of female leaders which will support and strengthen the adoption of leadership styles and approaches that are associated with effective police leadership outcomes. Police organizations need to ensure that they employ a formal, standardized and transparent system of eligibility for promotion and embrace the requirement for educational qualifications for both entry-level recruits and those seeking leadership positions. Promotional systems need to include an assessment of the leadership characteristics and competencies required of officers moving to the next level/rank within the organization, going beyond the assessment of current knowledge and skills.

The role and impact of police leaders

History reveals the critical role that police leadership can play in both major crises and periods of positive growth. A classic and stark example of poor leadership is evidenced in the two-year inquiry into police misconduct within the Queensland Police Service in Australia. The recommendations of the *Commission of Inquiry into Possible Illegal Activities and Associated Misconduct* (hereafter referred to as the Fitzgerald Inquiry) resulted in significant and profound structural and operational changes to policing in Queensland. Of particular relevance were revelations that the systemic problems uncovered were supported, reinforced and encouraged by senior police leaders. In fact, the Fitzgerald Inquiry led to the subsequent jailing of the then Police Commissioner, Sir Terry Lewis (for a comprehensive discussion, see Lewis, Ransley, & Homel, 2010). Tony Fitzgerald QC who led the inquiry noted,

The Queensland Police Force is debilitated by misconduct, inefficiency, incompetence, and deficient leadership (p. 200).... Much of the focus of concern in this Inquiry and in this report has been upon the structural, organizational and cultural malaises of the Police Force. Existing causes of misconduct and other cultural aberrations must be eliminated and wrong-doers identified and excluded or neutralized. Barriers to reintroduction and expansion of misconduct must be erected. A new influential leadership must be established which is committed to excellent ethical performance and discipline.

(Fitzgerald, 1989, p. 307)

From an operational perspective, many have recognized that leaders are crucial in the successful adoption of new and innovative policing strategies (Crothers & Vinzant, 1996; Henry, 2003; Willis, Mastrofski, & Weisburd, 2007). Brown and Scott (2007) examined the factors that impacted on response implementation within the problem-oriented policing framework, concluding,

Indeed, it often seems that a strong leader can make a success of even the weakest of responses due to his or her diligence, persistence, and perseverance in the implementation process.

(p. 10)

Further, Chief John Welter, Police Chief of the Anaheim Police Department (formerly, Deputy Chief of the San Diego Police Department), reflected on the adoption of community policing initiatives, stating,

one of the biggest barriers to implementing COPPS [Community Oriented Policing and Problem Solving training program] has been the lack of informed, experienced leadership in COPPS at all organizational levels.

(cited in Prince, Hesser, & Halstead, n.d., p. 2)

Clear evidence of the role of leadership in police reform can be found by examining the introduction by the New York Police Department (NYPD) of the COMPSTAT system. This approach to performance management has subsequently been widely adopted by police organizations across the world. It has been argued that the style of leadership brought to the NYPD by then-Chief William Bratton was a key factor in implementation of COMPSTAT and the transformation of culture and organizational structure of the NYPD. The reforms were linked to the dramatic decreases in crime rates in New York City that occurred at that time (Henry, 2003). Bratton concluded,

> ... my command staff and I made major changes in the manage-ment style of the NYPD. Precinct commanders were granted far more latitude in initiating their own operations and running their own shops.... Backed by sweeping changes in many department proce-dures and by a policy of decentralising management to precinct level, these strategies have achieved by far the largest drops in New York City felony crime in a quarter century.
>
> (cited in Henry, 2003, p. v)

The design of the COMPSTAT system itself directly impacted on lead-ership and management. Bratton recognized the role that managers and leaders play in achieving police effectiveness, efficiency and out-comes. COMPSTAT meetings between senior executives and precinct commanders were used to

> identify which mid-level managers should be replaced or transferred and which managers should be promoted to positions with addi-tional responsibilities. Within the new administration's first year, more than two thirds of the department's seventy-six precinct com-manders were been replaced. The key strategy here was to match up particular positions with the commanders who had the requi-site skills, experience, expertise and personality to manage them proficiently.... Compstat meetings proved to be an essential tool in identifying individual managers' strengths and weaknesses...
>
> (Henry, 2003, p. 11)

Given the impact, both positive and negative, that police leaders can have on the organization and its performance, the overarching ques-tion is, 'what is the "best" leadership style for police leaders to adopt?' Further, what style of leadership is needed that embraces change and adaptation to contemporary policing demands and produces optimally effective and efficient organizations?

Police leadership styles

Many 'lists' of police leadership skills or competencies have been pro-posed, typically based on 'professional' judgement rather than sound empirical investigation (Dobby et al., 2004). The following review discusses effective leadership style as a function of outcome measures, particularly subordinate outcomes. Whilst it has been concluded that leadership impacts on the success of police strategies in areas such as crime rates, community satisfaction and crime prevention, empirical testing of these relationship has rarely been undertaken (Schafer, 2010a). Police organizations and policing scholars need to rise to the challenge of building a stronger empirical evidence base that guides and assists police organizations to effectively translate the theory of effective leadership into operational practice. Research validating the linkages between leadership attributes and styles and policing outputs remains an area that requires further research (Dobby et al., 2004; Schafer, 2010a).

Transformational leadership

The empirical work that has been conducted on police leadership has provided mounting support for a transformational leadership style. The concept of 'transformational' and 'transactional' leadership styles were first proposed by Burns (1978). Transformational leaders are described as leaders who motivate followers, are a role model, foster a shared vision, are innovative, provide a supportive environment for their subordinates and have a strong sense of internal ideals and values (Northouse, 2010). Transactional leaders are those leaders who reward subordinates for their effort in an exchange process, closely monitor subordinates' rule violations and institute corrective action using negative reinforcement (Northouse, 2010).

Singer and Singer's (1990) study of 60 New Zealand police officers found that officers' satisfaction with supervision was correlated with transformational leadership behaviours. Similarly, Murphy and Drodge (2004) in a rank-diversified, interview-based study of Royal Canadian Mounted Police ($N = 28$) found supervisors displaying a transformational leadership style were most valued by officers. Andreescu and Vito's (2010) study of ideal leadership behaviour involving US police and a large-scale study of police drawn from across the rank structure of a number of UK police organizations was also supportive of transformational leadership behaviours (Dobby et al., 2004).

Dobby et al.'s (2004) research on police leadership is particularly important as it is one of the few studies to empirically examine the nature of police leadership and its impact on performance-related outcomes. The researchers found that many of the leadership behaviours

Table 7.1 Transformational leadership dimensions and additional characteristics

---

Transformational leadership dimensions

1. Genuine concern for others' well-being and their development	2. Clarifies individual and team direction, priorities and purposes
3. Empowers, delegates, develops potential	4. Creates a supportive learning and self-development environment
5. Transparency, honesty, consistency	6. Manages change sensitively and skilfully
7. Integrity and openness to ideas and advice	8. Charismatic, in-touch
9. Accessible, approachable	10. Encourages questioning and critical and strategic thinking
11. Inspirational communicator, networker and achiever	12. Analytical and creative thinker
13. Unites through a joint vision	14. Decisive/risk-taking

Additional leadership characteristics

1. Professional competence   2. Strategic and tactical competence
3. Commitment to high-quality service outcomes involving good service to the community, having a positive public image and continuous improvement

---

Source: Adapted from Dobby et al. (2004).

that were most highly related to effective leadership were those characteristic of the transformational leadership style (see Table 7.1). The transformational leadership characteristic of genuine concern for others' well-being and development had the strongest impact on psychological outcomes, positively influencing subordinates' job commitment, self-confidence, job fulfilment, self-esteem, organizational commitment and drive to achieve beyond expectations (Dobby et al., 2004).

Three additional constructs were also found. These constructs largely reflected the importance placed by subordinates on their leaders being able to competently provide operational and ethical direction when required. Given the nature of policing, in particular the requirement of police to quickly react and respond accurately to emergency situations, these additional constructs were not surprising (Dobby et al., 2004).

Coupled with empirical support, calls for the practical adoption of a transformational police leadership style have been made by such bodies as the UK-based Police Leadership Development Board (PLDB) (Silvestri, 2007). Interestingly, former Police Chief William Bratton, touted by many as one of the great US police chiefs of recent times, defined his success using transformational leadership principles.

> I think of myself as a transformative leader. I see crises as opportunities. People expect that leaders will create change and be risk takers.... My leadership style is that you can't do it alone. You have to get the right people in place as quickly as possible. You inspire them and they inspire you. You allow them to take risks, to make mistakes, and then you reward their successes.
>
> (Bratton, 2008, para. 4)

Leadership and rank

Given support for the transformational leadership style, the focus of the discussion must turn to the prevalence of transformational leadership within policing and what barriers may impact on its adoption. The answers to these questions require consideration of the structure of contemporary police organizations.

The hierarchical structure of policing impacts on how leadership is organized. The police organization is characterized by layers of supervision, management and leadership. At the executive level, police leaders are expected to craft and share their vision for the police organization, providing a performance framework that seeks to achieve both short-term and longer-term strategic objectives (Andreescu & Vito, 2010; Baker, 2008). Those police who hold middle-management positions fulfil a liaison role between senior managers and direct supervisors, building teams, coaching, planning and rewarding performance (Baker, 2008; Casey & Mitchell, 2007; Coleman, 2002). At the lowest level of leadership are front-line supervisors, typically at the rank of sergeant (Baker, 2008). Supervisors at the front-line take on a more traditional management role which involves leading by example, directing and supervising tactical and operational strategies and directly managing day-to-day officer performance. While the decisions and plans developed and communicated by senior leaders influence the whole organization it is at the middle, and perhaps even more so, at the front-line levels of management that operational execution occurs (Baker, 2008; Heidingsfield, 2002).

From these descriptions it is apparent that the nature of effective leadership is likely to differ as a function of both context and rank (Schafer, 2010b). The way in which police leadership roles are currently described implies a leadership-management dichotomy. The description, particularly of front-line officers, emphasizes tasks that are aligned with a more transactional, directive or managerial style. The description of the role of senior leaders clearly infers a more transformational leadership style.

Whilst it cannot be definitively concluded, this may be one important reason why recent studies have found that police leaders predominantly employ transactional and autocratic leadership behaviours (Silvestri, 2007; Villiers, 2003). It is not proposed that transactional leadership, particularly at lower-level leadership is redundant, rather that the balance between transactional and transformational leadership behaviours needs to be considered and addressed. Research supports the need for front-line and middle-level managers to employ transactional or directive leadership behaviours in certain situations such as emergencies (Andreescu & Vito, 2010; Terry, 2009). However, the key issue is that for the majority of time, leaders are simply engaged in managing routine tasks and managing police personnel, and in these circumstances and regardless of leadership level or rank, subordinates prefer leaders who are transformational (Dobby et al., 2004). Therefore, the current articulation of layers of police leadership may encourage officers, particularly front-line officers, to rely too heavily on directive and transactional approaches.

Neyroud's (2010) review of police leadership and training in the United Kingdom concluded that 'great police leadership' involves choosing the right leadership style for the right situation. Police organizations need to embrace the notion that a single decision-maker, supervisor, manager or leader must embody knowledge and skills that allow that officer to simultaneously and seamlessly juggle the roles of management and leadership (Anderson et al., 2000).

The following discussion turns its attention to how police organizations can practically support the goal of maximally effective and efficient police leadership. The discussion takes into account the influence of the hierarchical structure of policing on the approach of police organizations to the recruitment, professional development and promotion of leaders. It is through this analysis that a number of best practice principles for police leadership are derived.

Recruitment and development of police leaders

Recruitment

Police recruitment has come a long way from the selection systems of old, which primarily relied on sex, height, weight and age restrictions. Most contemporary police organizations now accept that their recruitment systems must be rigorous, demand high educational standards and meet equity and diversity objectives (Drew & Prenzler, 2010). Failure to select quality applicants results in the inability of officers to effectively carry out strategic objectives of the organization at the coal face, translating senior police objectives into operational practice. Further, effective recruitment and selection systems are vital and have a substantial impact on quality of the pool of officers from which police leaders of the future are selected.

Education. Historically, recruitment processes used by police organizations have placed emphasis on the physical standards required for police entry (Baker, 2008). However, contemporary police organizations have begun to acknowledge the significance of a range of characteristics beyond physicality including intelligence, problem-solving, innovation, flexibility and emotional and social intelligence (Baker, 2008; White & Escobar, 2008; Youngs, 2010). The increasing complexities of the policing role and the policing organization itself demand different types of employees and leaders than those recruited in previous police eras (Jones, Moulton, & Reynolds, 2010; Pagon, 2003; White & Escobar, 2008). The emphasis has shifted to recruiting 'smarter' police rather than those who simply have the 'muscle power' (Silvestri, 2007), a move aligned with the push towards greater professionalization of policing (Jones et al., 2010). This change is underpinned by the belief that highly educated officers are likely to be more effective and are better prepared for the environment of policing. Studies have found that college-educated police are less authoritarian, are more flexible in their belief system, are more culturally and socially aware, more professional, more ethical, have a higher service standard and receive more positive job performance evaluations from their supervisors (see Roberg & Bonn, 2004, for a list of individual studies). These studies suggest that at recruitment, educational standards are useful in the identification of those officers who are likely to perform better on a range of performance indicators.

Recommendations regarding education, handed down in the Fitzgerald Inquiry in Queensland, were underpinned by the increasing complexities of policing duties with a view to decreasing the susceptibility of officers to unethical behaviour.

Police need more education to cope with their increasingly complex role. Officers should be encouraged to undertake higher education in colleges of advanced education and other tertiary institutions, along with students from other disciplines. There should be a long-term move to recruit more graduates.

(Fitzgerald, 1989, p. 365)

Consistent with research conducted with other professions, police studies are supportive of educational qualifications of police leaders. For example, Krimmel and Lindenmuth's (2001) research with police chiefs in Pennsylvania found that leaders who were more highly educated (i.e. held a college degree) received better performance and leadership ratings (35 leadership attributes and performance indicators were examined). Based on a review of the performance of the Lakewood Police Department in Denver, Youngs (2010) concluded that it is not essential for police chiefs to hold a degree in order to be successful. However, those who have tertiary-level education are 'more qualified' and achieve better outcomes. As discussed later in respect to promotional systems, some police organizations already work on the assumption that education leads to better police leaders, requiring those seeking promotion to complete an undergraduate or postgraduate degree and/or professional qualifications (Carter, Sapp, & Stephens, 1989; Neyroud, 2010; White & Escobar, 2008).

Diversity. Traditionally, policing has been a male-dominated occupation with the numbers of female police remaining small (Brown & Heidensohn, 2000; Raganella & White, 2004). The representation of female police has been slowly changing due to legislative mandates focused on gender and ethnic diversity, along with the advent of community policing and the push to make police organizations more reflective of the communities they serve (Raganella & White, 2004; Zhao, He, & Lovrich, 2006). Recent research in Australia and the United Kingdom found that approximately 25 per cent of police personnel were female (Home Office, 2010; Prenzler, Fleming, & King, 2010)). The numbers of female police in local US police departments is around 12 per cent, 6.5 per cent in state police departments and 20 per cent across federal law enforcement agencies (Langton, 2010).

Research generally supports an increase in the representation of female police. It is proposed that police organizations that achieve representative diversity compared to that of the communities they serve will enact more effective and fair policing services. It has been argued that a lack of diversity is linked to scandals involving excessive force and discrimination in the provision of policing services (Raganella & White, 2004; Skolnick & Fyfe, 1993). Research has also demonstrated that female police are more committed to a service-orientation consistent with modern police practice, are more likely to de-escalate violent encounters, attract less misconduct complaints (particularly, assault allegations), are no less capable in violent encounters compared to male officers and increasing women police numbers is negatively correlated with corruption (Balkin, 1988; Fleming & Lafferty, 2003; Fleming & McLaughlin, 2010).

Despite the relative success of many police departments in increasing female police numbers and positive findings regarding performance, female police remain disproportionately overrepresented in the lower ranks (Boni, 2005; Lonsway, Carrington, Aguirre, Wood, Moore, Harrington, Smeal, & Spillar, 2002). The numbers of females in leadership positions is clearly limited (Silvestri, 2007). In Australia, for example, movement up the ranks of female police is painstakingly slow and clearly needs to be improved (Prenzler et al., 2010). A more positive picture is reported for the United Kingdom with a doubling of females at the sergeant rank and above. However, female officers were found to be less likely than male police to be promoted from constable to sergeant (Home Office, 2010).

Given the small numbers of senior female police, the opportunity to study their leadership has been understandably limited (Osterlind & Haake, 2010; Silvestri, 2007). Despite this, a small number of interesting studies have been published. Interview research conducted with senior British policewomen found they tend to employ consultative and participatory approaches to leadership and display leadership skills aligned with transformational leadership characteristics (Silvestri, 2007). Similarly, Osterlind and Haake's (2010) small-scale study of female police leaders in Sweden identified transformational leadership behaviours as crucial to leadership effectiveness: specifically communication, participation and involvement, and creating and maintaining good relationships. Female leaders were able to appropriately employ transactional leadership behaviours such as giving orders and making tough decisions when required.

This research is consistent with research conducted in other professions. A meta-analytic review involving 45 studies of transformational, transactional and laissez-faire leadership styles found that female leaders were more likely to employ a transformational leadership style. Further, female leaders compared to male leaders produced better outcomes, defined as inspiring extra effort from subordinates, satisfaction of others with leadership style and effectiveness in leading. It was concluded that numerous benefits can be obtained by ensuring that female leaders have equitable access to leadership positions (Eagly, Hohannesen-Schmidt, & vanEngen, 2003).

Professional development

Miller, Watkins and Webb (2009) contend that police leadership development is crucial in order to meet the current and emerging challenges of policing and to achieve leadership excellence. Australia, the United Kingdom and United States all have professional development programmes specifically designed for police. In Australia, the Australian Institute of Police Management (AIPM) offers a range of leadership courses, including course offerings such as Police Executive Leadership, Developing Future Leaders and Intelligence Management Development Course and also, Graduate Certificate and Graduate Diploma programmes (see http://www.aipm.gov.au/index.html). These courses are typically complemented by leadership development programmes offered by each State-based police organization, who conducts in-house leadership development programmes for its officers. In the United States, the Federal Bureau of Investigation (FBI) offers programmes such as the Law Enforcement Executive Development Seminars (LEEDS) and sponsors regional programmes, modelled on the LEEDS curriculum, through 16 command colleges across the United States (Miller et al., 2009). In the United Kingdom, the National College of Police Leadership offers leadership programmes addressing the three key leadership domains of business, professional and executive policing skills (see http://www.npia.police.uk/en/5249.htm).

Research conducted by Krimmel and Lindenmuth (2001) supports the positive impact that professional development can have on leader effectiveness. Their study of Pennsylvanian police chiefs found that those police chiefs who had undergone some leadership 'grooming' (defined as participation in the FBI National Academy programme) rated themselves comparatively higher across 22 positive leadership indicators than those who did not attend the programme. Officers who had undertaken leadership development were more responsible, capable, intelligent, sophisticated, conscientious, motivating and had a clearer vision.

Although professional development programmes are available and can achieve positive outcomes, engagement statistics are difficult to obtain. It is unclear whether the current offerings are adequate for handling the numbers of police who are in leadership positions and whether professional development is equally accessible across ranks. The need to better understand the availability of leadership development is reinforced by mandate that 'every officer is a leader'. The International Association of Chiefs of Police (IACP) strongly promotes the need to develop leaders at all levels in the police organization.

> The unique and distinguishing feature of the IACP model is its focus on the systematic development of leaders at all levels of an organization – the concept of 'every officer a leader.' A police organization can no longer rely on a single leader or a small group of leaders. In order to develop leaders, law enforcement executives must first create a culture in their organizations that is supportive of dispersed leadership. This means establishing expectations that officers will take leadership actions at their level of responsibility, and it means providing training, support, and rewards to those who do.
>
> (IACP, 2011, para. 2)

Further, and perhaps even more fundamental, are questions surrounding the current curriculum of leadership development programmes. Drawing on the work of Haberfeld (2006), Schafer (2010b) reiterates the concern that management and leadership are often confused, resulting in the devotion of resources to management training or the mechanical aspects of supervision opposed to leadership theories and styles. It was suggested that police organizations need to consider the role descriptions of leadership positions to realign the behaviour of leaders to emphasize transformational leadership and employ transactional, management and directive leadership in contexts where it is required. Similarly, police organizations need to ensure that the curriculum of professional development programmes reinforces the types of leadership behaviours that have been identified as most effective.

Promotion systems

Promotion systems constitute a key issue that is inextricably linked to police leadership. However, more research examining the direct impact of promotion processes on identifying effective leaders is needed (Hughes, 2010). This is concerning as it appears that most police leaders attain their leadership position by promotion through the ranks.

Historically, in police organizations this approach has resulted in the implementation of a system of promotion by seniority not merit. As concluded by Tony Fitzgerald QC in the course of the Fitzgerald Inquiry in Queensland, Australia,

The effectiveness of an officer does not at present seem to be of primary importance in the promotional process. There is little indication of importance attached to the personal educational standard, particular experience and proven efficiency and skills of an appointee. There is no assessment of a particular appointee's aptitude for appointment to higher rank generally, let alone an appointee's aptitude to perform the specific tasks which appointment to the higher rank will require other than the internal courses mentioned above.

(Fitzgerald, 1989, p. 267)

While police organizations have largely moved towards a system of promotion-by-merit, the challenge now is on their ability to develop suitably qualified candidates from which to select supervisors, managers and senior leaders (Haberfeld, 2006; Schafer, 2010b; Rowe, 2006). One solution is for police organizations to embrace lateral transfers, which would involve the selection of leaders from across any police organization and not rely on promotion from within their ranks. However, police organizations appear to have largely resisted this solution.

An alternate approach involves tying promotion to educational attainment (Carter et al., 1989; Neyroud, 2010). A major review of the UK police training and development system by Neyroud (2010) strongly recommended a structured approach to developing police leaders through the completion of mandated professional qualifications (which includes a significant emphasis on management and leadership) for promotion to the ranks of Sergeant and Inspector. White and Escobar (2008) conclude that college education makes police applicants more attractive and, once employed within policing, promotion should be linked to the completion of an undergraduate or postgraduate degree.

Police organizations also struggle with implementing the most effective method for selecting the right officers for promotion. Traditional systems of police promotion based on seniority were plagued by allegations of cronyism, nepotism and corruption (Drew & Prenzler, 2010). Whilst today's police promotion systems based on merit inject more objectivity and fairness into promotion decisions, a criticism of many contemporary systems is that promotion is based on current functioning (Schafer, 2010a). Officers are typically promoted based on their proficiency and skill as an operational officer, using only vague or subjective assessments of leadership skills (Schafer, 2010b). Therefore, police promotion systems have been criticized for their myopic assessment of procedural knowledge and reliance on previous perfor-mance evaluations which focused on technical competence and task performance (Schafer, 2010a). Krimmel and Lindenmuth (2001) con-clude that police supervisors themselves can feel overwhelmed when promoted as they are unprepared for the leadership and management demands that are placed upon them in their new roles.

Police organizations need to use a variety of different assessment tools within their promotion systems, including examinations, competency-based assessment inclusive of role-play scenarios and assessment centres. Assessment tools that have traditionally been used for promotion overemphasize the assessment of technical or operational competen-cies and skills. Police organizations need to embrace the need to assess potential police leaders according to their current and potential managerial and leadership skills and behaviours (Neyroud, 2010).

Conclusions

Based on the review presented in this chapter, a number of best practice principles have been developed. They have been crafted as a guide to police organizations in meeting the challenge of improv-ing organizational outcomes and efficiency through effective leadership practices.

> **Principle 1.** Commitment to increasing educational standards of police officers is consistent with achieving more effective leader-ship outcomes. It is recommended that police organisation should require recruits to hold or have made significant progress towards the attainment of post-secondary qualifications.

> **Principle 2.** Commitment to increasing the representation of female police within police organisations will serve to support and strengthen the adoption of leadership styles and approaches that have been found to be associated with effective police leadership outcomes.

> **Principle 3.** Professional development opportunities are essential to developing effective leaders:

> a. the curriculum of leadership programs should be carefully con-sidered to ensure that they are developing the characteristics of effective leaders, not just managers;

b. development should be available and encouraged at all ranks given that each rank or leadership layer within the police organisation is likely to play a role in influencing effective police performance.

Principle 4. Promotional systems are crucial to establishing and maintaining effective leadership at all levels in the police organisation:

a. Police organisations should employ a formal, standardised and transparent system of eligibility for promotion. Educational and/or professional qualifications in the areas of management and leadership are relevant to this aim. It is recommended that police organisations should require police officers seeking promotion to leadership positions, particularly senior leadership positions, to have obtained the equivalent of a postgraduate, tertiary-level qualification in the area of leadership.
b. Promotional systems need to include an assessment of the leadership characteristics and competencies required of officers moving to the next level/rank within the organisation, going beyond assessment of current knowledge and skills.

These best practice principles make a contribution to current knowledge and serve as a starting point for further research. Police organizations and policing scholars need to broaden their research agenda in the area of leadership. Greater understanding needs to be gained of the predictive relationship between police leadership and performance outcomes and the factors that are able to support the enhancement of leadership effectiveness. Undoubtedly, police organizations are faced with a number of substantial challenges in the area of leadership. Research has suggested that transformational leadership behaviour provides a framework that is likely to improve leadership effectiveness across all leadership positions in the police hierarchy (Dobby et al., 2004). In turn, it has been argued that engagement of transformational leaders is likely to produce better performance outcomes (Schafer, 2010a). However, a major challenge for police organizations is how best to reconcile the introduction and translation of this style of leadership into an organizational system that encourages, or at least emphasizes (though its demography, structure, descriptions of leadership roles and developmental and promotional processes), a transactional, managerial and directive leadership approach.

References

Anderson, T. D., Gisborne, K. D., Hamilton, M., Holliday, P., LeDoux, J. C., Stephens, G., & Welter, J. (2000). *Every officer is a leader: Transforming leadership in police, justice, and public safety.* Boca Raton: St Lucie Press.

Andreescu, V., & Vito, G. F. (2010). An exploratory study on ideal leadership behaviour: The opinions of American police managers. *International Journal of Police Science and Management, 12*(4), 567–583.

Baker, T. (2008). *Effective police leadership: Moving beyond management* (2nd ed.). New York: Looseleaf Law Publications, Inc.

Balkin, J. (1988). Why policemen don't like policewomen. *Journal of Police Science and Administration, 16,* 29–38.

Boni, N. (2005) Barriers and facilitating factors for women in policing: Considerations for marking policing an employer of choice. *The Journal of Women and Policing, 17,* 13–18.

Braga, A. A., & Weisburd, D. (2006). Conclusion: Police innovation and the future of policing. In D. Weisburd & A. A. Braga (Eds.), *Police innovation: Contrasting perspectives.* Cambridge: Cambridge University Press.

Bratton, W. (2008). *Los Angeles Police Chief William Bratton delivers major address on police leadership at John Jay College.* Retrieved from http://www.jjay.cuny.edu/1894.php.

Brown, J., & Heidensohn, F. (2000). *Gender and policing: Comparative perspectives.* London: Mcmillan Press.

Brown, R., & Scott, M. S. (2007). *Implementing responses to problems.* Problem-Oriented Guides for Police Problem-Solving Tools Series, No. 7. Washington, D.C.: U.S. Department of Justice, National Institute of Justice.

Burns, J. M. (1978). *Leadership.* New York: Harper & Row.

Carter, D. L., Sapp, A. D., & Stephens, D. W. (1989). *The state of police education: Policy directions for the 21st century.* Washington: Police Executive Research Forum.

Casey, J., & Mitchell, M. (2007). Requirements of police managers and leaders from sergeant to commissioner. In M. Mitchell & J. Casey (Eds.), *Police leadership and management.* Sydney: The Federation Press.

Coleman, J. L. (2002). *Operational mid-level management for police* (3rd ed.). Illinois: Charles C Thomas Publisher Ltd.

Crothers, L., & Vinzant, J. (1996). Cops and community: Street-level leadership in community-based policing. *International Journal of Public Administration, 19*(7), 1167–1191.

Dobby, J., Anscombe, J., & Tuffin, R. (2004). *Police leadership: Expectations and impact.* Home Office Online Report 20/04. London: Research Development and Statistics Office.

Drew, J. M., & Prenzler, T. (2010). The evolution of human resource management in policing. In C. Lewis, J. Ransley, & R. Homel (Eds.), *The Fitzgerald legacy: Reforming public life in Australia and beyond.* Brisbane: Australian Academic Press.

Eagly, A. H., Hohannesen-Schmidt, M. C., & vanEngen, M. L. (2003). Transformational, transactional, and laissez-faire leadership styles: A meta-analysis comparing women and men. *Psychological Bulletin, 129*(4), 569–591.

Fitzgerald, G. E. (1989). *Report of the commission of inquiry into possible illegal activities and associated police misconduct.* Brisbane, Australia: Government Printer.

Fleming, J., & Lafferty, G. (2003). Equity confounded: Women in Australian police organisational. *Labour and Industry, 13*(3), 37–50.

Fleming, J., & McLaughlin, E. (2010). The public gets what the public wants? Interrogating the 'public confidence' agenda. *Policing: A Journal of Policy and Practice, 4*(3), 199–202.

Haberfeld, M. R. (2006). *Police leadership.* Upper Saddle River, NJ: Pearson Prentice Hall.

Heidingsfield, M. J. (2002). Bumps in the road to advancement: A chief's perspective. In W. G. Doerner & M. L. Dantzker (Eds.), *Contemporary police organization and management: Issues and trends.* Boston: Butterworth Heinemann.

Henry, V. E. (2003). *The COMPSTAT paradigm: Management accountability in policing, business and the public sector.* Flushing, NY: Looseleaf Law Publications, Inc.

Home Office. (2010). *Assessment of women in the police service.* Home Office, London: Research Development and Statistics Office.

Hughes, P. J. (2010). Increasing organizational leadership through the police promotional process. *Law Enforcement Bulletin, 79*(10). Retrieved from http://www.fbi.gov/stats-services/publications/law-enforcement-bulletin/October-2010/copy_of_confronting-science-and-market-positioning.

International Association of Chiefs of Police (IACP). (2011). Leadership model. Retrieved from: http://www.theiacp.org/LeadershipandTraining/LeadershipinPoliceOrganizations/LeadershipModel/tabid/161/Default.aspx.

Jones, M., Moulton, E., & Reynolds, J. K. (2010).The 'universality' of leadership and management in policing. In J. A. Schafer & S. Boyd (Eds.), *Advancing police leadership: Considerations, lessons learned, and preferable futures.* Vol. 6. Proceedings of the Futures Working Group, Quantico, Virginia.

Krimmel, J. T., & Lindenmuth, P. (2001). Police chief performance and leadership styles. *Police Quarterly, 4*(4), 469–483.

Langton, L. (2010). *Women in law enforcement, 1987–2007.* Crime Data Brief, Bureau of Justice Statistics. Washington: US Department of Justice.

Lewis, C., Ransley, J., & Homel, R. (2010). *The Fitzgerald legacy: Reforming public life in Australia and beyond.* Brisbane: Australian Academic Press.

Lonsway, K., Carrington, S., Aguirre, P., Wood, M., Moore, M., Harrington, P., Smeal, P. E., & Spillar, K. (2002). *Equality denied: The status of women in policing 2001.* California: National Center for Women and Policing.

Miller, H. A., Watkins, R. J., & Webb, D. (2009). The use of psychological testing to evaluate law enforcement leadership competencies and development. *Police Practice and Research, 10*(1), 49–60.

Moore, M., Sparrow, M., & Spelman, W. (1997). Innovation in policing: From production lines to job shops. In A. Altshuler & R. Behn (Eds.), *Innovations in American government: Challenges, opportunities, and dilemmas.* Washington: Brookings Institution Press.

Murphy, S. A., & Drodge, E. N. (2004). The four Is of police leadership: A case study heuristic. *International Journal of Police Science and Management, 6*(1), 1–15.

Neyroud, P. (2010). *Review of police leadership and training.* London: UK Home Secretary.

Northouse, P. G. (2010). *Leadership: Theory and practice* (5th ed.). Los Angles: Sage Publications.

Osterlind, M., & Haake, U. (2010). The leadership discourse amongst female police leaders in Sweden. *Advancing Women in Leadership Journal, 30*(16). Retrieved from http://advancingwomen.com/awl/awl_wordpress/.

Pagon, M. (2003). The need for a paradigm shift. In R. Adlam & P. Villiers (Eds.), *Leadership in the twenty-first century: Philosophy, doctrine and developments.* Winchester: Waterside Press.

Prenzler, T., Fleming, J., & King, A. (2010). Gender equity in Australian and New Zealand policing: A five-year review. *International Journal of Police Science and Management, 12*(4), 584–595.

Prince, H. T., Hesser, L., & Halstead, J. (n.d.). *Leadership in police organizations.* International Association of Police Chiefs, training bulletin 1. Retrieved http://www.theiacp.org/LinkClick.aspx?fileticket=Ci%2fCB1uNKPA%3d& tabid=164.

Raganella, A. J., & White, M. D. (2004). Race, gender, and motivation for becoming a police officer: Implications for building a representative police department. *Journal of Criminal Justice, 32,* 501–513.

Roberg, R., & Bonn, S. (2004). Higher education and policing: Where are we now? *Policing: An International Journal of Police Strategies and Management, 27*(4), 469–486.

Rowe, M. (2006). Following the leader: Front-line narratives on police leadership. *Policing: An International Journal of Police Strategies and Management, 29*(4), 757–767.

Schafer, J. A. (2010a). Effective leaders and leadership in policing: Traits, assessment, development, and expansion. *Policing: An International Journal of Police Strategies and Management, 33*(4), 644–663.

Schafer, J. A. (2010b).On leaders and leadership: The on-going dialogue within policing. In J. A. Schafer & S. Boyd (Eds.), *Advancing police leadership: Considerations, lessons learned, and preferable futures.* Vol. 6. Proceedings of the Futures Working Group, Quantico, Virginia.

Skolnick, J. H., & Fyfe, J. J. (1993). *Above the law.* New York: The Free Press.

Silvestri, M. (2007). 'Doing' police leadership: Enter the 'new smart macho'. *Policing & Society, 17*(1), 38–58.

Singer, M. S., & Singer, A. E. (1990). Situational contraints on transformational versus transactional leadership behaviour, subordinates' leadership preference and satisfaction. *The Journal of Social Psychology, 130*(3), 385–396.

Terry, D. D. (2009). Leadership perception in police organisations. *Law Enforcement Executive Forum, 9*(1), 11–20.

Villiers, P. (2003). Leadership by consent. In R. Adlam & P. Villiers (Eds.), *Leadership in the twenty-first century: Philosophy, doctrine and developments.* Winchester: Waterside Press.

White, M. D., & Escobar, G. (2008). Making good cops in the twenty-first century: Emerging issues for the effective recruitment, selection and training of police in the United States and abroad. *International Review of Law Computers and Technology, 22*(1–2), 119–134.

Willis, J. J., Mastrofski, S. D., & Weisburd, D. (2007). Making sense of COMPSTAT: A theory-based analysis of organizational change in three police departments. *Law & Society Review, 41*(1), 147–188.

Youngs, A. (2010). Leadership development creates chiefs of police. In J. A. Schafer & S. Boyd (Eds.), *Advancing police leadership: Considerations, lessons learned, and preferable futures*. Vol. 6. Proceedings of the Futures Working Group, Quantico, Virginia.

Zhao, J. S., He, N., & Lovrich, N. P. (2006). Pursuing gender diversity in police organizational in the 1990's: A longitudinal analysis of factors associated with the hiring of female officers. *Police Quarterly, 9*(4), 463–485.

8

Corruption Prevention and Complaint Management

Louise Porter and Tim Prenzler

Policing is now widely recognized as a high-risk occupation for diverse types of misconduct, including financial corruption, legal process corruption and excessive force. Police work also tends to attract large numbers of complaints, many of which concern lower-level customer service issues. This chapter reports on current developments in police integrity systems, which increasingly are adopting a complex array of misconduct prevention techniques. The chapter addresses the challenging issue of the division of labour between internal professional standards departments and external oversight agencies. Attention is also paid to measuring misconduct, refining codes of conduct, integrity-related recruitment and training methods, compulsory reporting and whistleblower protection, integrity testing, drug and alcohol testing, covert tactics and recording police activities. The chapter concludes by setting out best practice principles in responding to complaints, including local resolution, mediation and early intervention.

Police misconduct and complaints against police

Police work is subject to numerous pressures and temptations towards misconduct. Unethical behaviour can involve classic corruption – in terms of soliciting or accepting bribes for not enforcing the law – as well as legal process corruption – including fabricating, altering or hiding evidence. Inquiries in numerous countries – including advanced democracies such as Britain, the United States, Canada and Australia – have uncovered organized police 'protection rackets' related to illegal gambling, the supply of alcohol, prostitution and other forms of vice; along with routine violations of due process rights resulting in numerous miscarriages of justice (e.g. McDonald, 1981; Mollen, 1994; United

States Commission on Civil Rights, 2000; Wood, 1997). Police in some jurisdictions are also notorious for using excessive force as a preferred method of pre-empting suspect resistance or meting out 'street-level justice', as well as forcing confessions from suspects held in custody (Christopher, 1991; Prenzler, 2009; Punch, 2009). Police can also be negligent in failing to respond sensitively or speedily to victims of crime or failing to investigate crimes properly. They can also engage in racial or sexual harassment and discrimination – for example, through practices such as 'racial profiling' of groups targeted for questioning and searches. Policing is also vulnerable to internal forms of corruption and misconduct not uncommon in many occupations, including favouritism or bribery in assignments and promotion, cheating in exams, misuse of company equipment, embezzlement, and harassment and internal discrimination. Police have been adept at evading accountability through their knowledge of the law and closing ranks behind a 'blue curtain of silence' (Skolnick, 2002). Cycles of reform and corruption indicate how difficult it is to establish long-term probity in police organizations (Mollen, 1994).

Policing is also associated with large numbers of complaints from the public. For example, in England and Wales, with approximately 143,000 police, in 2009/10 there were 33,854 complaints, representing an 8 per cent increase over the previous year, including 58,399 separate allegations (Home Office, 2010; Independent Police Complaints Commission, 2010b). The complaints involved 35,557 police officers, and there were also 5584 appeals against decisions, representing a 21 per cent increase on the previous year. Typically, complaints are concerned less with financial or legal process corruption than with neglect of duty, rudeness and excessive force. Nonetheless, complaints against police provide a considerable challenge for authorities. Often they lack probative value – formal investigations usually achieve substantiation rates of only 10 or 20 per cent – but they are indicative of conflict and misunderstanding between police and citizens. What is more, surveys of the public indicate that many people who would like to make a complaint do not take action because they think nothing will be achieved (e.g. Independent Police Complaints Commission, 2010a, p. 30). If everyone with a grievance against police made a formal complaint, then the volume of complaints would probably be increased by threefold in many places. Most surveys of complainants show that between 70 and 90 per cent are dissatisfied with the way their complaint was handled, and they tend to be especially dissatisfied with the lack of independence in in-house police complaints and discipline systems (e.g. Brown, 1987; Hayes,

1997; Prenzler, Allard, Curry, & Macintyre, 2010). Inquiries into police internal affairs departments have also frequently exposed a system that intimidates complainants, facilitates biased investigations and produces weak disciplinary outcomes. While policing in many places has undergone periods of reform following earlier scandals and Commissions of Inquiry, cases of misconduct still surface and perceptions of biased complaints systems remain. All these factors tend to undermine public trust and confidence in the police.

The historical problem of police misconduct and public dissatisfaction is intimately related to the nature of police duties and the traditional structures of policing. Porter (2005) summarized influences on police misconduct as 'organizational' and 'social'. Organizational obstacles to ethical conduct include a culture that values the ends rather than the means (e.g. crime clear-up rates rather than professional standards), as well as inadequate policies and rules, poor or absent leadership, and a lack of investigative capacity or consequences for misconduct. Social influences include hostility to those who report misconduct; poor role modelling; and associations with criminals, including criminal informants, or others who may encourage inappropriate behaviour. Police work uniquely combines a number of additional factors – including high levels of discretion and power, and low visibility activities with vulnerable populations – that create opportunities and pressures for misconduct. The broader social and political environment of policing can also place crime clear-up rates and public order above due process rights and adequate scrutiny.

Integrity systems

In response to these problems many jurisdictions across the world have established advanced systems for the management of misconduct risks and the promotion of ethical policing. It is standard practice for police departments to have internal police professional standards (or 'internal affairs') units, with an increasing incidence of external oversight agencies specifically established to monitor police integrity. There are, therefore, a variety of agencies dedicated to reducing police misconduct, and integrity systems are increasingly adopting a complex array of techniques, some of which are quite sophisticated and intrusive. Getting the mix of strategies right is a difficult task, including the mix of responsibilities of internal and external agencies. From there, more specific, tailormade integrity strategies need to be developed across these two sites.

Balance of internal and external responsibility

Independent oversight of police varies significantly across jurisdictions. Some agencies have no substantive powers and simply audit police investigations and make recommendations for modifications to procedures or disciplinary outcomes. Others are much more actively involved in conducting independent investigations, with powers to compel testimony or conduct covert operations (Prenzler, 2009). A strong consensus exists regarding the need for oversight, and there is a discernable trend world-wide to greater external involvement in police complaints and discipline and input into police reform. Nonetheless, there is also considerable resistance to externalization, often from police themselves, and each jurisdiction needs to find the most appropriate arrangement. It would seem to be the case that the more scandal-prone police departments need fairly close scrutiny and direct involvement in investigations by external agencies. An independent response is also very important to complainants and many members of the public, even when police departments are generally fairly well managed. While some oversight agencies report that the quality of police internal investigations have improved in recent decades (Porter & Prenzler, 2011a), complainants still generally call for external investigation of their complaints.

The United Kingdom is instructive in having three police oversight agencies across a scale of types (Porter & Prenzler, 2011b). The Police Ombudsman for Northern Ireland (PONI), established in 2000 in the wake of decades of civil unrest and biased policing, is amongst the most advanced oversight agency in the world in conducting almost all complaint investigations itself, with a large number of investigators from outside a police background. The Police Complaints Commissioner for Scotland (PCCS), established in 2009, can only review complaints and make recommendations, but puts considerable energy into improving police practices at the policy level. The Independent Police Complaints Commission (IPCC) for England and Wales, established in 2004, is an intermediate type of oversight agency. It carries out investigations of serious incidents, such as deaths or serious injuries inflicted by police; all serious allegations, such as those involving 'organized corruption' or process corruption; all allegations involving senior police; and it responds to complainants who are dissatisfied with the police response to their complaint. Other matters may be dealt with by police but subject to varying degrees of IPCC direct 'management' or more detached 'supervision', depending on their seriousness. While the PONI appears most likely to satisfy key criteria for independence, most jurisdictions appear to be extremely reluctant to take so much responsibility for complaints and discipline out of the hands of police. In such cases, the IPCC provides a model that at least specifies the levels and types of alleged misconduct that will be handled externally.

Measurement

Integrity strategies should be developed that match the risk-profile for each police department. Some departments may have problems with highly secretive drug corruption; others may have more of a problem with excessive force and abuse of human rights. Finding out the misconduct types and their level of risk is, therefore, a crucial first step. Judicial inquiries can provide important base-line data, but after that on-going information feeds are required. As with many types of research, no one data source is likely to provide a comprehensive or adequate picture of a topic. 'Triangulation' – the overlapping of data sources – is likely to provide the best picture. Because things change it is also important to ensure that the same, or only slightly modified, 'repeated measures' are used, such as on an annual basis. In policing, the following are some key data sources that have been used to measure misconduct and integrity levels and the impact of integrity strategies.

Complaints, as we have seen, are a major but problematic source of information about police. Some complaints will be proven if investigations are thorough, but many others will come down to a 'he said/she said' standoff between complainants and officers. Survey research shows, nonetheless, that most complainants are not belligerent but are genuine in their complaints and, of course, complaints are also important because they represent only the 'tip of the iceberg' of public dissatisfaction. Overall, it can be said that analysing complaint allegations by type (assault, rudeness, etc.), over time, can provide a picture of possible problem behaviours and changes in police practices. Analysing complaints by subject officers and units can also allow for the identification of 'problem officers' or problem units, although it should be kept in mind that some research shows that high numbers of complaints can be related to more productive officers willing to directly engage with suspects (Terrill & McCluskey, 2002). Public opinion surveys, and surveys of arrestees, can also provide useful information about perceptions and experiences of police conduct.

Another source is surveys of police. If these are conducted anonymously, respondents are often candid and results can be quite reliable.

Surveys can be used to identify officers' views about types and levels of misconduct, and also their views about the utility and acceptability of different integrity strategies. The other main type of survey is an 'ethical climate' survey that measures respondents' understanding of the seriousness of a range of misconduct behaviours as well as the perceived consequences for these behaviours and officers' likelihood of reporting them (e.g. Klockars, Ivkovic, & Haberfeld, 2004).

Codes of conduct

Police professional standards are typically prescribed through codes of conduct. Police codes of conduct have been criticized for being too vague or too descriptive, without sufficient connection to real-life situations and without sufficient allowance for officer discretion. However, given the right mix of principles and examples, codes can be very useful for identifying expectations of the organization and for developing training scenarios (e.g. International Association of Chiefs of Police, 2002). Codes need to be kept up to date to address emerging ethical risks – such as police use of social networking websites or off-duty recreational drug taking.

Recruitment

Most advanced police departments now employ a large battery of tests and recruitment criteria to ensure they select trainees most likely to resist misconduct pressures. Psychological tests can assess personality and attitudes, coping mechanisms, and susceptibility and reactions to stress; as well as underlying psychological conditions or problems such as addiction or depression that may present vulnerabilities. The value of these tests is well supported. For example, in Australia, Lough and Ryan (2005, 2010) showed that recruits who were selected using the Australian Institute of Forensic Psychology profiling system went on to outperform those who were selected using more conventional means. Screened officers had a lower drop-out rate, and were less likely to make errors that resulted in formal disciplinary action or investigation. Other integrity-related screening mechanisms include criminal and financial checks, home visits, behavioural interviewing, and ethical dilemma questions or scenarios.

A number of other selection criteria have been shown to contribute to improved integrity. For example, increasing emphasis is being placed on developing a personnel profile that more closely resembles community demographics. In the case of women, an added benefit is that they have been shown to attract fewer complaints, and are more likely to reduce conflict with members of the public in comparison to males (Waugh, Ede, & Alley, 1998). Research also supports the view that college educated police are less likely to attract complaints and have lower use of force rates (Harris, 2010; Paoline & Terrill, 2007).

Training

Ethics components of police training have increased in recent years in most jurisdictions, with the recognition that ethics is a core component to training that should be interwoven into all subjects. While basic ethics training may be designed to help new members understand organizational codes of conduct, values, rules and policies, more advanced ethics training encourages the application of ethical principles to decision-making (Alexandra & Miller, 2010). Officers' knowledge of ethics needs to be maintained through refresher training and as officers advance through the ranks they need an increasingly sophisticated knowledge of integrity strategies and their role in maximizing organizational values. These are training principles, with more research needed about what types of ethical training are demonstrably effective in assisting ethical practice.

Compulsory reporting and witness support

A variety of studies have reported on the obstacle that police solidarity presents to the disclosure of misconduct. This culture of secrecy often extends to the harassment and persecution of internal witnesses (or 'whistleblowers'). One basic legislative response to this situation is to mandate reporting of misconduct, making failure to report a disciplinary offence. More sophisticated and sensitive additions to this include confidential reporting lines, computerized reporting systems, and support networks and protection for whistleblowers. However, one review of a confidential telephone reporting line in the Western Australia Police – the 'Blue-line' – found that, while survey respondents were generally supportive of an internal reporting system, they tended to lack trust in the Blue-line and its promise of confidentiality, preferring instead to report matters to their supervisor (Sellenger Centre, 2010).

Compulsory reporting systems should also include penalties for harassing or threatening witnesses. Support may informally be offered through an officer's supervisor, or more formally through staff support services to offer advice and counselling for whistleblowers. Some anti-corruption agencies also provide witness support mechanisms for more serious cases, similar to criminal witness protection, including new identities and relocations. There should also be a legal facility for prosecuting harassing or malicious complainants (New South Wales Ombudsman, 2002).

Integrity testing

Integrity testing can take several forms and can be used to identify more secretive forms of corruption, as well as to measure integrity and deter misconduct. The New York Police Department is famous for its pioneering use of a type of 'random integrity testing', which was used in areas where there were some indicators of particular types of misconduct that were difficult to expose through conventional investigations (KPMG, 1996). These tests involve creating scenarios where police officers are randomly presented with a situation in which their integrity is tested, for example by an undercover officer offering a bribe or handing in a lost wallet full of cash. The subject officers' reactions are monitored, often by covert videorecording. Unethical and illegal responses – such as accepting the bribe or pocketing the cash – lead to disciplinary action. Random testing can contribute to deterrence if officers are aware that their organization has a testing programme and any opportunity offered for misconduct or corruption could be monitored. Random testing can also be used to test lower-level customer service-type conduct, similar to 'mystery shopper' programmes in the retail and services areas (e.g. New South Wales Police, 2009, p. 47).

'Targeted integrity testing' is also used by some jurisdictions. Here, tests are tailored towards an individual officer or small group suspected of specific types of misconduct. These tests, again, are a type of 'last resort' action where there is a strong indication of serious misconduct but an absence of adequate evidence to allow charges to be brought. Targeted integrity tests are said to be fairer than random integrity tests, due to the suspicion that the subject has already engaged in the activity (rather than indicating a general mistrust of employees). However, the techniques are still sometimes criticized in regard to issues of potential entrapment. Targeted testing has been shown to be successful in exposing corruption in a number of jurisdictions. For example, data from New South Wales (NSW), following the introduction of targeted testing in the 1990s, showed that out of 90 operations, 37 per cent identified misconduct, 27 per cent showed no misconduct, 12 per cent were forwarded on for further investigation and 24 per cent were inconclusive or were discontinued. The 'failed' tests led to 51 criminal charges: 54 per cent against police, 23 per cent against police staff and 23 per cent against civilians (Prenzler & Ronken, 2001).

Drug and alcohol testing

Drug and alcohol problems among police clearly present performance issues, where members are impaired by substances while on duty; as well as exposing officers to potential criminal activity and corruption in the case of illicit drug use (both on and off duty). Addiction problems can also present significant welfare issues. Many jurisdictions have now legislated random drug testing of sworn officers. Some are also able to test unsworn employees and also recruits at the police academy (Porter & Prenzler, 2011a). The aim of random drug testing of officers is to deter inappropriate behaviour before it occurs, rather than actually detect a member's drug use. Deterrence works through the knowledge that one could be drug tested at any time, even in the absence of any evidence or suspicion, and, thus, could be caught under the influence. Random testing must, therefore, be visible, unpredictable and likely, in order to have a deterrent effect. For example, the Australian Federal Police reports publicly that it drug tests around 80–90 per cent of its workforce each year at a randomly chosen time (AFP, 2009, 2010). In comparison, other departments randomly drug test approximately 10–20 per cent of members (Committee on the Office of the Ombudsman and the Police Integrity Commission, 2002).

Targeted drug and alcohol tests, on the other hand, are more focused on detection of misuse. Tests can be carried out when there is reason to believe that an officer may have used illegal drugs or be under the influence of alcohol while on duty. Many targeted drug testing programmes only permit police forces to drug test their members when they are on duty. However, the use of illegal drugs off-duty is a criminal offence and impacts on the integrity of the officer. The Police Integrity Commission (2005) reported on drug use in the NSW Police and noted that some drug types can be very difficult to detect if officers take them early in their off-duty time. Several jurisdictions have, therefore, introduced legislation allowing officers to be recalled to duty in order for a targeted drug test to be conducted. Hair testing has also been the subject of recommendation, but remains to be accepted or implemented. Alcohol and drug testing are also mandated in some police departments following all incidents involving death or serious injury (Prenzler & Ronken, 2001).

Covert operations

Covert methods of evidence collection for corruption and serious misconduct are in use by both police and anti-corruption agencies. These include undercover officers, covert surveillance, listening devices and telephone intercepts, as well the 'controlled operations' or integrity tests described above. Many jurisdictions have seen recent strengthening in these areas with the introduction of legislation to support covert tactics, and some anti-corruption/oversight agencies have resourced specialist units to carry out this work (Porter & Prenzler, 2011a). The results of covert methods can be quite dramatic, for example when covert footage of an assault by police is revealed during a hearing or trial.

Recording police activities

The recording of police activities by devices such as audiotapes, videotapes and CCTV also appear to be useful in detecting and reducing misconduct. CCTV can be located in high-risk areas. For example, CCTV is often used in police watchhouses where there are risks of assaults or neglect of detainees. Many police now have cameras in their vehicles and officers are also wearing 'head-mounted' or 'body-worn video'. Video evidence can be used to test allegations against police and can be of great value in protecting police from false complaints (Home Office, 2007). The recording of police interviews with suspects and witnesses appears particularly valuable in reducing the coercion and fabrication of confessions and other evidence common in traditional police process corruption (Dixon, 2006; Royal Commission, 1993).

Complaints management and reduction

As we have seen, policing tends to attract large numbers of complaints. Rigorous formal investigations would seem to be required for accountability, but these are usually expensive, time consuming and inconclusive, with both complainants and subject officers alienated and dissatisfied at the end of the process. While formal investigations will be required for some or even many complaints, there are a number of alternatives to the traditional 'investigate, prosecute and punish' model. The three main alternatives – or complementary approaches – are forms of (1) 'alternative dispute resolution', (2) early intervention systems and (3) learning from complaints. When applied systematically, these methods should help improve the speedy and satisfactory resolution of complaints and also contribute to reductions in complaints.

Surprisingly, perhaps, many police departments do not have an explicit complaints reduction policy. This would seem necessary as a first step to developing a plan to reduce complaints. However, an important caveat must be applied here. The goal of reducing complaints can motivate police to return to the bad old days when complaints were 'lost' or downgraded, or when complainants were intimidated. At one level, therefore, potential complainants need to be encouraged, with easy access and a positive reception. The presence of strong external oversight should also prevent police undermining the complaints recording process because aggrieved persons always have an alternative agency where they can lodge their complaint or appeal a decision by police.

Alternative resolution of complaints

While investigations of serious allegations usually require sophisticated detection methods, as described earlier, the majority of complaints against police concern less serious matters that may not warrant such an intensive approach. This situation, combined with widespread dissatisfaction with formal investigative procedures, has prompted many police departments to introduce various forms of alternative dispute resolution. At the high end, this involves face-to-face mediation. Although this is clearly the preference of many complainants, police seem to be reluctant to commit to this somewhat demanding process (Walker, Alpert, & Kenney, 2002). However, there have been reports of successful mediation of police complaints. For example, relatively high rates of satisfaction with mediation were reported by both citizens and police officers in Portland, Oregon. Indeed, even where participants were not directly satisfied with the outcome they still felt positive about the process, particularly regarding fairness, the opportunity to be heard, understanding 'the other side' and bringing 'humanity to the situations' (Independent Police Review, 2004, p. 53).

The more popular options occur at the lower end of the spectrum: through forms of 'local resolution' by police managers. This usually entails a quick assessment of a complaint, an apology to the complainant, often by telephone, and an undertaking that the officer in question has been subject to some form of 'managerial guidance'. This approach can attract higher complainant and police satisfaction – up to 75 per cent in some studies – and is generally much cheaper and faster than more formal disciplinary procedures (Ede & Barnes, 2002; Maguire and Corbett, 1991). However, there are dangers that it becomes just a convenient way for police managers to account for complaints without taking complainants seriously and doing anything substantive about systematic behavioural or procedural problems.

Below are two examples of the local resolution of complaints considered to be successful by the Police Ombudsman for Northern Ireland (2011, p. 25):

> *Case study 1.* A member of the public contacted the Office [of the Police Ombudsman] to complain about the lack of contact from a PSNI (Police Service of Northern Ireland) Investigating Officer in relation to an alleged assault on a juvenile. Over two months had passed since the juvenile had provided police with a statement and neither the juvenile nor the parents had received any update from police. The complainant agreed to engage in local resolution and a PSNI Inspector was appointed to look into the matter. The Inspector discussed the complaint with the complainant and then spoke to the officer subject of the complaint. The officer stated that he had forgotten to update the family and was sorry about this. The complainant was provided with up-to-date details of how police were progressing the matter and expressed satisfaction with the local resolution process. The complaint was then closed by the Office.

> *Case study 2.* A member of the public contacted the Office to make a complaint about the alleged incivility of a PSNI Constable who had stopped them for an alleged traffic offence. The complainant stated that they found the attitude of the officer to be unpleasant and rude. The complainant agreed to engage in local resolution. The complainant wanted a senior police officer to speak to the officer and advise him of the issue with him and if this was done the complainant would not want any further action to be taken. A PSNI Inspector was appointed to conduct the local resolution and spoke to the officer as requested by the complainant. The complainant was satisfied that the local resolution had been successful once made aware that the officer had been spoken to. The complaint was then closed by the Office.

Early intervention systems

Early intervention, or 'early warning' systems, developed from the slippery slope theory of corruption, which proposes that minor behavioural infractions can lead to more serious misconduct. Early intervention is also built on statistical evidence that some officers and some units attract excessive numbers of complaints or lodge more use of force reports (Walker, Alpert, & Kenney, 2000). Pioneering programmes to address this phenomenon focused on interventions with officers who attracted repeat complaints. A 'flag' would be triggered when officers passed a threshold, such as more than three complaints in one year. Counselling and re-training interventions were found to be effective in many cases in stopping repeat complaints. Because a small proportion of officers often accounted for a large proportion of complaints, this led to large overall reductions in complaints. Significant benefits also often accrued to the officers whose careers were saved as a result of timely interventions. Contemporary early intervention systems are now more sophisticated, with specialist computer software that allows for the collection and analysis of diverse behavioural 'indictors' of at-risk conduct – including traffic accidents, sick leave and supervisor reports – with a focus on welfare as well as disciplinary issues. Providing local-level managers with this information, as well as the responsibility to deal with the issues, allows problematic behaviour to be addressed directly and quickly.

Learning from complaints

When complaints are properly recorded and analysed, they can be a rich source of information about the causes of police–citizen conflict and areas of police conduct that might be considered inappropriate or unethical. This is an area where some police departments have shown considerable initiative in attempting to learn from complaints. It is also an area where external oversight agencies have been particularly active. Many now have research and policy development built into their governing legislation, and they have established sophisticated research units that utilize a variety of social science methods to better understand and address police conduct issues (Porter & Prenzler, 2011a, 2011b). Many also provide reports, often readily accessible at their websites, which provide unprecedented amounts of detailed information about complaints. These reports often include focused studies on topical issues, such as racial profiling, police high-speed pursuits, police shootings and complaints processing options, that make use of complaints and other data sources such as surveys, interviews and incident reports. The focus of this activity is scientifically based police reform.

An example of a learning outcome is provided below from an account by the Independent Police Complaints Commission (2010a, p. 20) in the United Kingdom:

Examples of cases where we have identified organisational learning.
The findings of our investigation released in December 2009 revealed
a number of failings on the part of Greater Manchester Police (GMP),
as well as individual officers and staff, in their dealings with Katie
Boardman (also known as Summers). Ms Summers was stabbed to
death by Brian Taylor on 9 October 2008. There had been a history
of domestic abuse in her relationship with Mr Taylor and GMP officers had dealt with a number of incidents involving the couple. GMP
recognised the shortcomings in their dealings with Ms Summers and
acted promptly to learn lessons. Their response included additional
training for Domestic Violence Unit staff (DVU), a review of logs to
ensure that they have been completed correctly, and dip sampling of
incidents reviewed by DVU staff.

Complaint reduction

A combination of traditional investigations and discipline, and alternative complaint-handling processes, should theoretically lead to
reduced complaints – indicative of reduced police–citizen conflict and
improved citizen satisfaction. Alternative complaints resolution tends
to be focused more on improved stakeholder satisfaction, but even
this – when properly conducted through internal assessment and feedback processes – should reduce problem police behaviours and repeat
complaints. Typically the lessons learnt relate to police being more
polite, less discriminatory, more respectful of citizens' rights and better
at obtaining cooperation without the use of force.

There are a number of case studies available in the literature showing
that a combination of measures can be highly effective when managers
make an explicit commitment to reducing complaints. For example,
in the 1990s in New York City the world-famous crackdown on crime
was accompanied by large increases in complaints. Two Bronx precincts
went against the trend, with large decreases in both crime and complaints (Davis, Mateu-Gelabert, & Miller, 2005). In the 42nd Precinct,
complaints declined by 54 per cent over a 6-year period and in the
44th Precinct complaints declined by 64 per cent. Researchers related
the reduction in complaints to the introduction of a 'courtesy, professionalism and respect policy' ('CPR'), a 'verbal judo' course designed to
improve police negotiation skills, and close supervisor monitoring of
staff with complaints histories. Similarly, Portland Police Bureau saw a
64 per cent reduction in excessive force complaints over a seven-year
period following the introduction of better training in alternatives to

the use of force, mandatory reporting of use of force, a Use-of-Force Review Board with citizen representation and an early intervention system (Independent Police Review, 2004, 2010).

In Australia, the Tasmania Police has also seen substantial reductions in complaints of assault and excessive force, as well as a decrease in the number of repeat complaints that officers received (Porter, Prenzler, & Fleming, 2011). Figure 8.1 displays the rate of complaints against Tasmania Police per 100 officers from 1994/95 to 2008/09. While the rate of complaints decreased by 79 per cent from 1996/97, the decline was primarily due to a remarkable 87 per cent drop in complaints from members of the public – from a high of 23 per 100 officers in 1996/97 to a low of 3 per 100 officers in 2008/09. What is also notable is that the rate of internally generated complaints increased by 85 per cent from a low of 0.38 per 100 officers in 1995/96 to a high of 2.57 in 2005/06. Since that time the rate has fluctuated but remained relatively high. While public complaints are said to be indicative of problematic officer behaviour, internal complaints have been seen as a potentially positive indicator of a police culture that is intolerant of misconduct.

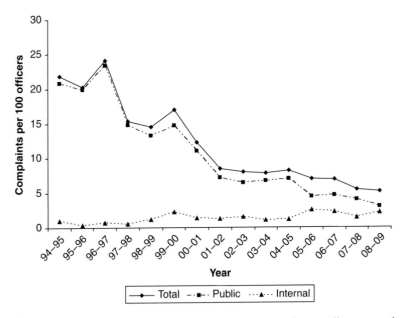

Figure 8.1 Rate of total complaints, public complaints and internally generated complaints against Tasmania Police per 100 officers
Source: Adapted from Porter et al. (2011).

Porter et al. (2011) concluded that a number of strategies instigated by Tasmania Police during this period were likely to have influenced the large decline in complaints. These included the introduction of a psychological recruit screening test, enlarged ethics training and improvements to use of force training. The training in use of force included an emphasis on de-escalation and communication techniques, demonstrating accountability, and greater validity of training through the use of simulated scenarios. The Tasmania Police also introduced an early intervention system focused on addressing multiple complaints against individual officers (and targeting multiple complaints of the same allegation type). Complaint handling was also made more rigorous, with improved training in complaint management and a focus on learning lessons from complaints. Reductions in complaints also allowed for closer scrutiny of individual cases and more personal communication with complainants.

Conclusion

While considerable advances in police integrity systems have been made in recent decades, reform is often highly uneven and jurisdictionally specific. However, case studies show that a variety of techniques can be applied to reduce misconduct and make police more accountable. Complaints can be reduced through targeted efforts aimed at officers who attract multiple complaints and through better training and supervision, especially in the area of negotiation skills and reduced use of force. Strategies should be tailored to the key underlying risk areas of both the organization (its structures, systems, policies and procedures) and the members within the organization (including individuals and the collective culture). A comprehensive integrity system will have proactive strategies (e.g. education, research and analysis, and risk assessment) and reactive strategies (such as complaints receipt and investigation, and performance assessments). While each allegation of misconduct requires a response, there is a positive move apparent in many jurisdictions towards agencies addressing systemic misconduct issues with a variety of prevention strategies.

References

Alexandra, A., & Miller, S. (2010). *Integrity systems for occupations.* Farnham, Surrey: Ashgate.
Australian Federal Police (AFP) (2009). *Annual report for 2008–9.* Canberra: Australian Federal Police.

Australian Federal Police (AFP) (2010). *Annual report for 2009–10.* Canberra: Australian Federal Police.

Brown, D. (1987). *The police complaints procedure: A sur\vey of complainants' views.* London: Home Office.

Christopher, W. (1991). *Report of the independent commission on the Los Angeles Police Department.* Los Angeles: Independent Commission on the LAPD.

Committee on the Office of the Ombudsman and the Police Integrity Commission. (2002). *Research report on trends in police corruption.* Sydney: New South Wales Parliament.

Davis, R., Mateu-Gelabert, P., & Miller, J. (2005). Can effective policing also be respectful? Two examples in the South Bronx. *Police Quarterly, 8*(2), 229–247.

Dixon, D. (2006). A window into the interviewing process? The audio-visual recording of police interrogation in New South Wales, Australia. *Policing & Society, 16*(4), 323–348.

Ede, A., & Barnes, M. (2002). Alternative strategies for resolving complaints. In T. Prenzler & J. Ransley (Eds.), *Police reform: Building integrity* (pp. 115–130). Sydney: Federation Press.

Harris, C. J. (2010). Problem officers? Analyzing problem behaviour patterns from a large cohort. *Journal of Criminal Justice, 38*(2): 216–225.

Hayes, M. (1997). *A Police Ombudsman for Northern Ireland?* Belfast: Home Office Stationery Office.

Home Office. (2007). *Guidance for the use of body-worn video devices.* London: Home Office.

Home Office. (2010). *Police officer strength in England and Wales by police force area on 31 March 2010.* Retrieved from www.homeoffice.gov.uk/publications/science-research-statistics/research-statistics/police-research/hosb1410/apo09 10-tabs?view=Binary.

Independent Police Complaints Commission. (2010a). *Annual report 2009/10.* London: Independent Police Complaints Commission.

Independent Police Complaints Commission. (2010b). *Police complaints: Statistics for England and Wales 2009/10.* London: Independent Police Complaints Commission.

Independent Police Review. (2004). *Annual report.* Portland, OR: Office of the City Auditor.

Independent Police Review. (2010). *Annual report.* Portland, OR: Office of the City Auditor.

International Association of Chiefs of Police. (2002). *Police chiefs' desk reference.* Washington, D.C.: International Association of Chiefs of Police and Bureau of Justice Assistance.

Klockars, C., Ivkovic, S., & Haberfeld, M. (Eds.). (2004). *The contours of police integrity.* Thousand Oaks, CA: Sage.

KPMG. (1996). *Report to the New York City Commission to combat police corruption: The New York City Police Department random integrity testing program.* New York: NYC Commission to Combat Police Corruption.

Lough, J., & Ryan, M. (2005). Psychological profiling of Australian police officers: An examination of post-selection performance. *International Journal of Police Science and Management, 7*(1), 15–23.

Lough, J., & Ryan, M. (2010). Research note: Psychological profiling of Australian police officers: A three-year examination of post-selection performance. *International Journal of Police Science and Management, 12*(3), 480–486.

Maguire, M., & Corbett, C. (1991). *A study of the police complaints system.* London: Her Majesty's Stationery Office.

McDonald, D. (1981). *Freedom and security under the law: Report of the commission of inquiry into certain activities of the Royal Canadian Mounted Police.* Ottawa: Minister of Supply and Services Canada.

Mollen, M. (1994). *Commission to investigate allegations of police corruption and the anti-corruption procedures of the police department: Commission report.* New York: City of New York.

New South Wales Ombudsman. (2002). *Improving the management of complaints: Identifying and managing officers with complaint histories of significance.* Sydney: New South Wales Ombudsman.

New South Wales Police. (2009). *Annual report 2008/09.* Sydney: New South Wales Police.

Paoline, E., & Terrill, W. (2007). Police education, experience, and the use of force. *Criminal Justice and Behavior, 34*(2), 179–196.

Police Integrity Commission. (2005). *Operation Abelia: Research and investigations into illegal drug use by some NSW police officers. Volume 1: Summary report.* Sydney: Police Integrity Commission.

Police Ombudsman for Northern Ireland. (2011). *Local resolution pilot project report for PSNI D District, June 2010–November 2010.* Belfast: Police Ombudsman for Northern Ireland.

Porter, L., & Prenzler, T. (2011a). *A stocktake study of police integrity strategies in Australia.* Brisbane: Australian Research Council Centre of Excellence in Policing and Security.

Porter, L., & Prenzler, T. (2011b). *Police oversight in the United Kingdom.* Brisbane: Australian Research Council Centre of Excellence in Policing and Security.

Porter, L. E. (2005). Policing the police service: Psychological contributions to the study and prevention of police corruption. In L. J. Alison (Ed.), *Offender profiling and criminal investigation: A forensic psychologist's casebook* (pp. 143–169). Cullumpton, Devon: Willan.

Porter, L., Prenzler, T., & Fleming, J. (2011). Complaint reduction in the Tasmanian Police. *Policing and Society.* Available online: http://www.tandfonline.com/doi/pdf/10.1080/10439463.2011.641548.

Prenzler, T. (2009). *Police corruption: Preventing misconduct and maintaining integrity.* Boca Raton FL: CRC Press-Taylor and Francis.

Prenzler, T., Allard, T., Curry, S., & Macintyre, S. (2010). Complaints against police: The complainants' experience. *Journal of Criminal Justice Research, 1*(1), 1–18.

Prenzler, T., & Ronken, C. (2001). Police integrity testing in Australia. *Criminal Justice: The International Journal of Policy and Practice, 1*(3), 319–342.

Punch, M. (2009). *Police corruption.* Cullumpton, Devon: Willan.

Royal Commission. (1993). *The Royal Commission on criminal justice: Report.* London: HMSO.

Sellenger Centre. (2010). *Evaluation of the blueline.* Perth: Sellenger Centre for Research in Law, Justice and Policing; Edith Cowan University.

Skolnick, J. (2002). Corruption and the blue code of silence. *Police Practice and Research: An International Journal, 3*(1), 7–19.

Terrill, W., & McCluskey, J. (2002). Citizen complaints and problem officers: Examining officer behavior. *Journal of Criminal Justice, 30*(2), 143–155.

United States Commission on Civil Rights. (2000). *Revisiting who is guarding the guardians?*. Washington, D.C: United States Commission on Civil Rights.

Waugh L., Ede, A., & Alley, A. (1998). Police culture, women police and attitudes towards misconduct. *International Journal of Police Science and Management 1*(3), 288–300.

Walker, S., Alpert, G. P., & Kenney, D. J. (2001). *Early warning systems: Responding to the problem police officer*. Washington, D.C.: National Institute of Justice.

Walker, S., Archbold, C., & Herbst, L. (2002). *Mediating citizen complaints against police officers: A guide for police and community leaders*. Washington, D.C.: United States Department of Justice.

Wood, J. (1997). *Royal Commission into the New South Wales Police Service: Final report*. Sydney: Government of the State of NSW.

9

Public–Private Crime Prevention Partnerships

Tim Prenzler and Rick Sarre

Partnerships between the public and private sectors – including police and private security – are promoted as providing a synergetic effect in crime prevention. This chapter considers both the potential benefits and risks of these partnerships, and reports on diverse examples from the United Kingdom, the Netherlands and Australia, most of which have demonstrated large reductions in target crimes. Despite the fact that police and private security operate on quite different principles of private and public interests, there does seem to be scope for enhanced relationships that provide wide benefits to diverse stakeholders. With this in mind, the chapter concludes with a set of guiding principles for ensuring accountability and optimal outcomes in crime prevention partnerships.

Partnerships

Public–private partnerships are very much on the agenda of governments today. Partnerships represent something of a moderate policy option in contrast to the more controversial policy of complete privatization of public assets and services. Public–private partnerships come in many forms, including operating leases on government-owned infrastructure or simply contractual arrangements for direct service delivery. Partners can be businesses, concerned with profit, or community-based groups, concerned with non-profit service delivery. The alleged benefits of partnerships for governments include buying in expertise to meet a temporary or urgent need, serving a public interest by augmenting the work of established organizations, ensuring compliance through enforceable contracts, spreading risk, obtaining investment without burdening taxpayers and stimulating employment (Commission of the European Communities, 2009; Van Buuren & den Boer, 2009).

Criminal justice is an area of government service delivery that has largely been shielded from privatization, with the partial exception of prison management and related custody functions including prisoner transport (Sarre & Prenzler, 2012). To some extent the retention of public ownership of prison infrastructure means these arrangements are more in the form of public–private partnerships than full privatization. The 'privatization' of policing has been a major development in policing internationally since the 1960s. However, the available evidence suggests this is primarily the result of market forces – the demand for private security – rather than deliberate policies of reducing police numbers or selling off or 'contracting in' police services (Sarre & Prenzler, 2011).

The growth of private security has been attributed to a large number of factors, including increased litigation and workplace safety legislation – both of which place obligations on property owners to protect customers and visitors. Improvements in security technology have been another factor. However, the main driver of growth in private security was arguably the steep increases in crime experienced in many countries from the 1960s to the 1990s, associated with rising prosperity and freedom (van Dijk, 2008). The much lower costs of security guards vis-à-vis police and the potential omnipresence of technologies such as intruder alarms and CCTV have also been major attractors. Increasing crime rates and the failure of traditional policing influenced local government involvement in crime prevention in countries (such as Britain and Australia) where this has not been a traditional task of local authorities. The local response frequently involves the outsourcing of security to private contractors (Wilson & Sutton, 2003). Since crime rates have levelled off (or fallen in many instances), the on-going growth of security has been associated with a new culture of 'securitization' (van Dijk, 2008) or 'self-protection' (Sarre & Prenzler, 2009) that recognizes the limits of public policing and the need for tailor-made security.

Securitization and self-protection are not intrinsically private sector phenomena. Any government department or project – such as public housing – can self-manage their security, including employing security officers and installing security equipment. 'Pluralization' of policing is, in fact, a more appropriate description of changes in policing, including growth in the number of public sector specialist policing and regulatory agencies (Van Buuren & den Boer, 2009). Nonetheless, private security is a key player, largely because of its size and number of specializations. In one of the most recent reviews, van Dijk (2008, p. 15) estimated that, in the mid-2000s, 'worldwide, more people are employed as a private security officer (348 per 100,000) than as a police officer (318 per 100,000)'. In some countries, especially emerging economies and new democracies with significant crime problems, private security personnel substantially outnumber public police. However, despite some convergence of roles, currently it appears that security is still largely focused on providing a preventive presence, while police have a more dominant role in arrests, investigations and prosecutions, including interdictions in crisis situations (Pastor, 2003).

The pros and cons of public–private cooperation

The growth of private security has led to calls for greater co-operation with police and for formal public–private partnerships (Golsby & O'Brien, 1996). However, there are numerous obstacles to a closer working relationship. In the first instance, the two groups operate on fundamentally opposing principles. Police have a duty to serve the public equally on the basis of need, whereas private providers are, for the most part, obliged only to their employer or principal. The latter can be a government agency, and contractual arrangements can require police-like duties to the public, but the basis of engagement remains selective. For example, the limits of private security have at times been highlighted in the media, who have reported cases where private guards have refused to come to the aid of citizens endangered outside the guards' proprietorial zone (Sarre & Prenzler, 2009). Furthermore, forms of cooperation between police and private security firms could potentially involve a skewing of public resources towards particular firms and their customers.

There have also been significant cultural differences between the two groups (Shearing, Stenning, & Addario, 1985). Police have generally looked down on private guards and investigators as less professional. Despite some high skill levels in private security, this situation derives in part from the lower training, selection and salary standards that generally apply to security officers. False intruder alarm activations have been another source of alienation. Typically up to 98 per cent of activations are false, causing a significant waste of police resources in response. Some police departments have had to introduce fines for repeat false alarm calls and charge a fee for call outs (Sampson, 2001). Furthermore, police are usually in possession of crime data that can be broken down by location, time of day and method; but they typically do not make this information available to security managers and security firms, let alone the general public (Prenzler, 2009a). This is despite the fact that these data are often highly valuable for effective security risk assessments.

Despite these problems the calls for greater cooperation continue, based largely on a shared mission for crime prevention and the idea of a public interest benefit from private security operations. For example, the greater ubiquity of security guards and surveillance technology means that direct lines of communication and sharing of intelligence between police and private security should improve the speed of interdictions and arrest of offenders. In that regard there is some research evidence indicating that informal and formal communication between police and private security tends to be more one way in benefitting police (Golsby & O'Brien, 1996). A Spanish study (Gimenez-Salinas, 2004) found that police and private security could productively work together on a routine basis – in this case through a communications coordination room – in relation to procedures such as licence checks on suspect vehicles, information about suspect persons, recovery of stolen vehicles, back-up assistance to security officers and intelligence about organized crime. However, the police seemed to be the main beneficiaries of these arrangements.

The need for basic labour-intensive front-line measures against terrorism at critical infrastructure locations has been a major factor behind recent expansions of public–private arrangements. In 2005 the United States Department of Justice issued a report, 'Engaging the Private Sector to Promote Homeland Security: Law Enforcement-Private Security Relationships', which included a strong recommendation to

> Prepare Memorandums of Understanding (MOUs) and formal coordination agreements between public and private agencies. MOUs should describe mechanisms for exchanging information about vulnerabilities and risks, coordination of responses, and processes to facilitate information sharing and multijurisdictional preemption of terrorist acts.
>
> (National Institute of Justice, 2005, p. 6)

One example of cooperation in this area is Project Griffin, established by the London Metropolitan Police in 2004, involving specialist 'Griffin-trained' private security officers available to assist police with major incidents, such as a terrorist attack, in areas such as perimeter access control (CoESS, 2010). Refresher training and intelligence updates are designed to maintain interest and preparedness, and the model has been adopted widely in the United Kingdom and overseas.

However, the need to reduce more traditional types of crimes has continued to be a prominent consideration. For example, the Security Industry Authority (SIA) in the United Kingdom, established in 2003, was charged with both improving industry professionalism and facilitating public–private cooperation in crime prevention:

> One of the reasons we came into being was to contribute as effectively as possible to a fundamental Government objective – reducing crime and the fear of crime...But there is still a long way to go before the private security industry is viewed with trust by the general public, as a partner by other law enforcement authorities, and as making a real contribution to the fight against crime.
>
> (Security Industry Authority, 2004, p. 2)

Recently CoESS (2010) – the Confederation of European Security Services – released a discussion paper and set of guidelines titled 'Critical Infrastructure Security and Protection: The Public-Private Opportunity', which promotes partnerships well beyond basic counter-terrorism operations.

Partnerships in practice

Venue security and mass-transit security are arguably the most obvious public–private crime prevention partnerships for most people. Both formats now cover many decades of experience, and there are well-established contractual arrangements, divisions of labour and protocols for cooperation between police and security. This is an area of limited research, however. There are certainly many cases where it appears that arrangements work optimally with very few adverse incidents. In other cases, there would appear to be room for some improvement. The 1996 Atlanta Olympic Games marked something of a watershed after the event was marred by the 'Centennial Olympic Park bombing'. The bombing triggered criticisms of the cooperative security arrangements in place, including allegations of poor communication and inadequate personnel standards (Forst & Manning 1999, p. 35). The lessons learnt were evident in the 2000 Sydney Olympics, which proved a high point in the effective deployment of diverse security services. The New South Wales Police Service had overall command, with approximately 4000 security officers working a combined total of 27,000 shifts along with police and security volunteers over a two-week period free of adverse incidents (Sarre & Prenzler, 2011, p. 84).

Many major sporting events have been marred by riots, brawls and assaults, related to poor security and police management. Stadium security has, however, become increasingly effective with the (more expensive) police officers adopting a back-up role to security personnel in situations requiring the application of criminal law. Closer planning between police and security is also evident, with review and feedback procedures, significant use of CCTV and plain clothes 'spotters' to remove troublemakers, better use of point-of-entry bag searches to exclude contraband, and the shared use of intelligence databases (Sarre & Prenzler, 2011, pp. 84–91). The on-going problem of alcohol-related violence has also shown the need for a more coordinated approach to policing clubs and pubs, including specialist training for security officers, mandated patron–security officer ratios and stakeholder management committees (Graham & Homel, 2008). Airport security arrangements have often been effective in many locations. However, security breaches have led to audits which have revealed numerous vulnerabilities in areas such as criminal infiltration of security staff, poor communication between partners, inadequate system tests and outdated security technology (e.g. Prenzler, Lowden, & Sarre, 2010; Wheeler, 2005).

Sometimes crime prevention partnerships are maintained at significant public cost despite the absence of a demonstrable crime-reduction effect. Criteria such as greater feelings of safety, more arrests and enhanced forensic values, or faster emergency response times, are sometimes used to justify continuation (Fairfield City Council, 2002; Wilson & Wells, 2007). CCTV projects – many involving formal partnerships between police and private security firms – have been particularly popular in the last two decades and attract enormous amounts of public money despite the fact that very few have been able to show reductions in crime (Farrington, Gill, Waples, & Argomaniz, 2007). A final major criticism of crime prevention partnerships is that they fail to include a wide range of stakeholders in their management structure and consultation processes, especially vulnerable groups, such as young people, who might be adversely affected by project strategies (Mazerolle & Prenzler, 2004).

UK case studies

The United Kingdom has seen considerable innovation and experimentation in crime prevention partnerships, with particular success in burglary reduction (Prenzler, 2009a). In the Safer Merseyside Partnership, for example, 105 businesses received free security audits and advice, and were offered subsidized security (Bowers, 2001). Some businesses improved lighting. Others installed 'target hardening' devices, such as window locks and roller shutters. Amongst participating businesses, attempted burglaries declined from 49 per cent to 25 per cent between survey periods. Successful burglaries were reduced from 31 per cent (33 burglaries) to 13 per cent (14 burglaries) – representing a 58 per cent reduction in offences. No significant changes were recorded in offences against non-participating businesses.

The Leicester Small Business and Crime Initiative provides another example, this time focusing specifically on reducing repeat commercial burglaries (Taylor, 1999; Tilley & Hopkins, 1998). The initiative was managed by a committee that included members of the City Council, Police and Chamber of Commerce; and was funded by a charity trust. Security audits were carried out by a project officer following a police burglary report. A mix of security measures was usually recommended, including alarms and CCTV. Portable alarms could be shared with other premises once risk periods for repeat offences had expired. Silent alarms were selected with a view to capturing and incapacitating offenders after research found numerous offenders could complete a burglary following the activation of an audible alarm. The project resulted in very few arrests, but offences in the target areas were reduced by 41 per cent from the year before the project to the final year of evaluation.

A similar project targeting prolific burglars in Boggart Hill was more successful in arresting repeat offenders in an initial 'crackdown' period, using profiling techniques that matched known offender methods with offence characteristics. Typically, in a traditional police operation, 'the response to the burglary problem would have ended there' (Farrell, Chenery, & Pease, 1998, p. 7). However, the project included a 'consolidation phase' that saw the installation of security hardware on burgled homes. The approach generated a 60 per cent reduction in burglaries from an average 44.9 per month pre-project to 18.5 in the consolidation phase. A 'hallow effect' was evident in a 36 per cent drop in burglaries in adjoining areas.

Dutch case studies

The Netherlands has also been a leader in the area of formal crime prevention partnerships, with particular success with commercial burglary. The Department of Crime Prevention in the Dutch Ministry of Justice adopted a policy of initiating and supporting partnerships (Van den Berg, 1995). A three-step process involved (1) a feasibility study of potential sites (including profiling the crime problem and gauging business support); (2) developing site-specific plans, establishing a coordinating committee, selecting a security firm and signing a master contract; and (3) implementing the plan, typically through operationalizing on-site security and police alarm responses.

In an early example, in the late 1980s, the Area Entrepreneur Association of the Dutch Enschede-Haven industrial site requested police to provide increased patrols to counter criminal activity (Van den Berg, 1995). The police produced a crime profile for the area and suggested a partnership arrangement in which they supported private security patrols. The Association established a cooperative with membership from the majority of the 410 companies on the site, and police set up a Project Agency to coordinate the work of the cooperative, the police and the local government. A submission was successful in securing start-up funds from the national government. Further assistance was provided by a government employment agency which subsidized the appointment of unemployed people as security guards, with training provided by police. The key element of the project was the stationing of a security guard on the estate outside business hours, who checked alarm activations before contacting police. The local council also improved lighting and the amenity of the area, while signage about the project was designed to deter offenders.

A formal evaluation of the Enschede-Haven project found that security incidents were reduced by 72 per cent, from 90 per month in the 18 months before the project to 25 per month in the 18 months after it was established. The partnership continued as a self-funded project once the initial subsidy expired (Van den Berg, 1995). A similar project on the Dutch Vianen Industrial Site saw commercial burglary reduced by 52 per cent from 75 incidents in the year before the project to 36 in the year after the project's commencement. All crime incidents were reduced by 41 per cent from 133 to 78 (Van den Berg, 1995).

Australian case studies

Australia has also been the site of various experiments in public–private partnerships. The following five case studies demonstrate some of the potential diversity of partnerships, and successes and failures that relate in part to differing implementation strategies and evaluation methods.

Perth 'Eyes on the Street'

'Eyes on the Street' is a crime prevention initiative involving working partnerships between the Western Australia Police, local government, businesses and the security industry. The programme primarily involves local businesses and staff in gathering and reporting information to police (Crime Research Centre, 2008). Partners receive training in recording and reporting suspicious persons or events. Reports are made to an 'Eyes on the Street' team, who then follow up the report, typically through police action. Regular feedback is provided to the partners to ensure they are kept motivated to continue to report incidents. The programme is widely promoted, including by displaying the Eyes on the Street logo on vehicles and shop windows. Advertising is designed to encourage participation, deter offenders and stimulate feelings of safety. Security personnel are considered key players, both those employed directly by businesses and those working for contract security firms. They require less training, are more likely to recognize and report a relevant incident, and they provide more detailed and useful information in their reports (Crime Research Centre, 2008). Security personnel have the option of either reporting to an Eyes on the Street Team or directly to police.

In 2007 the programme included over 100 participating organizations, with over 4000 employees and over 500 vehicles branded with the Eyes on the Street logo. Between 2004 and 2007, 2555 reports were made and over 200 arrests were attributed to Eyes on the Street intelligence. A formal evaluation of the programme found strong support from participants. However, there was no objective evidence of a crime-reduction effect. The report concluded that

> In order for a more comprehensive quantitative evaluation to be conducted, a 'controlled' implementation of the (Eyes on the Street) program would need to be undertaken by selecting an area in which to implement the program, and making a crime rate comparison over a specific time period with a demographically similar control area, while attempting to control as many other factors as possible. This needs to be a carefully designed prospective study rather than a retrospective examination of crime rates.
>
> (Crime Research Centre, 2008, p. 29)

Ipswich Safe City

The Ipswich (Queensland) Safe City Program was established in 1994 in response to an upsurge in alcohol-related crime and disorder, mainly in the city centre (City of Ipswich, 2010). The programme is centred on a CCTV system managed 24/7 by a contracted security firm. The monitoring facility is linked by radio to security officers and police on the beat – as well as connecting with other security firms, the police operations centre and other services. By 2010 the programme had a network of 181 cameras extending beyond the city centre to neighbouring suburbs and potential hotspots for crime such as bikeways and bus stops. The programme invests heavily in the latest technology with pan, tilt and zoom camera functions, high picture definition and full digital recording and archiving. Live feeds can be transmitted to the main police radio room. The programme includes a crime prevention through environmental design (CPTED) advisory service for businesses. Apart from law enforcement interventions, the programme also provides welfare referrals, including for young people, drug-affected persons and missing persons.

The Ipswich Safe City Program is 'widely recognised as one of the best private/police partnership anywhere in Australia' (ASIAL, 2010). It has also been described as 'the benchmark for a fully integrated crime prevention program that is not solely reliant on cameras and utilises a co-ordinated approach of all agencies' (City of Ipswich, 2010). It receives numerous visits from interested parties across Australia and overseas. Over the years a number of dramatic claims have been made for the benefits of the programme, including directly leading to '5,475 arrests from 1994 to 2008' (*Ipswich News*, 2009). A 2010 magazine article reported that Safe City had 'reduced crime by 78 per cent over the last 15 years, and in some cases...by 90 per cent' (cited in Cowan, 2010, p. 23). Despite such claims, there are no formal evaluations on the public record. Inquiries by the chapter authors to the Queensland Police Service also revealed there are no historic, nor contemporary, crime data available for the areas covered by the cameras. Figure 9.1 shows recorded crimes against property and the person from 1990 to 1991 in the police district of Ipswich – an area that goes well beyond the inner city. The data clearly show that there is no correlation between the roll out of the camera programme from 1994 and offences at this level. A closer examination was made of specific relevant offences – such as good order offences, assault, theft, burglary, property damage and motor vehicle theft – again with no evidence of a positive effect from the camera programme over the long term. More detailed data are available from 2001 for the smaller police division of Ipswich, which more closely approximates the city centre where the majority of cameras are located. These data also show no appreciable benefits from the Safe City Program. The rates of reported property and violent crimes are well above those for Queensland and neighbouring police divisions.

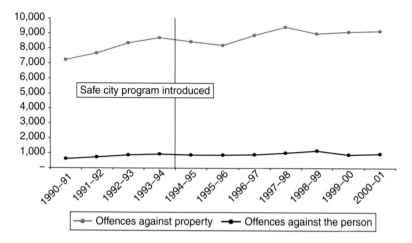

Figure 9.1 Offences recorded by police, Ipswich division, rate per 100,000 population
Source: Queensland Police Service (1990/91–2000/01).

Strike Force Piccadilly 1

Strike Force Piccadilly is a New South Wales Police initiative designed to address an outbreak in ram raids targeting automatic teller machines (ATMs) in the greater Sydney area, beginning in 2005. An evaluation (Prenzler, 2009b) found that the project was highly successful in its core mission. The initial increase in ram raids was halted, and the number was reduced from 69, in the 12 months before the nine-month intervention implementation period, to 19 in the final 12 months of the post-intervention period. This represented a 72 per cent reduction in incidents. For the same periods, successful raids (where cash was obtained) were reduced from 30 down to one – representing a 97 per cent reduction (Prenzler, 2011). Although Strike Force Piccadilly was a 'natural experiment', developed in a crisis without a control group, there was no evidence of displacement to related crimes such as armed robbery, commercial burglary and motor vehicle theft.

The evaluation also found that the reduction in ram raids was attributable to interventions developed in an ad hoc partnership between police and industry stakeholders, including security managers from the Australian Bankers' Association, the Shopping Centre Council of Australia, cash-in-transit firms and the ATM Industry Association. A consultation and development process began with a large forum and was followed by smaller meetings. It was discovered that all stakeholders were engaged in different prevention efforts. The consultation process allowed for a coordinated approach and led to the implementation of six main strategies:

1. The introduction of a police 1-800 phone hotline. Alarm monitoring companies would only use the system when two or more alarms in a multiple alarm system would indicate a high probability of a ram raid in progress. Police made the calls a priority (subject to triage) and despatched patrol cars with sirens and lights. In most cases this closed off the offenders' window of opportunity.
2. Companies were engaged in development and installation of cut-resistant and ramming-resistant bollards; internal bollards around machines; and other technologies for securing ATMs, such as shock absorbing base plates.
3. Companies relocated machines to areas inaccessible to vehicles wherever possible.
4. Police developed and disseminated a risk assessment and reduction tool, which included information on many of the measures at (2) and (3) above.
5. Police also made available Crime Prevention Officers to carry out risk assessments and make recommendations for security upgrades.
6. Regular intelligence reports were circulated by e-mail with detailed data on factors associated with successful and unsuccessful raids, and contributions about prevention measures from all stakeholders.

Strike Force Piccadilly 2

A follow-up study to the Strike Force Piccadilly 1 evaluation found that the reductions in ram raids were sustained over a further two years of data (Figure 9.2) (Prenzler, 2011). As noted, all raids had been reduced by 72 per cent from 69 in the 12 months before the-nine month intervention to 19 in the first-year post-intervention. Raids were subsequently reduced by 91 per cent (from the pre-intervention period) to six in the second year, and by 94 per cent to four in the third and final year. There were 30 successful raids in the 12 months before the intervention. This had been reduced by 97 per cent to one in the first post-intervention year, then by 100 per cent to zero in the second year and by 96.6 per cent to one in the third year.

However, the tapering off of ram raids saw displacement to an innovative new type of crime threat. Gas attacks – sometimes called

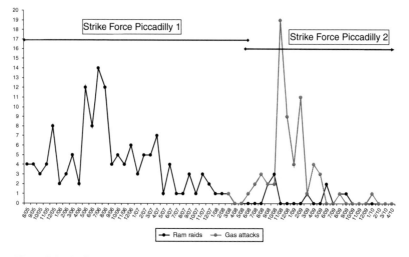

Figure 9.2 Strike Force Piccadilly: All ram raids and gas attacks
Source: Adapted from Prenzler (2011).

'bam raids' – were a growing phenomenon internationally, and Australian incidents were probably copied from methods reported in the Netherlands. Gas attacks involve pumping accelerant gases into an ATM and then setting the gases alight, resulting in an explosion intended to provide access to the cash canister. A category of 'gas attack' was introduced into the Strike Force Piccadilly database after the first incident recorded in March 2008 (Figure 9.2). The attacks peaked from 2008 to 2009, including 19 attacks in November 2008.

In July 2008 Strike Force Piccadilly was restructured as Strike Force Piccadilly 2, primarily in response to the upsurge in gas attacks. The strategies adopted by Strike Force Piccadilly 1 were maintained, including participant meetings, along with the introduction of gas detection devices by ATM operators and the rapid enlargement of police personnel. The detection equipment normally triggered (1) a back-to-base alarm that alerted police on the priority response system, (2) an audible alarm and release of smoke designed to act as deterrents and (3) the release of a gas that mixed with the explosive gas making it inoperable. Strike Force staff were increased from 6 to 50 during the peak of operations, including detectives, intelligence analysts and forensic specialists.

Across 14 months of data, there was a 91 per cent reduction in all gas attacks from 54 in the first 12 months to 5 in the final 12 months of data included in the evaluation (Figure 9.2). For the same periods, successful attacks were reduced by 100 per cent from 22 to 0. (There were also some minor instances of ATM attacks by burglaries and with cutting equipment.) Again, there was no evidence of displacement to related crimes, which were stable or showed modest declines.

Data on gas detection alarm activations and the number of times activations foiled attacks were not available, due to confidentiality concerns. Furthermore, the deterrent effect of these measures could not be measured, although ATMs with gas detection equipment have signs to that effect. The 1800 hotline and other features of Strike Force Piccadilly 1 may have contributed to the disruption of attacks. However, the effect of security strategies dominant in Strike Force Piccadilly 1 appeared less important than police investigations and the incapacitation of a small group of specialist offenders, but these investigations were facilitated by CCTV footage from ATM operators and assistance from partners in the preservation of crime scenes that provided forensic data.

Centrelink's outsourced surveillance programme

Covert or 'optical' surveillance was adopted as an 'Enhanced Investigation Initiative' by Centrelink – Australia's main welfare distribution agency – in 1999 (Sarre & Prenzler, 2011, p. 97). This is a partnership between government and private security with little involvement from police. Cases of suspected benefit fraud amenable to surveillance are outsourced to a panel of private investigation firms. In the first year of operation, 1063 cases were finalized with 70 per cent leading to $3.9 million in payments targeted for recovery. In 2008–2009, 1023 surveillance operations were completed; with 589 or 57.5 per cent considered 'actionable', leading to annualized gross reductions in payments of $5.5 million and debt of $21.2 million. Total savings were estimated at $26.7 million or $26,126 per investigation.

In 2010 Centrelink had 11 surveillance providers on its panel. Cases are allocated for fixed amounts of surveillance, although complex cases can lead to extended surveillance periods. Surveillance is conducted in accordance with the Privacy Commissioner's *Covert Surveillance in Commonwealth Administration: Guidelines*, which include a requirement for qualified operatives. As part of an evaluation of the programme (Sarre & Prenzler, 2011), Centrelink was asked to provide a breakdown of all costs in the surveillance programme, including contract, administration and recovery costs. Only the surveillance contract costs were reported, at AU$1,003,998 for 2009/10. 'Total annualized savings' were estimated at $28,007,961. These figures suggest a net return of approximately AU$27.0 million, or AU$27.89 saved for every dollar spent, not including administration and debt recovery. However, it must be kept in mind that actual recoveries were not reported, only 'debt raised', which was listed at $22.8 million. In relation to the benefits of outsourcing, Centrelink reported that an in-house unit would not be cost-effective. The irregular nature and location of operations meant that surveillance was more effectively contracted out to specialist firms with availability in targeted locations. At the same time, it was reported that video footage was rarely used in court cases.

Best practice in public–private crime prevention partnerships

The case studies outlined above show some of the potential benefits and pitfalls of public–private partnerships. Some quite dramatic reductions in crimes were reported and these were at least in part attributable to the sharing of resources, knowledge, skills and information across a range of public and private sector participants. Process evaluation data indicate the following ingredients are important for successful partnerships (Sarre & Prenzler, 2011):

- a common interest in reducing a specific crime or crime set;
- effective leadership, with personnel with authority from each partner organization driving participation;
- mutual respect;
- information sharing based on high levels of trust and confidentiality;
- formal means of consultation and communication, such as committees, forums and e-mail networks;
- willingness to experiment and consider all ideas;
- formal contractual relationships are not always essential;
- additional legal powers are not always necessary on the security side;
- data-rich projects appear more likely to generate effective interventions and demonstrate success.

The case studies also demonstrated a number of weaknesses. Most obvious was the failure to show a reduction in target crimes in some instances. The Centrelink surveillance case was interesting in showing the contribution of a private provider to secondary prevention – identifying and stopping fraud, and assisting with recovering losses – but not in primary prevention – stopping the onset of offences. In a number of cases, such as the Strike Force Piccadilly ATM crime prevention partnerships, it was difficult to precisely identify specific effective strategies, in part because of confidentiality concerns about operational details. There also tended to be a lack of financial cost-benefit data included in most evaluations.

Most importantly, there has to be a large question mark over any partnership that is ongoing but does not show a clear reduction in crime. This is especially the case where significant public money is involved. According to situational crime prevention theory, the failure of an intervention to reduce crime should result in further research, modifications to the programme and further evaluation (Clarke, 1997). This approach does not appear to have been followed in at least some of the case studies reported here. As indicated, crime reduction is not the sole criterion applied when evaluating partnerships. Feelings of safety, bringing offenders to justice and improving emergency responses are other criteria that have been applied. Nonetheless, crime reduction should be paramount on the assumption that crime entails harm, often to a wide range of victims.

Overall, the evidence presented in this chapter lends cautious support to the idea of public–private crime prevention partnerships, including partnerships involving police and private security, subject to qualifications and a public interest test. A number of sources now provide principles and guidelines to assist in developing projects (CoESS, 2010; Marks, Meyer, & Linssen, 2005; Mazerolle & Prenzler, 2004; National Institute of Justice, 2005). Police and other government authorities should seek to reduce crime in their jurisdictions by scoping possible partnerships with the private sector. Once potential sites are identified, a coordinating committee is most likely to be essential to organize diagnostic research, the development and implementation of strategies and protocols for cooperation, and oversighting contracts. The committee should make an early commitment to systematic process and impact evaluations across all aspects of a project, including a financial cost-benefit assessment. Governments should also consider providing start-up funds and subsidizing security upgrades for participating partners, especially in high-risk economically deprived areas. A number of other strategies can be developed to enhance cooperation with private security, including developing alarm response protocols (Sampson, 2001), educating police about crime prevention and private security, and improving security industry professionalism (see Chapter 12). Partnerships can also be facilitated by local governments establishing crime prevention units with specialist staff. And consultation processes and stakeholder management committees should be as inclusive as possible.

Conclusion

The private sector is a key player in the fight against crime, including at critical infrastructure sites and through the reach of the private security industry into almost every aspect of people's lives. Despite different operating principles, it does appear to be possible to develop public–private partnerships that address crime problems in ways that benefit a variety of stakeholders, including the general public and taxpayers. Considerable caution should be exercised in moving to private involvement in policing, especially in regard to ensuring that the universal mission of the police is not compromised. Nonetheless, available evidence indicates that a variety of very productive relationships can be established and maintained that are capable of showing success across a range of criteria, including significant reductions in victimization.

References

ASIAL. (2010). *Partners in crime.* Retrieved from http://www.aprs.com.au/australian-government-news/partners-in-crime.

Bowers, K. (2001). Small business crime: The evaluation of a crime prevention initiative. *Crime Prevention and Community Safety: An International Journal, 3*(1), 23–42.

City of Ipswich. (2010). *Safe city program.* Retrieved from http://www.ipswich.qld.gov.au/community/safety/safe_city_program/index.php.

Clarke, R. (Ed.). (1997). *Situational crime prevention: Successful case studies.* Guilderland, NY: Harrow and Heston.

CoESS. (2010). *Critical infrastructure security and protection: The public-private opportunity.* Wemmel, Belgium: Author.

Commission of the European Communities. (2009). *Mobilising private and public investment for recovery and long-term structural change: Developing public private partnerships.* Brussels: Author.

Cowan, R. (2010). Security makeover saves city. *Security Insider, 14*(6), 20–23.

Crime Research Centre. (2008). *Evaluation of the eyes on the street program.* Perth: Crime Research Centre, University of Western Australia.

Fairfield City Council. (2002). *Cabramatta townsafe 5 year review.* Sydney: Author.

Farrell, G., Chenery, S., & Pease, K. (1998). *Consolidating police crackdowns: Findings from an antiburglary project.* London: Home Office.

Farrington, D., Gill, M., Waples, S., & Argomaniz, J. (2007). The effects of closed circuit television on crime: Meta-analysis of an English national quasi-experimental multi-site evaluation. *Journal of Experimental Criminology, 3*(1), 21–38.

Forst, B., & Manning, P. (1999). *The privatization of policing: Two views.* Washington, D.C.: Georgetown University Press.

Gimenez-Salinas, A. (2004). New approaches regarding private/public security. *Policing and Society, 14*(2), 158–174.

Golsby, M., & O'Brien, R. (1996). *A co-operative approach to crime prevention: Police and security working together.* Perth: Australian Institute of Security and Applied Technology, Edith Cowan University.

Graham, K., & Homel, R. (2008). *Raising the bar: Preventing aggression in and around bars, pubs and clubs.* Cullompton, UK: Willan.

Ipswich News. (2009). Eyes on crime threat. Retrieved from http://ipswich-news.whereilive.com.au/news/story/eye-on-crime-threat/.

Marks, E., Meyer, A., & Linssen, R. (2005). *Beccaria-standards for ensuring quality in crime prevention projects.* Hannover: Council for Crime Prevention of Lower Saxony.

Mazerolle, L., & Prenzler, T. (2004). Third party policing: Considering the ethical challenges. In M. Hickman, A. Piquero, & J. Greene (Eds.), *Police integrity and ethics* (pp. 163–187). Belmont, CA: Wadsworth.

National Institute of Justice. (2005). *Engaging the private sector to promote homeland security: Law enforcement-private security partnership.* Washington, D.C.: US Department of Justice.

Pastor, J. (2003). *The privatization of police in America.* Jefferson, NC: McFarland & Company.

Prenzler, T. (2009a). *Preventing burglary in commercial and institutional settings: A place management and partnerships approach.* Washington, D.C.: ASIS Foundation.

Prenzler, T. (2009b). Strike Force Piccadilly: A public-private partnership to stop ATM ram raids. *Policing: An International Journal of Police Strategies and Management, 32*(2), 209–225.

Prenzler, T. (2011). Strike Force Piccadilly and ATM security: A follow up study. *Policing: A Journal of Policy and Practice, 5*(3), 236–247.

Prenzler, T., Lowden, C., & Sarre, R. (2010). Aviation security issues in Australia post-9/11. *Journal of Policing, Intelligence and Counter-Terrorism, 5*(2), 9–22.

Queensland Police Service. (1990/91–2000/01). *Statistical reviews.* Brisbane: Queensland Police Service.

Sampson, R. (2001). *False burglar alarms.* Washington, D.C.: Community Oriented Policing Services, US Department of Justice.

Sarre, R., & Prenzler, T. (2009). *The law of private security in Australia* (2nd ed.). Sydney: Thomson Reuters.

Sarre, R., & Prenzler, T. (2011). *Private security and public interest: Exploring private security trends and directions for reform in the new era of plural policing.* Adelaide: University of South Australia.

Sarre, R., & Prenzler, T. (2012). Issues in courtroom security: The new role of the private sector in Australia and New Zealand. *Security Journal, 25*(1), 25–37.

Security Industry Authority. (2004). *SIA annual report 2003/4.* London: Author.

Shearing, C., Stenning, P., & Addario, S. (1985). Police perceptions of private security. *Canadian Police College Journal, 9*(2), 127–154.

Taylor, G. (1999). Using repeat victimization to counter commercial burglary: The Leicester experience. *Security Journal, 12*(1), 41–52.

Tilley, N., & Hopkins, M. (1998). *Business as usual: An evaluation of the small business and crime initiative.* London: Home Office.

Van Buuren, J., & den Boer, M. (2009). *A report on the ethical issues raised by the increasing role of private security professionals in security analysis and provision.* Oslo: International Peace Research institute and European Commission.

Van den Berg, E. (1995). Crime prevention on industrial sites: Security through public-private partnerships. *Security Journal, 6*(1), 27–35.

van Dijk, J. (2008). *The world of crime.* Thousand Oaks, CA: SAGE.

Wheeler, J. (2005). *An independent review of airport security and policing for the Government of Australia.* Canberra: Department of Transport and Regional Services.

Wilson, D., & Sutton, A. (2003). *Open-street CCTV in Australia: A comparative study of establishment and operations.* Canberra: Report to the Criminology Research Council, Australian Institute of Criminology.

Wilson, P., & Wells, H. (2007). What do the watchers watch? An Australian case study of CCTV monitoring. *Asian Policing, 5*(1), 49–60.

10
Safety in Policing and Security

Tim Prenzler

Police and security work are both widely perceived as dangerous, and the deaths of police officers or security officers attract major headlines. Despite this high profile, there is surprisingly little in-house research on safety, and basic safety measures are frequently neglected. This chapter summarizes international research, showing that both groups are at considerable risk from workplace violence and are also at risk from workplace accidents. There is also a major problem with preventable deaths and injuries to members of the public as a result of the actions of police and security officers. Analysis of the circumstances of deaths and injuries for all stakeholders indicates a wide scope for improved safety, often through simple changes to procedures, along with the guided adoption of current and emerging technologies.

Police and security officers: Deaths and injuries

Interest in comparing policing and security has been influenced by the dramatic growth of the private security sector since the 1960s. In many countries the number of security officers approximates or exceeds that of police (see Chapter 9). While security appears more oriented towards a preventive presence and police remain more focused on investigations and arrests, there are numerous points of overlap that generate similar risk profiles (Ferguson, Prenzler, Sarre, & de Caires, 2011). For example, crowd control work at pubs and clubs puts security officers into direct physical confrontation with members of the public, as occurs in policing. Nonetheless, overall, the variety of police work would seem to put police officers at greater risk, especially when investigating serious crimes, intervening with high risk offenders and responding to emergency situations.

There is considerable variability in estimates for police and security officer fatalities and injuries, and published research is biased towards US sources. However, some general points can be made. Both groups often have workplace accident rates as much as twice that of the average for all occupations – although the rates are much lower than some occupations, such as construction and transportation. At the same time, when it comes to violence, available reports consistently place police and security at or near the top 3–5 occupations for injuries and fatalities (Budd 1999; Kraus, Blander, & McArthur, 1995; National Occupational Health and Safety Commission, 1999; Smith & Webster, 2005; Sygnatur & Toscano, 2000). The reports also show that police are more likely to be the victims of workplace violence than security officers. These differences are not entirely consistent, however. For example, a recent study in Australia (Ferguson et al., 2011), that examined workers' compensation data, found the rate of occupational violence was slightly higher for security officers – 399 claims per 100,000 workers compared to 383 per 100,000 workers for police. Both security and police were in the top three highest claiming occupations for work-related injuries and deaths from occupational violence, with security officers at number one in both instances. The study also found that lost work time per claim for police averaged 586.9 hours for workplace violence, while the losses for security officers averaged 823.9 hours.

Another recent Australian study adds some details about the experiences of security officers. A survey found that 58 per cent of respondents had experienced a major assault at least once in their career (Sarre & Prenzler, 2011). The main types of physical injuries reported were cuts, scrapes, bruises and scars (54 per cent); 13 per cent had experienced broken bones or fractures; and 5 per cent reported permanent or ongoing injuries. Furthermore, 41 per cent of respondents reported anxiety as a result of workplace violence. One area of security work that seems particularly prone to assaults is that of crowd controllers ('door staff' or 'patron protectors'). In the same survey, this group reported much higher rates of violence than other security officers. For example, 57 per cent of crowd controllers reported they had experienced a major physical assault once or more in the past year compared to 24 per cent of security officers. Similar results were found in a recent UK survey (Security Industry Authority, 2010, p. 53):

Two thirds of Door Supervisors had been assaulted at work, with 60 per cent reporting being abused verbally and more than half (54 per cent) reporting a physical assault. For those who had worked in the sector for more than five years, 94 per cent reported being attacked. Door Supervisors are significantly more likely to have been subjected to verbal or physical assault compared to the Security Guarding sector (where only 48 per cent of staff report being assaulted).

Policing and security are characterized by exposure to assault-related injuries. However, police deaths tend to generate the most attention and alarm. Without detracting from the importance of security officer safety, some available statistics on police fatalities illustrate the seriousness of the problem. As one example, the South African Police Service (2010) lost an extraordinary 118 officers on duty in 2009–2010 alone. The United Nations has reported that in one of the worst years on record, 2008, 130 police officers died on peacekeeping missions (United Nations Secretary General, 2009). In the United States in 2010 162 officers were killed in the line of duty – an increase of 40 per cent on 2009 (National Law Enforcement Officers Memorial Fund, 2010, p. 1): 'The average age of the officers killed in 2010 was 41; the average length of their law enforcement service was nearly 12 years and on average each officer left behind 2 children' (2010, p. 1). Summary statistics for the United States make for sobering reading:

> There are more than 900,000 sworn law enforcement officers now serving in the United States... Since the first recorded police death in 1792, there have been nearly 19,000 law enforcement officers killed in the line of duty... A total of 1,626 law enforcement officers died in the line of duty during the past 10 years, an average of one death every 53 hours or 163 per year... On average, more than 58,000 law enforcement officers are assaulted each year, resulting in approximately 16,000 injuries... The 1970s were the deadliest decade in law enforcement history, when a total of 2,286 officers died... The deadliest day in law enforcement history was September 11, 2001, when 72 officers were killed while responding to the terrorist attacks on America.
>
> (National Law Enforcement Memorial Fund, 2009)

Overall though it should be said that the main threat to the lives of police officers comes from ill-health, especially heart disease and cancer. Ill-health can account for up to 85 per cent of police in-service deaths (Swanton & Walker, 1989; also Parsons, 2004). While work-related stress may play a part – including psychological conditions leading to suicide – much of the blame for these deaths is likely to lie with lifestyle factors, including sedentary work (Swanton & Walker, 1989, p. 48). In other words, inaction and bad habits are probably more dangerous for police than action on the job.

Members of the public: Deaths and injuries

Fatalities and injuries are also common at the other end of police–citizen encounters. Selected examples indicate a problem of some magnitude. In the United States, the most recent survey of police–citizen interactions by the Bureau of Justice Statistics for the year 2005 included over 60,000 respondents. Nineteen per cent had had contact with police on a face-to-face basis. Of these, 90 per cent 'felt police acted properly'. However, 1.6 per cent 'had force used or threatened against them during their most recent contact', and 83 per cent of these people thought that the amount of force was excessive (Durose, Schmitt, & Langan, 2005, p. 1). Among those who said they experienced force, 55 per cent indicated the force was 'physical' in nature, such as 'pushing, pointing a gun, or using chemical spray'; 14.8 per cent of persons who said they experienced any type of force also said they were injured (pp. 8–9). Although the proportion of people claiming to be injured in these encounters was quite small, the total number was large. The study authors projected the responses from the sample to the whole population. This meant that, in the one year, approximately 696,000 people experienced force or threats by police, and 103,008 claimed to have been injured.

Alpert and Dunham (2010), in their review of use of force issues, confirm that most studies show police use of force generally occurs at very low levels as a proportion of all police–citizen contacts. Nonetheless, they assert that while force is 'a rare event in routine police work, its study is important because its use can cause injuries to officers and/or citizens and is the major police issue that leads to community unrest and negative attitudes toward the police' (p. 236).

Policing is of course notorious for fatal injuries caused by officers in two main areas: shootings of suspects and deaths in custody. Fatalities in these areas often trigger crises in law enforcement that lead to major inquiries and reform agendas imposed on police (see below). The policing of protest is also a high risk area for injuries (Chapter 4). High-speed vehicle pursuits also often result in injuries and deaths to members of the public, as well as police (Hoffman, 2003).

In terms of injuries to the public, the security industry is most notorious for assaults by crowd controllers at nightclubs and pubs. Injuries can also result from the failure of crowd controllers to protect patrons. There is little in the way of accurate information on the scale of the problem. However, a 1990 study from Victoria (Australia) illustrates some of the issues (Victorian Community Council Against Violence, 1990). The study identified a major problem with fights and assaults in and around nightclubs and hotels. It was estimated that about 20 per cent of all reported serious assaults in the state were associated with licensed premises – approximately 818 per year. A survey of nightclub patrons found a large majority had witnessed violence. Thirty per cent claimed to have been victims themselves, and 37 per cent of this group claimed the violence was perpetrated by crowd controllers. Patron drunkenness and aggressiveness also meant that crowd controllers themselves were frequently harassed and assaulted.

Causes of deaths and injuries

As we have seen, there are a number of obvious dangers in policing and security work which make sense of high rates of injuries and deaths, especially from workplace violence. Officers from both groups have frequent contact with people engaged in criminal activity or who may be mentally unstable, aggressive, under the influence of drugs and alcohol, or injured. This contact exposes officers to physical injury due to manual handling, assaults or accidents (Guthrie, 2009; National Occupational Health and Safety Commission, 2003; WorkCover NSW, 2007). An important general finding from police research is that the more officers engage in direct physical contact with suspects, the more likely it is that injuries will result to both groups (Alpert & Dunham, 2010). Police – and security officers to a lesser extent – are also involved in protecting people in non-criminal emergency response and rescue situations, including in natural disasters, where there are risks from a great variety of sources, including fire and flood, explosions and landslides.

Research on causes of deaths and injuries has some longevity in police studies. In security studies, research is in its infancy, although the lack of compulsory training of security officers and weak government regulation of private security companies and liquor outlets are often cited as major contributors to violence and injuries (Sarre & Prenzler, 2011). Another area that receives some attention is the cash-in-transit sector, where guards are often highly exposed to attacks in armed robberies (Smith & Louis, 2010).

When it comes to the high-profile area of police officer deaths, the 'causes' can be categorized in different ways. Table 10.1 shows one

Table 10.1   Causes of law enforcement deaths, United States, 2001–2010

Cause of death	Number	Percent
Shot	572	35.1
Auto accidents	469	28.8
Job-related illness	156	9.5
Struck by vehicle	153	9.3
Motorcycle accident	80	4.9
Terrorist attack	78	4.7
Aircraft accidents	33	2.0
Drowned	23	1.4
Beaten	10	0.6
Fall	13	0.7
Stabbed	8	0.4
Bomb-related incident	7	0.4
Struck by falling object	6	0.3
Struck by train	5	0.3
Boating accident	4	0.2
Bicycle accident	3	0.1
Electrocuted	3	0.1
Poisoned	2	0.1
Horse-related accident	1	0.0
Strangled	1	0.0
Total	1,627	~100

Source: Adapted from National Law Enforcement Memorial Fund (2011).

format adopted by the US National Law Enforcement Memorial Fund. It is clear that accidents are prominent in the profile, and other research shows the majority of police deaths typically result from accidents rather than attacks (Allard & Prenzler, 2009; Mumola, 2007). Available data indicate that the majority of accidental deaths result from high-speed vehicle pursuits and dangerous or careless driving (Allard & Prenzler, 2009; NLECTC, 2009; Payne & Fenske, 1997). In their study, Pinizzotto, Davis and Miller (2002) found that 'diminishing physical skills' – in areas such as emergency driving and traffic stop procedures – were a major contributing factor to police accidental deaths (p. 10; also Boylen & Little, 1990). When it comes to fatal attacks on police, available data indicate that the large majority of incidents involve firearms and occur in arrest situations; at traffic stops; while responding to robberies, disturbances and domestic violence calls; and while investigating reports of suspicious persons (Allard & Prenzler, 2009; Carderelli, 1968; Edwards, 1996; Federal Bureau of Investigation, 2007). Mayhew (2001) reported that police homicides also frequently involve offenders with personality disorders. In these fatal encounters officers underestimated the risks they faced and were either overly reliant on negotiation or breached procedures – such as failing to wait for back-up (see also Chapman, 1997; Kurby, 2004).

One might think that preventing officer deaths and injuries would be a key priority for governments, as well as for police and security managers, and also police and security officer unions. At the very least, the financial costs of litigation and workers' compensation should motivate action to address the problem. One might also assume that officers entering a dangerous field of work would be especially careful about protecting themselves. It is perhaps surprising therefore to discover that a key implication of research in this area is that management neglect and officer risk-taking behaviours are major factors in high death and injury rates. The circumstances of many injurious encounters are in fact reminiscent of the suicidal full frontal charges of old-fashioned set piece warfare (Boylen & Little, 1990; Prenzler, 2010). And management neglect is evidenced in part by the lack of agency research on the topic. If police departments and security firms and associations were serious about safety, they would conduct in-house research, combining the lessons from the literature with data from their own working environments. The institutional failure to identify, enact and enforce appropriate safety procedures has been fundamental to officer injuries and fatalities over many decades.

The alleged macho culture of policing provides one explanation for self-harming risk-taking behaviour by police officers and also for assaults by police (Silvestri, 2003). This probably also has application to the male-dominated field of security. The idea of danger and combat adds to the mystique and bravado of the job – a perspective confirmed by the occasional loss. One corollary of this is that the danger and physical demands of police work have repeatedly been used as arguments to exclude women. However, studies comparing the performance of male and female officers show women are just as effective as men and just as likely to be involved in arrests (Lunneborg, 1989). There is mixed evidence on male/female injury rates but some evidence that female officers may receive less severe injuries and may be more likely to report injuries (Criminal Justice Commission, 1996; VISU, 2009). Women police, proportionately, are also much less likely to kill offenders and much less likely to be murdered (Boylen & Little, 1990; Brown & Langan, 2001). This makes sense because women tend to adopt a more conciliatory style that requires less force. For example, an observation study carried out in South Australia (Braithwaite & Brewer,

1998) found that male officers were twice as likely as female officers to engage in threatening behaviour and physical contact with members of the public, which in turn elicited greater resistance and aggression. Women are also less likely to attract complaints of assault. For example, another Australian study found that allegations of assault against police in Queensland averaged 9.2 per 100 male officers compared to 3.7 per 100 female officers (Waugh, Ede, & Alley, 1998).

There are a number of other specific reasons for injuries and fatalities in police work. The chapter on public order policing in this volume describes a variety of inappropriate tactics in relation to political protests that can lead to violence, including a failure to negotiate with protestors or plan containment strategies. Of course, many of the injuries experienced by protestors and dissidents at the hands of police in repressive regimes are deliberate – designed to eliminate, incapacitate or intimidate opposition to the ruling elite. Similarly, police shootings and deaths in police custody often result from the deliberate policies of repressive regimes. At the same time, these adverse events are also a feature of policing in many democracies. Fatal shootings by police have frequently been attributed to deficits in training and supervision and a 'firearms-dependent culture' with inadequate safety procedures (Office of Police Integrity, 2005, p. ii). Deaths in custody have also been associated with deficits in training, supervision and procedures related to the well-being of detainees (Independent Police Complaints Commission, 2010). This often includes failure to ensure inmates do not commit suicide.

Preventing deaths and injuries

Deaths and injuries on a large scale are not inevitable in policing and security. Risks are intrinsic to the job and elimination of danger is probably impossible. At the same time, there is good evidence that safety can be significantly improved, both for officers and members of the public, and that this can be achieved without compromising the mission for law enforcement and crime prevention.

Most of the research on prevention is, again, in the policing area. For security, some survey research indicates support for the proposition that enhanced regulation can improve safety – particularly mandatory training, disqualifying offences that exclude inappropriate persons and spot checks on licensed premises. One recent survey of the owners and managers of security firms found that 72 per cent agreed regulation was effective in 'promoting safe work practices and minimising injuries', while 66 per cent believed regulation had reduced assaults by security personnel, and 60 per cent believed it was effective in reducing injuries to security personnel (Sarre & Prenzler, 2011, pp. 57–58). A similar survey of security operatives found 57 per cent felt that better regulation helped reduce assaults by security officers on members of the public. However, only 24 per cent believed it had helped reduce assaults on officers (p. 131). It is possible, given the dearth of research on safety in security, that useful lessons can be drawn from the larger field of police officer safety. Examples include defensive tactics and negotiating skills – especially for crowd controllers – or body armour for cash-in-transit guards. However, the main lesson is that much more industry-specific and task-specific research needs to be done in this area.

In the area of police fatality prevention there do not appear to be any classic intervention studies with control groups. Nonetheless, evidence of the impact of various strategies can be deduced, if not precisely, from reductions and associated preventive innovations. A good example of this is the trend in police fatalities in Australia. Figure 10.1 shows that across 17 decades, from 1841 to 2010, the rate of police deaths per 10,000 officers fell by 97.4 per cent from a peak of 23.3 in the decade 1861–1870 to 0.6 in the most recent decade. In the nineteenth century many police deaths were related to the frontier environment, including fatal horse riding accidents and some cases of officers being speared by Indigenous people. In the post-World War II period, motor vehicle accidents were the main cause of death,

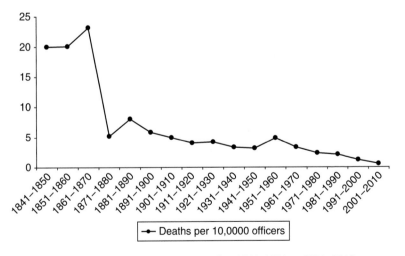

Figure 10.1 Police deaths on duty in Australia, 1841–1850 to 2001–2010
Source: Updated from Allard and Prenzler (2009).

but at this time all deaths declined by 87.7 per cent from a peak of 4.9 per 10,000 officers in 1951–1960 (67 deaths) to 0.6 in 2001–2010 (30 deaths). Police deaths in Australia (and other jurisdictions) have declined despite increases in crime from the 1970s to the 1990s, and despite the availability of firearms and increased high-risk activities such as drug raids. The circumstances in which this decline has occurred suggest a cumulative effect from improvements in areas such as training, procedures (e.g. delaying entry to premises, calling for back up) and technology (e.g. body armour) (Brown & Langdon, 2001; Mayhew, 2001; National Institute of Justice, 1998; Swanton & Walker, 1989). The literature also suggests that general improvements in road safety appear to have directly affected police officer safety. These measures include the compulsory wearing of seat belts and motorcycle helmets and greater restrictions on speeding (Allard & Prenzler, 2009).

Body armour is one specific technology which has reputedly saved many lives. In the United States, between 1975 and March 2006, there were 3000 documented cases of officers saved from death or serious injury because they were wearing armour (NLECTC, 2006, p. 5). However, police should not take false comfort from this. In 2009, for example, 36 of 48 officers recorded as 'feloniously killed' in the United States were wearing body armour (Federal Bureau of Investigation, 2010). Most were shot in the head, but some were shot in the upper chest and back. These findings support the view that police must take a highly systematic and cautious approach to all high-risk activities – such as raids, sieges and arrests – including the use of criminal intelligence, setting up perimeters and calling in special operations teams where appropriate (Prenzler, 2010).

The discussion so far has been largely about protecting officers. A key finding of recent work on the effects of OC ('pepper') spray and conducted electricity devices (CEDs) is that the deployment of these devices can reduce injuries to both police and the public (Taylor & Woods, 2010; Thomas, Collins, & Lovrich, 2010). For example, a study supported by the Police Executive Research Forum compared injuries across 24,380 encounters between police and citizens in which police employed force against suspects (Alpert & Dunham, 2010). Injury rates to officers were as follows: 21.2 per cent when officers used 'hands-on' physical force to control a suspect, 14.0 per cent when OC spray was used and 7.6 per cent when a CED was deployed. Injury rates to suspects were 48.9 per cent when officers used physical force, 22.1 per cent when OC spray was used and 25.1 per cent when a CED was deployed.

Of course, OC spray and CEDs can also cause injuries, and research has also informed the design of guidelines intended in part to prevent 'overuse and abuse' (Alpert & Dunham, 2010, p. 251). The best policy option is to ban the use of CEDs and OC spray against 'passive resisters' and authorize their use only in response to 'active threats of resistance' (p. 251). It is also particularly important in the case of suspects subject to a CED charge that their condition is closely monitored and medical care provided if abnormal responses are evident. All officers should also have training in 'real-world and high-stress conditions' (p. 251). More generally:

> CED policies and training should require that officers evaluate the totality of the circumstances before using a CED, which would include the environment, age, size, gender, apparent physical capabilities, and health concerns (e.g., obviously pregnant women) of suspects...CEDs are often used against vulnerable populations, which can result in problematic outcomes. Department trainers should focus on alternative methods to control suspects who are members of these at risk populations. In cases where it is determined that CEDs are ineffective or create an unacceptable health risk, multiple applications of a CED should be prohibited. In addition, CED policies and training should prohibit the use of CEDs in the presence of flammable liquids or in circumstances where falling would pose unreasonable risks to the suspect (elevated areas, into water, adjacent to traffic, riding a bicycle, etc.). Finally, policies and training should address the use of CEDs against persons who are restrained (e.g., handcuffed or otherwise controlled) and should either prohibit such uses outright or limit them to clearly defined, aggravated circumstances. (p. 252)

International codes of practice in relation to minimum force should always apply in police use of force decisions. The International Association of Chiefs of Police (2002) *Law Enforcement Code of Ethics* provides one example:

> A police officer will never employ unnecessary force or violence and will use only such force in the discharge of duty as is reasonable in all circumstances. The use of force should be used only with the greatest restraint and only after discussion, negotiation and persuasion have been found to be inappropriate or ineffective. While the use of force is occasionally unavoidable, every police officer will refrain

from unnecessary infliction of pain or suffering and will never engage in cruel, degrading or inhuman treatment of any person.

(pp. 36–37)

Making the most of emerging technologies is one way to reduce injuries. But often the best solution to a problem is a fairly simple one. The evidence is building, as indicated in the section above on 'causes of deaths and injuries', that good old-fashioned courtesy and verbal skills are also important for safety. Chapter 8 – Corruption Prevention and Complaints Management – referred to three studies showing large reductions in complaints against police, including complaints about assaults and excessive force (Davis, Mateu-Gelabert, & Miller, 2005; Independent Police Review, 2004, 2010; Porter, Prenzler, & Fleming, 2011). Unfortunately, these studies do not include injury data, but reducing assault allegations is a good first step. The main ingredients in the interventions included (1) adoption of an explicit policy of reducing complaints and/or use of force incidents, (2) improved training in negotiation skills and minimum use of force and (3) application of an early warning system to intervene with officers associated with abnormal complaints or abnormal use of force incidents.

There is also evidence that simple changes in procedures can reduce deaths in police custody. In the United Kingdom, for example, deaths in police custody decreased by 69 per cent from 49 cases in 1998/99 to 15 in 2008/09 (a 72 per cent fall in the rate of deaths 'per 100,000 notifiable arrests') (Independent Police Complaints Commission, 2010, pp. 10–11). This reduction was attributed to improvements in cell design – with fewer points where inmates could hang themselves – as well as police taking persons directly to hospital instead of the watchhouse, custody sergeants taking action to address detainee health issues at the point of admission, the influence of custody visitors and better risk management procedures generally. These lessons are likely to be increasingly relevant for private security as governments outsource more prisoner transportation and detention services (Sarre & Prenzler, 2012).

Fatal shootings by police is another area where major reductions can be achieved, although these can be hard to sustain. An illustrative case is that of the Victoria Police in Australia. In the mid-1990s an escalation in police shootings generated a crisis that led to five separate reviews of police conduct. Figure 10.2 shows that fatal shootings increased in the late-1980s to a peak of six in 1988. The number then declined, but then rose again – to a peak of nine in 1994. The increase in the 1980s was

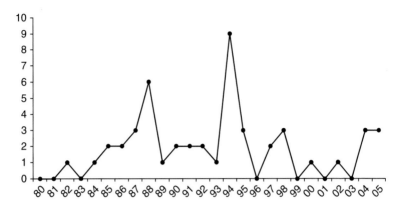

Figure 10.2 Fatal shootings, Victoria Police
Source: Office of Police Integrity (2005, p. 63).

attributed to the emergence of urban warfare between police and criminals, and the decline was attributed to improved training in 'methods of controlling violent criminals [with] a strong focus on firearms and defensive physical tactics' (Office of Police Integrity, 2005, pp. i–ii). The upsurge in the 1990s was related in part to police shootings of mentally ill people displaying aggressive behaviours in public. The reviews led to the introduction of 'Project Beacon' and the implementation of a 'Safety First Philosophy' in 1994, which included clearer policies and better training in 'communication, conflict resolution, risk assessment, tactical planning, decision-making and defensive tactics' (p. 1). These policies appeared to have a direct impact, with an average of 0.8 fatal shootings per year over the eight years from 1996 to 2003. The occurrence of three fatal shootings in 2004 and three in 2005 prompted another review of the situation. The Office of Police Integrity (2005, p. 55) found that:

> It appears that Victoria Police has lost some of the strategic focus on safety and avoiding the use of force which it developed during Project Beacon...The result is a lack of effective risk management, a culture in which self-assessment, review and improvement are given insufficient attention, and a diminution of essential police training.

Implementing safety

Across the whole policing and security environment there are two main ways in which improvements in safety can be implemented: (1) through government action at a broad social level and (2) through direct action by police departments and by security firms and associations. At the broader level of government action, a number of policies are apparent with likely direct benefits to officers and the public. Most importantly, governments should increase regulation of driving to minimize crashes. Chapter 6 reports on a wide range of successful measures in enforcing compliance with road rules covering speed, seat belts and alcohol and drugs. To these we can add improved roads (including dual carriageways), reduced speeds and higher safety standards in motor vehicle design. Governments can also reduce injuries and fatalities in policing and security by providing better public mental health services, including early diagnosis, treatment and institutionalization. Strong gun control measures are also likely to produce reductions in officer fatalities. And a less liberal approach to repeat violent offenders, including those facing outstanding charges, should help keep high-risk persons off the streets (Prenzler, 2010).

Police also need to take a much more cautious and planned approach to their work, with much stricter procedural controls than are generally evident, and the same could probably be said for security providers in many instances. With police, stricter controls are particularly relevant to vehicle-related safety (Allard & Prenzler, 2009). For example, police motorcycles figure prominently in fatal accident statistics and their use should be limited to operational necessity. Officers should always avoid approaching the driver of a stationary vehicle through the driver's side window where they can be hit by passing vehicles. Police should also obey all road rules except in emergency situations, when they should use emergency lights and sirens. Contemporary best practice standards now place strict limits on officer discretion in vehicle pursuits. There should be (1) a high threshold of grounds for a pursuit (likely serious offences) and (2) a low threshold of grounds for terminating a pursuit (risks to suspects, police and the public), as well as (3) absolute speed limits of 30–40 per cent above the posted limit, (4) radio supervision of drivers by a senior officer and (5) regular refresher training that includes research findings contradicting myths about the value of pursuits (Hoffman, 2003; see also Alpert, 1997; Rix, Walker, & Brown, 1997). Police should also follow strict safety procedures at road blocks, making use of barriers, reflective vests and emergency lights. Pre-service training in safety needs to be reinforced and advanced by in-service training that is informed by the latest research; and the latest proven protective technology needs to be adopted wherever possible subject to guidelines.

Both policing and security agencies also need to do research about the risks that apply in their jurisdictions and relate these to the literature in order to develop specific measures that can be implemented, evaluated and modified as required, including best practice in alternatives to the use of force. The relevance to security of best practice policing principles – in areas such as OC spray, CEDs, body armour, defensive tactics and custody procedures – all need to be tested through systematic research.

Conclusion

Police and security officers provide an essential service in protecting people from crime and violence. However, provision of this service often comes at an unacceptable cost in terms of injuries and fatalities. It is important therefore that greater efforts are put into protecting the welfare of officers engaged in the common tasks of crime prevention, order maintenance, law enforcement and emergency response. Policing and security operations also involve a substantial risk to members of the public, and there is an emerging body of research that shows that these risks can be reduced through proper research and planning and through the guided adoption of diverse technologies. However, improvements in negotiation, physical restraint and self-defence skills, involving minimal force, are also likely to yield safety benefits and should constitute a priority response in most circumstances.

References

Allard, T., & Prenzler, T. (2009). A summary analysis of police deaths in Australia: Implications for prevention. *International Journal of Comparative and Applied Criminal Justice, 33*, 61–81.

Alpert, G. (1997). *Police pursuit: Policies and training*. Washington, D.C.: National Institute of Justice.

Alpert, G. P., & Dunham, R. G. (2010). Policy and training recommendations related to police use of CEDS: Overview of findings from a comprehensive national study. *Police Quarterly, 13*(3), 235–259.

Boylen, M., & Little, R. (1990). Fatal assaults on United States law enforcement officers. *The Police Journal, 63*, 61–77.

Braithwaite, H., & Brewer, N. (1998). Differences in the conflict resolution tactics of male and female police patrol officers. *International Journal of Police Science and Management, 1*(3), 288–300.

Brown, J., & Langan, P. (2001). *Policing and homicide, 1976–98: Justifiable homicide by police, police officers murdered by felons*. Washington D.C.: US Department of Justice.

Budd, T. (1999). *Violence at work: Findings from the British Crime Survey*. London: Home Office.

Carderelli, A. (1968). An analysis of police killed in action 1961–1963. *Journal of Criminal Law, Criminology and Police Science, 59*, 447–453.

Chapman, S. (1997). *Murdered on duty: The killing of police officers in America*. Springfield IL: Charles C. Thomas.

Criminal Justice Commission. (1996). *Assault-related injuries reported by Queensland police officers.* Brisbane: Author.

Davis, R., Mateu-Gelabert, P., & Miller, J. (2005). Can effective policing also be respectful? Two examples in the South Bronx. *Police Quarterly, 8*(2), 229–247.

Durose, M. R., Schmitt, E. L., & Langan, P. A. (2005). *Contacts between police and the public.* Washington, D.C.: Bureau of Justice Statistics.

Edwards, T. (1996). Felonious killings of state police and highway patrol officers: A descriptive and comparative evaluation. *American Journal of Policing, 14,* 89–105.

Federal Bureau of Investigation. (2007). *Law enforcement officers killed and assaulted 2006.* Washington D.C.: Federal Bureau of Investigation.

Federal Bureau of Investigation. (2010). *FBI releases 2009 statistics on law enforcement officers killed and assaulted.* www.fbi.gov/about-us/cjis/ucr/leoka/2009/leoka-2009.

Ferguson, P., Prenzler, T., Sarre, R., & de Caires, B. (2011). Police and security officer experiences of occupational violence and injury in Australia. *International journal of Police Science and Management, 13*(3), 223–233.

Guthrie, R. (2009). *The industrial relations of sick leave and workers compensation for police officers in Australia.* Canberra: Regnet, Australian National University.

Hoffman, G. (2003). *Police pursuits: A law enforcement and public safety issue for Queensland.* Brisbane: Crime and Misconduct Commission.

Independent Police Complaints Commission. (2010). *Deaths in or following police custody.* London: Author.

Independent Police Review. (2004). *Annual report.* Portland, OR: Office of the City Auditor.

Independent Police Review. (2010). *Annual report.* Portland, OR: Office of the City Auditor.

International Association of Chiefs of Police. (2002). *Police chiefs desk reference.* Washington, DC: Author & Bureau of Justice Assistance.

Kraus, J. F., Blander, B., & McArthur, D. L. (1995). Incidence, risk factors and prevention strategies for work-related assault injuries: A review of what is known, what needs to be known, and countermeasures for intervention. *Annual Review of Public Health, 16,* 355–379.

Kurby, R. (2004). *End of watch: Utah's murdered police officers: 1853–2003.* Salt Lake City: University of Utah Press.

Lunneborg, P. W. (1989). *Women police officers: Current career profiles.* Springfield, IL, Charles C. Thomas.

Mayhew, C. (2001). *Occupational health and safety risks faced by police officers.* Canberra: Australian Institute of Criminology.

Mumola, C. J. (2007). *Arrest-related deaths in the United States, 2003–2005.* Washington, D.C.: Bureau of Justice Statistics.

National Institute of Justice. (1998). *Selection and application guide to police body armor.* Washington D.C.: National Institute of Justice.

National Law Enforcement Memorial Fund. (2009). Law enforcement facts. www.nleomf.org/facts/enforcement/.

National Law Enforcement Memorial Fund. (2011). Causes of law enforcement deaths. http://www.nleomf.org/facts/officer-fatalities-data/causes.html.

National Law Enforcement Officers Memorial Fund. (2010). Law enforcement officer deaths: Preliminary 2010. *Research Bulletin, December,* 1.

National Occupational Health and Safety Commission. (1999). *Work-related fatal-ities involving emergency service workers in Australia, 1989 to 1992.* Sydney: Author

National Occupational Health and Safety Commission. (2003). *National code of practice for the control of work-related exposure to Hepatitis and HIV (Blood-borne) Viruses.* Canberra: National Occupational Health and Safety Commission.

NLECTC. (2006). 30 years, 3,000 saves. *Techbeat, Fall* (National Law Enforcement and Corrections Technology Center).

NLECTC. (2009). *Police officer involved vehicular fatalities in 2009.* Rockville, MD: National Law Enforcement and Corrections Technology Center, National Institute of Justice.

Office of Police Integrity. (2005). *Review of fatal shootings by Victoria Police.* Melbourne: Author.

Parsons, J. R. L. (2004). *Occupational health and safety issues of police officers in Canada, the United States and Europe.* Retrieved from http://www.safetynet.mun.ca/pdfs/Occupational%20H&S.pdf.

Payne, D., & Fenske, J. (1997). An analysis of the rates of accidents, injuries and fatalities under different light conditions: Michigan emergency response study of state police pursuits. *Policing, 20*, 357–373.

Pinizzotto, A., Davis, E., & Miller, C. (2002). Accidentally dead: Accidental line-of-duty deaths of law enforcement officers. *FBI Law Enforcement Bulletin, 71*, 8–13.

Porter, L., Prenzler, T., & Fleming, J. (2011). Complaint reduction in the Tasmanian Police. *Policing and Society.* http://www.tandfonline.com/doi/pdf/10.1080/10439463.2011.641548.

Prenzler, T. (2010). Learning from police deaths on duty: A case study. *Policing: A Journal of Policy and Practice, 4*(4), 421–431.

Rix, B., Walker, D., & Brown, R. (1997). *A study of deaths and serious injuries resulting from police vehicle accidents.* London: Home Office.

Sarre, R., & Prenzler, T. (2011). *Private security and public interest: Exploring private security trends and directions for reform in the new era of plural policing.* Adelaide: University of South Australia.

Sarre, R., & Prenzler, T. (2012). Issues in courtroom security: The new role of the private sector in Australia and New Zealand. *Security Journal, 25*(1), 25–37. http://www.palgrave-journals.com/sj/journal/vaop/ncurrent/pdf/sj20113a.pdf.

Security Industry Authority. (2010). *The impact of regulation on the door supervisor sector.* London: Author.

Silvestri, M. (2003). *Women in charge: Policing, gender and leadership.* Cullompton, UK: Willan.

Smith, D., & Webster, D. (2005). The relative hazards of Australian police work. *Australian Police Journal, 59*, 41–43.

Smith, L., & Louis, E. (2010). Cash in transit armed robbery in Australia. *Trends and Issues in Crime and Criminal Justice, 397*, 1–6.

South Africa Police Service. (2010). *Roll of honour, 2009–2010.* Retrieved from http://www.saps.gov.za/saps_profile/honour/roll_honour2009_10.html.

Swanton, B., & Walker, J. (1989). *Police employee health.* Canberra: Australian Institute of Criminology.

Sygnatur, E., & Toscano, G. (2000). Work-related homicides: The facts. *Compensation and Working Conditions, Spring,* 3–8.

Taylor, B., & Woods, D. J. (2010). Injuries to officers and suspects in police use-of-force cases: A quasi-experimental evaluation. *Police Quarterly, 13*(3), 260–289.

Thomas, K. J., Collins, P. A., & Lovrich, N. P. (2010). Conducted energy device use in municipal policing: Results of a national survey on policy and effectiveness assessments. *Police Quarterly, 13*(3), 290–315.

United Nations Secretary General. (2009). *Message on international day of peacekeepers, 29 May 2009.* Retrieved from http://un2.amblique.net/files/files/peacekeepersday2009.pdf.

Victorian Community Council Against Violence. (1990). *Inquiry into violence in and around licensed premises.* Melbourne: Victorian Community Council Against Violence.

VISU. (2009). *Injury to police and security officers: January 2000 to December 2008.* Melbourne: VISU (Victorian Injury Surveillance Unit), Monash University.

Waugh, L., Ede, A., & Alley, A. (1998). Police culture, women police and attitudes towards misconduct. *International Journal of Police Science and Management, 1*(3), 288–300.

WorkCover NSW. (2007). *Fatigue management in the security industry.* Sydney: Author.

11
Making the Most of Security Technology

Roderick ('Rick') Draper, Jessica Ritchie and Tim Prenzler

Rapid growth in the number of private security personnel in the last few decades has been matched by enormous expansion and diversification in security technology. The drive to supplement or replace security guards with security devices has led to the availability of a very wide and potentially confusing array of options as the affordability and accessibility of security technology have improved. However, it could be argued that many organizations do not fully realize the available return on their investments in this area. Failure to adequately define objectives and functional requirements can lead to poor decision making that results in system vulnerabilities. Security technology should not be viewed as a stand-alone function served by discrete technology, but rather it should be located within a holistic framework where strategic objectives are supported by a range of overlapping systems and processes. With this in mind, the chapter explores ways of understanding the underlying considerations and improving the functionality and cost effectiveness of crime prevention technologies within a comprehensive risk management framework. A wide array of security devices is available – from anti-counterfeiting technologies, through advanced locking mechanisms, to anti-malware computer software. The chapter focuses on three of these – alarm systems, electronic access control and CCTV – but within a framework of generic principles that should inform the introduction and ongoing use of all security technologies.

Background: The growth in security and issues with security technology

As noted elsewhere in this book, the growth of private security has been recognized as one of the most significant developments in policing generally since World War II (Bayley & Shearing, 2001). A 2011 survey across 70 countries estimated there were 19.5 million people employed in the private security industry – with a projected total of 25.5 million across all countries (Small Arms Survey, 2011). The industry was valued at $US100–165 billion per annum, with an annual growth rate of 7–8 per cent. Across the 70 countries surveyed, private security personnel were estimated to outnumber police by a ratio of 1.8:1. It should also be kept in mind that non-police guarding and crime prevention services are extensive in the public sector, and the two sectors together can be variously described as 'protective security' or 'security services'.

Growth in this broad area, but especially the private sector, has been associated with numerous influences, including increased litigation, health and safety legislation, the modern terrorist threat and government policies of privatization (Small Arms Survey, 2011). Arguably the strongest influence was the large increases in crime that occurred in many countries from the 1960s to the 1990s. This period was marked by a shift in consciousness away from reliance on police towards the self-provision of protection through the management of tailor-made, site-specific, security. Protective security has continued to grow despite stable or declining crime rates from the turn of the century, and the growth and impact of the whole sector provides one of the best explanations for reductions in crime rates (van Dijk, 2008). At the same time, ongoing expansion of security services is partly driven by the fact that crime remains at high levels in many countries. The risk of becoming a victim of crime remains a constant negative feature of modern life – for ordinary citizens as well as businesses and public sector organizations.

The increases in crime that were especially marked in most Western countries in the 1970s and 1980s have been closely associated with the prosperity and freer lifestyles that went with the post-War economic boom (Cohen & Felson, 1979). In this period there were enormous increases in the number of light-weight, high-value, easily transportable goods that could be stolen. At the same time, more people worked away from home during the day, while workplaces were abandoned at night in the flight back to the suburbs. People also went out more and travelled more, exposing themselves to robbery and assault. Separation of guardians from targets was a key factor in the escalating crime problem. While the employment of security guards provided one form of substitute guardianship, the enormous growth in guarding services could still not provide adequate cost-effective protection. The obvious 'solution' was to seek cheaper, omnipresent and more reliable forms of proxy guardianship through technology.

Humans have, of course, always made use of technology, in the broad sense of the term, to protect their property and person (McCrie, 2006). Ancient non-human devices, that we would now term 'low-tech', have included dogs, walls, fences, trip wires and bells, and strong boxes and secret compartments. The use of mechanical locks has been traced back as far as ancient Egypt. The invention of the burglar alarm in the mid-nineteenth century was arguably the key development that drove growth in the technical side of modern security, while also stimulating the 'manpower' sector (McCrie, 2006). Originally, alarms were designed to alert persons on-site, but advances in alarm communication technology and the availability of telephone lines allowed monitoring and response by guards from off-site locations.

Alarms have remained a mainstay of protective security, with their scope enlarged by the application of motion and other sensors to supplement simple circuit breaker mechanisms, such as magnetic reed switches. In the United States, 92 per cent of retail firms use an alarm system (Hollinger & Adams, 2009, p. 23). The uptake in residential premises is much lower, at around 30 per cent. Globally, household alarm usage is more in the vicinity of 10 per cent, but steadily increasing (van Dijk, 2008, p. 132). Since the 1980s, alarms have increasingly been supplemented by closed circuit television (CCTV). In 2011 the number of CCTV cameras in the United Kingdom alone was estimated at 1.85 million (Reeve, 2011).

The use of physiological traits or behavioural characteristics, collectively called 'biometrics', has also provided a new dimension to security, mainly from the latter part of the twentieth century (McCrie, 2006). Despite the hype around biometric technologies, beyond fingerprints and hand geometry, other biometric traits – such as iris and retinal structures, gait, typing rhythm and posture – have not proved particularly popular to date for main stream use in physical or computer access control. Building on success with in-built fingerprint scanners, computer manufacturers have been refining the use of face recognition for automating log-in and security processes. The software involved uses the computer's in-built camera to monitor the face of the logged-in user, and if that face changes or is absent for a nominated period of time the computer automatically locks (Dell Inc., 2010). The use of facial recognition technology is also now in practice in fraud control and immigration control, following significant investment stimulated by the 9/11 terrorist attacks (Gates, 2006).

The rise of private security has long attracted concerns about inequalities in security and threats to civil liberties from an under-regulated profit-driven sector. Improved regulation – through licensing, mandated training, disqualifying offences, auditing and complaints investigation – has moderated some of these concerns (see Chapter 12). Security services also provide many public interest benefits, including in government housing, public hospitals and schools; as well as helping to free up police to concentrate on serious crimes. However, the industry continues to attract criticism in many locations, especially in regard to professional standards in both probity and competence (Prenzler & Sarre, 2008). Security technology and its management have also been targets of criticism. There is an obvious concern about the threats to privacy represented by CCTV and biometrics (Coleman & McCahill, 2011). The effectiveness of security has also come under scrutiny, with allegations that security firms often mislead clients with promises of a cheap and quick 'technical fix' for a crime problem (Prenzler, 2004). This issue has been particularly acute with CCTV. Governments and private companies have rushed to install expensive camera systems. Local governments have been particularly enamoured of CCTV for tackling public order problems in inner city areas. However, recent reviews of CCTV projects have found that very few were able to show reductions in crime (Farrington & Welsh, 2009; Farrington, Gill, Waples, & Argomaniz, 2007). The forensic value of CCTV has also been questioned, given very small numbers of properly documented successful cases of crimes being solved as a result of camera-based evidence (Hughes, 2009).

The intruder alarm industry is illustrative of the potential pitfalls and benefits of security technology. Since its inception, the industry has been plagued by problems of false alarm activations. Numerous studies have put false activation rates as high as 98 per cent, contributing to a significant waste of resources in police responses (Sampson, 2001). There is evidence, nonetheless, for the relative effectiveness of alarms. For example, a study of commercial burglary in Philadelphia found that the probability of a property without an alarm being burgled was 4.57 times that of an alarmed property (Hakim & Shachmurove, 1996b, p. 43). In another study, Hakim and Shachmurive (1996a) sought to factor in all the financial costs of alarms against all the potential savings from reduced burglaries and concluded that alarms were cost-effective in residential and commercial settings. However, alarms are rarely intended to work alone. They are usually seen as one element in a layered security system – or 'defence-in-depth' – designed to deter, delay and detect intruders through concentric rings of protection (Prenzler, 2009; Smith, 2006). Chapter 9 described a number of successful crime prevention projects that involved multiple security methods. A public–private partnership on the Dutch Enschede-Haven industrial area saw a 72 per cent reduction in security incidents, mainly burglary-related, through a collective alarm monitoring programme, along with improved lighting and signage (van den Berg, 1995). In the United Kingdom, the Leicester Small Business and Crime Initiative reduced commercial burglary victimization with a mix of security measures, including alarms and CCTV; while the successful Safer Merseyside Partnership was focused more on window locks, roller shutters and better lighting (Bowers, 2001; Taylor, 1999; Tilley & Hopkins, 1998). Security devices in combination have also been shown to reduce residential burglary. For example, the 2009–2010 British Crime Survey reported that:

> Households with 'less than basic' home security measures were six times more likely to have been victims of burglary (5.8%) than households with 'basic' security (0.9%) and ten times more likely than households with 'enhanced' home security measures (0.6%).
>
> (Flatley et al., 2010, pp. 2–3)

'Basic security' included 'windows and double/deadlocks'; while 'enhanced' security included these and one other device, such as sensor lights, security grills or an alarm.

Principles for ensuring best practice in the application of security technology

Security technology is, by its nature, a strategy directed at mitigating specific security-related risks. However, over time, and through lowered costs, some security technologies have become ubiquitous and are routinely deployed without clear objectives and with little or no regard to the security-related risks the technology is intended to address. Similarly, security technology is frequently installed without adequate consideration being given either to policy and procedural issues or to supporting infrastructure and other technology that may be required to derive the optimum benefit from the investment. For example, according to a recent British Chambers of Commerce crime survey, 44 per cent of respondents had never sought advice about how to protect their business against crime (2008, p. 20). It is also the case that most businesses obtain security advice or upgrade security only after they become a victim of crime (Bowers, 2001; Shury, Speed, Vivian, Kuechel, & Nicholas, 2005).

This is not to say that there are not generic risks that almost invariably lend themselves to the use of specific technology in the management of those risks. For example, most businesses have some level of exposure to the threat of theft. In response, many choose to install an intruder alarm and/or CCTV system, which, dependent upon a number of factors, may be a viable strategy. However, CCTV systems can serve different purposes, and these entail different technical configurations. A CCTV system can be configured to provide images that will assist in the identification of an offender (Cohen, Gattuso, & MacLennan-Brown, 2007, p. 9), but unless this objective is defined and communicated to the system installer, the likelihood of achieving this outcome is significantly reduced. Similarly, an alarm or CCTV system may be configured to detect and communicate the attempted removal of an asset, but this purpose needs to be well understood and translated into functional requirements in the alarm system design.

There are a number of useful guidelines now available for the selection, installation and management of security technologies based on the application of generic crime prevention methodologies. 'Situational crime prevention', 'problem-oriented policing', 'crime prevention through environmental design' (CPTED) and 'security management principles' all emphasize the importance of (1) initial assessments of a crime problem or threat; (2) tailoring interventions to the specific nature and level of risk; and (3) monitoring impacts and adjusting interventions in a process of continuous feedback (Clarke, 1997; Crowe, 2004; Goldstein, 1990; Standards Australia, 2006b; Walsh & Healy, 1990). These principles are also reflected in wider 'risk management' principles that attempt to identify and counter all threats to an organization, not just crime (e.g. ISO, 2009a, 2009b); but have also been usefully applied to specific security technologies, such as CCTV (e.g. Cohen et al., 2007 [UK Home Office]; Standards Australia, 2006a). A generic formulation – applicable to almost any security technology – follows:

1. Identify and assess risks.
2. Use quantifiable measures and a scale of risk wherever possible.
3. Identify vulnerabilities that may be reduced or eliminated through security technology.
4. Document core objectives for security technology in the context of the identified risks and anticipated threat sources.
5. Develop functional requirements for security technology in line with core objectives and to address specific vulnerabilities.

6. Establish scope and range criteria for functional requirements to establish measurable outcomes.
7. Identify possible security technology options, including implementation considerations.
8. Identify and document dependencies for all functional requirements, including any policy and procedural matters, regulatory requirements, all necessary supporting technology and infrastructure, training and communication requirements, as well as interdependencies with external systems.
9. Identify possible counter-productive effects (e.g. excessive delays, compromised safety, alienation of customers).
10. Identify potential ethical and legal risks (e.g. breaches of privacy).
11. Translate functional requirements and dependencies into technical specifications and action plans.
12. Monitor impacts, using measures and categories at (2), (9) and (10) above, including cost-benefit ratios.
13. Modify systems in light of impact data and continue to monitor and adapt systems.

Establishing clear objectives and functional requirements will go a long way towards ensuring that the performance of security systems meets expectations and that the return on the investment is measurable. Making the most of security technology in this way can be assisted by reformulating this process as a series of questions. For example: Is the alarm system intended to detect an attempt to break into an area or to signal that a break-in has occurred? Is the intention to know that an item has been stolen or the identity of the thief? Under what conditions? When the mains power is unavailable? Even after the phone lines have been cut? And, when considering such questions, it must be kept in mind that there is usually more than one option available to meet functional requirements. In all cases, the principle of defence-in-depth should be followed, ensuring that, wherever possible, security is not reliant on a single mechanism (Smith, 2006). This approach also meshes with the legal duty of care attached to those with security responsibilities, given that, in certain circumstances, contract and regulatory law can hold security providers responsible for security breaches and associated losses (Sarre & Prenzler, 2009).

Making the most of specific technologies

The following sub-sections provide a more in-depth analysis of methods for optimizing the crime prevention benefits of three different security technologies: (1) alarm systems, (2) electronic access control and identification, and (3) CCTV.

Alarm systems

Alarms are popular because they offer the prospect of 24-hour continuous ubiquitous coverage of premises; along with major reductions in the financial costs, tedium and fatigue entailed in human guardianship. Alarms serve to deter would-be offenders, detect attempted intrusions and facilitate intervention by guardians. But alarm effectiveness is closely tied to contextual factors, particularly the nature of human guardianship or technical responses triggered directly by the alarm system (e.g. smoke generation, disorienting strobe lights and high decibel sirens). If an alarm is activated, then the response needs to be, or perceived to be, within the timeframe required for offenders to locate their target, seize it and escape. Well-organized criminals can be remarkably quick in getting in and out of a location before security officers or police arrive on the scene. Nonetheless, as outlined above, there is evidence that alarms can contribute to substantial reductions in crimes, mainly burglary. Interviews with burglars show that the large majority avoid alarmed premises (Cromwell, Olson, & Webster, 1991), and one study found that simply advertising the presence of alarms on commercial premises reduced the risk of burglary by 50 per cent – when compared to premises with alarms without advertising (Hakim & Shachmurove, 1996b, p. 451). Alarms have also been shown to help stop burglaries in progress. For example, in the Safer Merseyside Partnership (above), one-quarter of failed burglaries involved a member of the public being alerted by an alarm (Bowers, 2001, p. 36).

As noted, false activations and associated nuisance effects present one of the biggest challenges for alarm management. False activations are usually caused by low-grade equipment, faulty installation, environmental influences and user error (Gill & Hemming, 2003). In response to these problems the US Department of Justice developed a guide for minimizing false alarms, based on projects that reduced police call outs by up to 90 per cent. Recommendations included requiring monitoring companies make a visual inspection before contacting police, charging a fee for service for all activations, and fining companies responsible for repeat false alarms (Sampson, 2001). There are some obvious potential downsides to this approach, especially in contexts where police are expected to respond to all calls for service as a public service. Verifying alarms can involve excessive delays, and it can be dangerous for nonspecialists. Alarm verification was, nonetheless, an important part of the successful Enschede-Haven project (above) where companies pooled their resources to employ an on-site security officer. With the lowering of technology costs there is also an increasing trend to utilize secondary technology, such as video or still images from the location of the alarm, to provide increased capacity for interpretation of the alarm condition. This multiple technology approach has the added advantage in some cases of providing evidence to support investigations and prosecution of offenders (Jentoft, 2009). There is also increased capacity for this approach in residential situations with growth in Internet and smart phone technology (e.g. Figure 11.1), with capacity for home owners to take on the roles that have traditionally been contracted to alarm monitoring companies (Adão, Antunes, & Grilo, 2008).

Reducing false activations and improving detection can also be achieved by the installation of 'cross-zoning', involving coverage of one area with multiple detectors. A good example of this is the highly successful crime prevention partnership Strike Force Piccadilly 1, outlined

Figure 11.1   Example of iPhone alarm management application

in Chapter 9 (see Prenzler, 2011). The Strike Force was aimed at ATM ram raids in the greater Sydney area of Australia. False alarms were a major problem encountered by the stakeholder committee that drove the project. Monitoring companies were reluctant to call police because they could be fined for nuisance calls and there were up to 40 false ATM alarms per night. Alarms could be set off by cleaning equipment, passing trucks and construction. As a result, the firms tended to call police only after a visual inspection. This meant that the police often arrived on the scene up to half an hour after the ram raiders had departed with large quantities of cash. However, police intelligence found that offenders usually gave themselves an operating window of just two minutes. If they encountered a delay, they would abandon the raid. They also used scanners to listen in on the police radio system and would usually abandon the raid if they knew police were on the way. The solution to the problem of alarm verification and intervention was an agreement that police would prioritize calls received on a dedicated hotline with caller discretion given to control room operators based on multiple alarm activations (e.g. breach, vibration, power failure and smoke alarms). This methodology gave alarm operators the confidence to call police and allowed police to defeat the ram raiders' window of opportunity. The major reductions in ram raids that resulted from the Strike Force were assisted by the introduction of other security measures, including specialist bollards around ATMs and ATM re-locations.

Electronic access control and identification

A wide range of card access technologies have been developed since the original Hollerith cards (with punched holes) and embossed cards of the 1960s (Bowers, 1988). 'Smart cards' that store readable data in a computer chip are superseding mechanical keys and becoming the norm for both physical and computer/IT access controls. Smart card access control received a considerable boost from contemporary counter-terrorism programmes. In the aftermath of the 9/11 terrorist attacks US President George Bush (2004) issued *Homeland Security Presidential Directive 12 (HSPD-12)*. The directorate acknowledged that it was necessary to eliminate the 'wide variations in the quality and security of forms of identification used to gain access to secure Federal and other facilities where there is potential for terrorist attacks'. *HSPD-12* decreed that,

> It is the policy of the United States to enhance security, increase Government efficiency, reduce identity fraud, and protect personal privacy by establishing a mandatory, Government-wide standard

for secure and reliable forms of identification issued by the Federal Government to its employees and contractors.

(Bush, 2004)

HSPD-12 gave rise to the development of a standard for 'Personal Identity Verification (PIV) of Federal Employees and Contractors', published by the National Institute of Standards and Technology (NIST, 2006, 2011). NIST claimed that, as of 17 June 2009, over 2.5 million PIV cards had been issued to US government employees and contractors, and expected a further three million would be issued 'in the near future' (NIST, 2009). Other countries have built on the groundwork and investment made by the United States in refining the requirements for smart card technology. For example, the Australian government welfare agency, Centrelink, has invested over AU$500,000 in developing what it calls a 'Protocol for Lightweight Authentication of ID (PLAID)' (Centrelink, 2009), which was subsequently published as a formal Australian Standard. PLAID is being actively considered by a number of Australian government departments and agencies for access control applications, with trials already commenced.

The PIV initiative in the United States is having the effect of reducing the costs for smart cards in the wider market, which opens opportunities to leverage the technology for other applications. It is now feasible to have a single card that can be used for physical access to buildings (alone or in combination with a PIN and/or biometric data stored on the card), access to computers and other electronic devices, secure 'draw-down' printing from network connected printers, access to an electronic purse and secure storage of transactions and other data.

Organizations are also now taking advantage of developments in two-dimensional barcodes – incorporating a matrix rather than vertical lines. While there are a number of two-dimensional barcode formats that have been developed (Alapetite, 2010), the Quick Response (QR) code has been adopted in applications as diverse as product identification, marketing and entertainment (Broll et. al., 2009; Denso, undated). QR codes can be read by any smart phone with a camera and one of the many free applications available. Rapid advances in camera design in smart phones and the associated QR code reader applications have significantly improved the speed and reliability of QR codes for mobile interaction. A QR code, such as the one shown in Figure 11.2, can contain more than 4000 characters of text data, but more frequently stores details of a web page where more information can be obtained. For example, in an ID card application a QR code may provide a

Figure 11.2   Example of Quick Response code

link to a website that can establish the validity of the ID card being presented.

Developments in smart cards, particularly when combined with radio frequency identification (RFID) technology, have led to concerns about privacy (Slettemeås, 2009; Soppera & Burbridge, 2005). Privacy concerns have also hampered the implementation of biometric technologies in some access control applications, with users concerned that biometric data, such as fingerprints, could be accessed for other purposes (Ratha, Connell, & Bolle, 2001). If organizations are to make the most of these technologies, it is vital that these concerns are addressed through policy and practice, as well as through innovations in the technology itself. The PLAID standard discussed above is a technological approach to protecting the integrity of cards in terms of both their functionality and access to the data they hold. The challenge remains to convince users that the device they are being asked to trust is indeed secure. This process will be facilitated by compliance with privacy legislation in relation to the collection, storage and dissemination of personal information (see Sarre & Prenzler, 2009, chapter 7).

CCTV

In theory, CCTV is useful for deterring offenders; interrupting their offences; and identifying, arresting and convicting them. As noted previously, however, there is very little scientific evidence to support these claims in terms of consistent substantive advantages from CCTV. For example, it is very easy for offenders to hide their identity with balaclavas or other items of clothing, and image quality is often extremely poor. A recent review of 44 studies of the crime prevention effects of public space CCTV systems (Farrington & Welsh, 2009) made the following, generally negative, findings:

> The results suggest that CCTV caused a modest (16%) but significant decrease in crime in experimental areas compared with control areas.

This overall result was largely driven by the effectiveness of CCTV schemes in car parks, which caused a 51% decrease in crime. Schemes in most other public settings had small and nonsignificant effects on crime: a 7% decrease in city and town centers and in public housing communities. Public transport schemes had greater effects (a 23% decrease overall), but these were still nonsignificant. Schemes evaluated in the UK were more effective than schemes evaluated in the USA and other countries, but this was largely driven by the studies in the car parks.

(p. 716)

One example of a fairly successful city centre CCTV project was in Newcastle upon Tyne in the United Kingdom (Brown, 1997). The project was managed by police, with a standard CCTV system linking control room operators to patrol officers and retailers. The evaluation identified a 57 per cent reduction in the average number of burglaries recorded by police after the introduction of the system (covering 26 months before the introduction of the scheme and 15 months after). There was also a 34 per cent reduction in criminal damage, a 47 per cent reduction in motor vehicle theft and a 50 per cent reduction in theft from motor vehicles. In the same evaluation, smaller reductions in burglary and other crimes were associated with CCTV in some other city centres. However, the stronger success of the Newcastle project was attributed to the concentrated nature of the business district, which allowed for close camera coverage and rapid coordination of police responses. In similar terms, the Farrington and Welsh (2009) study confirmed the findings of an earlier study (Farrington et al. 2007) that CCTV systems were 'most effective when the degree of coverage by CCTV was high and when CCTV was combined with other interventions' (p. 21). Other interventions, in this report, included direct communication with police and improved lighting.

One particularly interesting evaluation of CCTV, which demonstrates the point about context, involved the installation of cameras in English double-decker buses in order to prevent vandalism (Poyner, 1988). The operation of the cameras led to dramatic reductions in repairs and cleaning requirements for the buses, to the point where two-thirds of the cleaners had to be laid off. One of the keys to the success of the programme lay in the fact that school children on the buses wore uniforms. Video recordings were used to identify vandals, and disciplinary action was taken through their school principals. The presence of cameras was also widely publicized in the media and through school visits.

As the size and complexity of CCTV systems have increased, system owners and operators have sought to enhance the effectiveness of monitoring through employing advances in 'video analytics' (Velastin, 2010). While initially plagued by false alerts, the technology now delivers useful semi-automated assessments of a range of events requiring the attention of human operators for further analysis. Systems can now detect events such as a person loitering, an object left unattended or removed, vehicle or pedestrian traffic changing direction, the number of people within a given space, as well as detecting movement within a space. Automatic number plate recognition (ANPR, also known as ALPR) is also a form of video analytics that has found application in law enforcement, toll roads and car parking management. In order to support further development in video analytics, the UK Home Office (2010) has developed an 'Imagery Library for Intelligent Detection Systems' [known by the acronym 'i-LIDS'].

High-definition 'megapixel' cameras now also provide higher levels of image quality for CCTV systems. These high definition cameras are able to satisfy multiple objectives with a single camera – such as maintaining wide area situational awareness and 'virtually' zooming in on selected areas of the image to identify individuals, with this being possible on live vision or recorded video. Interactive systems also allow communication between control room operators and persons in view of cameras, including potential offenders and victims of crime. The public can use these systems to report crime or communicate their fears and ask for assistance. Warnings can also be broadcast to deter offenders or assist in public emergency situations. The value of CCTV and other security-related technologies can be further enhanced through integration, or high-level interfacing, of inter-related aspects of the systems (Taylor, 2005, p. 64). With all elements of modern systems now supported on network (TCP-IP) infrastructure there is significant opportunity to allow elements of the security-related systems to communicate with each other, as well as to share data. By using Electronic Data Interchange (EDI) between a central data repository and individual electronic security systems it is possible to improve the value and effectiveness of all systems.

Despite these exciting developments in CCTV, care still needs to be taken in adopting advanced technology. Consideration must always be given to the 'human factors' involved in interpreting and managing the technology, including lapses of attention, inability to multi-task and wrong interpretations of data (Stedmon, 2011). In order to make the most of CCTV technology, organizations must address the factors that have been identified as reducing the effectiveness of systems, including, blind spots...camera signals affected by poor weather...faulty equipment...pointing cameras in bad positions...high camera-to-operator ratio...lack of familiarity with surveillance areas...poor quality video recording...too many audio sources...[and] poor communication between radio users [e.g., different accents and specialist terminology].

(Keval & Sasse, 2010, pp. 145–149)

Conclusion

Human beings are characterized by the use of technology, and smart people make the most of available technologies to improve their lives, including their security. Technical innovation is also part of the human process. Consequently, security technology and new security technology are not things to be afraid of – at least not in a liberal democracy with protections on privacy and regulation of security services in the public interest (Chapter 12). Security technology has a lot to offer in the way of potentially user-friendly crime prevention tools. But when an organization – public or private – makes the decision to introduce or expand security technology the choices can be confusing. A clear understanding of the risks and objectives the technology is intended to address is essential for making defensible decisions and obtaining the optimum return. Risk management and crime prevention guidelines and standards are an important aid in conducting site-specific risk assessments, developing site-appropriate security systems, and evaluating and refining systems.

Acknowledgements

The authors wish to acknowledge the contribution of Richard P. Grassie, CPP, in the area of security systems design and engineering. Rich Grassie's systematic approach to risk management through security technology is a guiding influence that underpins this chapter.

References

Adão H., Antunes, R., & Grilo, F. (2008). Web-based control & notification for home automation alarm systems. *World Academy of Science, Engineering and Technology, 37*, 152–156.

Alapetite, A. (2010). Dynamic 2D-barcodes for multi-device web session migration including mobile phones. *Personal and Ubiquitous Computing, 14*(1), 45–52.

Bayley, D., & Shearing, C. (2001). *The new structure of policing*. Washington, D.C.: National Institute of Justice.

Bowers, D. (1988). *Access control and personal identification systems*. Stoneham, MA: Butterworths.

Bowers, K. (2001). Small business crime: The evaluation of a crime prevention initiative. *Crime Prevention and Community Safety: An International Journal, 3*(1), 23–42.

British Chambers of Commerce. (2008). *The invisible crime: A business crime survey*. London: British Chambers of Commerce.

Broll, G., Rukzio, E., Paolucci, M., Wagner, M., Schmidt, A., & Hussmann, H. (2009). Perci: Pervasive service interaction with the internet of things. *IEEE Internet Computing, 13*(6), 74–81.

Brown, A. (1997). CCTV in three town centres in England. In R. Clarke (Ed.), *Situational crime prevention: Successful case studies* (pp. 167–182). Guilderland, NY: Harrow and Heston.

Bush, G. (2004) *Homeland Security Presidential Directive-12: Policies for a common identification standard for federal employees and contractors*. Retrieved from http://www.dhs.gov/xabout/laws/gc_1217616624097.shtm#1.

Centrelink. (2009). *Protocol for Lightweight Authentication of ID (PLAID)*. Retrieved from http://www.centrelink.gov.au/internet/internet.nsf/filestores/press_kits_5_a/$file/PLAID_backgrounder_0409en.pdf.

Clarke, R. (Ed.). (1997). *Situational crime prevention: Successful case studies*. Guilderland, NY: Harrow and Heston.

Cohen, L., & Felson, M. (1979). Social change and crime rate trends: A routine activity approach. *American Sociological Review, 44*, 588–608.

Cohen, N., Gattuso, J., & MacLennan-Brown, K. (2007). *CCTV operational requirements manual (version 4.0)*. London: Home Office

Coleman, R., & McCahill, M. (2011). *Surveillance and crime*. Los Angeles: SAGE.

Cromwell, P., Olson, J., & Webster, D. (1991). *Breaking and entering: An ethnographic analysis of burglary*. Los Angeles: SAGE.

Crowe, T. (2004). Crime prevention through environmental design strategies and applications. In L. Fennelly (Ed.), *Handbook of loss prevention and crime prevention* (pp. 82–142). Oxford: Elsevier, 19–43

Dell Inc. (2010). *A blockbuster marriage of form and function*. Retrieved from http://www.dell.com/downloads/global/casestudies/1504_2010-caa-10008170.pdf.

Denso. (undated). *About 2D code*. Retrieved from http://www.denso-wave.com/qrcode/aboutqr-e.html.

Farrington, D., & Welsh, B. (2009). Public area CCTV and crime prevention: An updated systematic review and meta-analysis. *Justice Quarterly, 26*(4), 716–745.

Farrington, D., Gill, M., Waples, S., & Argomaniz, J. (2007). The effects of closed circuit television on crime: Meta-analysis of an English national quasi-experimental multi-site evaluation. *Journal of Experimental Criminology, 3*(1), 21–38.

Flatley, J., Kershaw, C., Smith, K., Chaplin, R., & Moon, D. (2010). *Crime in England and Wales 2009/10*. London: Home Office.

Gill, M., & Hemming, M. (2003). *Causes of false alarms*. Leicester: Perpetuity Press.

Gates, K. (2006). Biometrics and access control in the digital age. *NACLA Report on the Americas, 39*(5), 35–40.

Goldstein, H. (1990). *Problem-oriented policing*. New York: McGraw-Hill.

Hakim, S., & Shachmurove, Y. (1996a). Social cost benefit analysis of commercial and residential burglar and fire alarms. *Journal of Policy Modeling, 18*(1), 49–67.

Hakim, S., & Shachmurove, Y. (1996b). Spatial and temporal patters of commercial burglaries: The evidence examined. *American Journal of Economics and Sociology, 55*(4), 443–456.

Hollinger, R., & Adams, A. (2009). *2008 National Retail Security Survey*. Gainesville, FL: Department of Sociology and Criminology and Law, University of Florida.

Home Office. (2010). *Imagery Library for Intelligent Detection Systems*. Retrieved from Http://Www.Homeoffice.Gov.Uk/Science-Research/Hosdb/I-Lids/.

Hughes, M. (2009). CCTV in the spotlight. *The Independent*. Retrieved from http://www.independent.co.uk/news/uk/crime/cctv-in-the-spotlight-one-crime-solved-for-every-1000-cameras-1776774.html?service=Print.

ISO. (2009a). *ISO 31000: 2009 risk management – Principles and guidelines*. Geneva: International Organisation for Standardisation.

ISO. (2009b). *ISO 31010: 2009 risk management – Risk assessment techniques*. Geneva: International Organisation for Standardisation.

Jentoft, K. (September 2009). Affordable construction security: 40 apprehensions in 4 months. *Modern contractor solutions*, 40. Retrieved from http://www.moderncontractorsolutions.com/articlesdetail.php?id_articles=627&id_artcatg=7.

Keval, H., & Sasse, M. A. (2010). 'Not the usual suspects': A study of factors reducing the effectiveness of CCTV. *Security Journal, 23*(2), 134–154.

McCrie, R. D. (2006). A history of security. In M. Gill (Ed.), *The handbook of security* (pp. 21–44). Houndmills, Basingstoke: Palgrave Macmillan.

NIST. (2006). *FIPS PUB 201-1 Personal Identity Verification (PIV) of federal employees and contractors*. Gaithersburg, M.D.: National Institute of Standards and Technology.

NIST. (June 2009). *Personal Identity Verification (PIV) of federal employees and contractors*. Retrieved from http://www.nist.gov/itl/csd/set/piv.cfm.

NIST. (2011). *FIPS PUB 201-2 Personal Identity Verification (PIV) of federal employees and contractors draft*. Gaithersburg, M.D.: National Institute of Standards and Technology.

Poyner, B. (1988). Video cameras and bus vandalism. *Security Administration, 11*, 44–51.

Prenzler, T. (2004). The privatisation of policing. In R. Sarre & J. Tomaino (Eds.), *Key issues in criminal justice* (pp. 267–296). Adelaide: Australian Humanities Press.

Prenzler, T. (2009). *Preventing burglary in commercial and institutional settings: A place management and partnerships approach*. Washington, D.C.: ASIS Foundation.

Prenzler, T. (2011). Strike Force Piccadilly and ATM security: A follow up study. *Policing: A Journal of Policy and Practice, 5*(3), 236–247.

Prenzler, T., & Sarre, R. (2008). Developing a risk profile and model regulatory system for the security industry. *Security Journal, 21*(4), 264–277.

Ratha, N. K., Connell, J. H., & Bolle, R. M. (2001). Enhancing security and privacy in biometrics-based authentication systems. *IBM Systems Journal, 40*(3), 614–634.

Reeve, T. (2011). How many cameras in the UK? Retrieved from http://www.securitynewsdesk.com/2011/03/01/how-many-cctv-cameras-in-the-uk/.

Sampson, R. (2001). *False burglar alarms*. Washington, D.C.: U.S. Department of Justice.

Sarre, R., & Prenzler, T. (2009). *The law of private security in Australia*. Sydney: Thomson Lawbook Company.

Shury, J., Speed, M., Vivian, D., Kuechel, A., & Nicholas, S. (2005). *Crime against retail and manufacturing premises: Findings from the 2002 commercial victimisation survey*. London: Home Office.

Slettemeås, D. (2009). RFID – The 'next step' in consumer-product relations or Orwellian nightmare? Challenges for research and policy. *Journal of Consumer Policy, 32*(3), 219–244.

Small Arms Survey. (2011). *Small arms survey 2011*. Retrieved from http://www.smallarmssurvey.org/publications/by-type/yearbook/small-arms-survey-2011.html.

Smith, C. (2006). Trends in the development of security technology. In M. Gill (Ed.), *The handbook of security* (pp. 610–628). Houndmills, Basingstoke: Palgrave Macmillan.

Soppera, A., & Burbridge, T. (2005). Wireless identification – Privacy and security. *BT Technology Journal, 23*(4), 54–64.

Standards Australia. (2006a). *AS 4806.2: Closed circuit television (CCTV) Part 2: Application guidelines*. Sydney: SAI Global.

Standards Australia. (2006b). *HB 167: Security risk management*. Sydney: SAI Global.

Stedmon, A. (2011). The camera never lies, or does it? The dangers of taking CCTV surveillance at face-value. *Surveillance & Society, 8*(4), 527–534.

Taylor, G. (1999). Using repeat victimisation to counter commercial burglary: The Leicester experience. *Security Journal, 12*, 41–52.

Taylor, M. (2005). Integrated building systems: Strengthening building security while decreasing operating costs. *Journal of Facilities Management, 4*(1), 63–71.

Tilley, N., & Hopkins, M. (1998). *Business as usual: An evaluation of the Small Business and Crime Initiative*. London: Home Office.

Van den Berg, E. (1995). Crime prevention on industrial sites: Security through public-private partnerships. *Security Journal, 6*(1), 27–35.

Van Dijk, J. (2008). *The world of crime*. Thousand Oaks, CA: SAGE.

Velastin, S. (2010). CCTV video analytics: Recent advances and limitations. In H. Badioze et al. (Eds.), *Visual informatics: Bridging research and practice* (pp. XX). Berlin: Springer-Verlag.

Walsh, T., & Healy, R. (1990). *Protection of assets*. Santa Monica, CA: Merritt Co.

12
Optimizing Security through Effective Regulation: Lessons from Around the Globe

Mark Button

Most countries have recognized that to optimize security, a major provider of it, the private security industry, needs to be subject to additional and specialist regulation to maximize its performance (Button, 2007a; CoESS/ UNI Europa, 2004; Hemmens, Maahs, Scarborough, & Collins, 2001; International Alert, 2005; Prenzler, Baxter, & Draper, 1998; Prenzler & Sarre, 2008; Sarre & Prenzler, 2005; Yoshida, 1999). There are only a few countries which do not have such regulation, but the regulatory systems which exist vary significantly on a variety of criteria (Button & George, 2006; George & Button, 1997; Prenzler & Sarre, 1999). However, even with some of the most basic regulatory systems, like the United Kingdom's, there has been evidence of improvement for both licence holders and purchasers of security (Security Industry Authority [SIA], 2010a, 2010b; White, 2010; White & Smith, 2010). This chapter will seek to review the experience of regulation from around the globe and identify best practice. Before we embark upon this, however, this chapter will begin by examining what optimum security is, before moving on to consider some of the factors which contribute to that. It will then explore briefly why regulation is required before examining the challenges of identifying best practice. The chapter will end with a consideration of proposals in England to reform regulation and the significance of these for the rest of the globe.

What is optimum security?

Optimal security could be defined as maximizing objective and subjective feelings of safety from risks emanating from crimes and related

204

behaviours and reducing the experience of those risks to an absolute minimum. The delivery of security is provided by a wide array of actors and entities which include citizens, the police, the military, corporations and the private security industry to name the most significant. It is also important to note there are a variety of other factors which contribute to security beyond this security infrastructure, such as economic factors, the degree of social cohesion, the degree of security equity, the culture amongst many others over which there is much debate over their influence (see Button, 2008; Johnston & Shearing, 2003; Loader & Walker, 2007; Reiner, 2007; Wood & Shearing, 2009). This chapter will concentrate upon optimizing the private security industry's contribution to security. Central to maximizing the performance of the industry is regulation, but also important is the professional infrastructure, which will also be explored in this chapter.

Why regulate?

It might seem strange to start by considering why regulation should be applied to private security, when so many countries already regulate the industry. However, in the United Kingdom (or rather England and Wales) the weakening of already light regulation of private security is a serious item on the political agenda. For this reason it is worth briefly examining this debate. Opponents of regulation have traditionally argued that private security is no different from any other industry and as such should not be singled out for special attention (Murray, 1996). It is argued that the provision of security guard services is no different from cleaning services, and the installation of an intruder alarm is no different to fitting a new boiler. However, as Stenning and Shearing (1979, p. 263) have argued:

> If private security personnel are in reality no different from ordinary citizens, a law which treats them alike seems most appropriate. But if in reality they are not, and the law still treats them as they are, it becomes inappropriate...

Security personnel aren't like ordinary citizens. A security officer guarding a factory could engage in or help others to steal the products of the factory. Critics might argue so could the ordinary workers, but the security officers are supposed to be the 'thin blue line' protecting the factory and as such will be trusted and have positions which enable them to conduct theft much more easily if that way inclined. Many occupations in the private security industry can and do draw upon such privileges (Button, 2007b; Sarre & Prenzler, 2005). Many security officers regularly detain shoplifters and use powers (Button, 2007a; Crawford, Lister, Blackburn, & Burnett, 2005; Wakefield, 2003), door supervisors frequently use force (Hobbs, Hadfield, Lister, & Winlow, 2003; Lister, Hadfield, Hobbs, & Winlow, 2001; Rigakos, 2008) and some security guards in cash-in-transit vehicles are armed (Hakala, 2007).

For some security occupations there is access to information or roles which could be exploited or abused (Prenzler & Sarre, 2008). Many security occupations in public/client facing positions will be seen as agents of help and support in a security-related situation. If a person is assaulted, robbed or there is some kind of accident, the public (and client on private space) will invariably turn to the person in a position of authority and particularly the uniformed person (Bushman, 1984). Finally, many security-related occupations have implications for public safety if they do not function effectively. If an intruder alarm is not fitted properly, this could result in a burglary or some other form of illegal entry: rape, kidnap, assault, robbery and so on which then involves police and possibly wider criminal justice system resources to deal with it. It may at a lesser level activate falsely, which means a drain on police resources responding to it.

It is also important to note the dominant decision-making process which underpins most security purchases: that it is a 'grudge cost' (George & Button, 2000; Goold, Loader, & Thulma, 2010). The private security industry is a very diverse industry encompassing a wide variety of products and services (George & Button, 2000; Jones & Newburn, 1998). Decisions to purchase security by individuals and organizations are taken for a variety of reasons, but one of the recurring themes in many sub-sectors of the industry is that it is treated as a grudge, a tax on the bottom line, which provides little benefit. As such many will buy the cheapest. Thus if minimum standards are taken away, there is a temptation to lower standards to win business with all the potential implications that has of a poorer quality security sector. As Goold et al. (2010, p. 12) argue:

> In short, cost rules: so long as the security purchased does the job of 'distancing the bad guys from your key assets' (Security consultant), or a buyer can tick the 'I've managed that risk box' (Security company manager), there seems little point in paying for products the selling point of which is quality. This basic fact is viewed by many in the industry as having a large determining effect on the trajectory and

fate of different security products and, specifically, as the primary cause of what one security company director called the 'cut-throat' nature of the industry, and its attendant low pay and standards.

Private security regulation around the globe: The good, the bad and the average

There are a number of challenges to identifying best practice in private security regulation. The first is that although there have been attempts to develop model systems of regulation and key principles, there is often a lack of clearly available data for judging regimes (Button & George, 2006; Prenzler & Sarre, 2008). One is therefore left with more subjective assessments of the private security industry. There is also the challenge of keeping up to date with the standards and controversies from so many countries, as well as state governments in federal countries. In some countries one relies on what is written down in laws, in documents and on websites, but the reality of what happens on the ground is different. So these caveats must be remembered when assessing the experience. Most countries regulate private security (the Czech Republic and Cyprus some of the few exceptions). There is, however, wide variation in regulatory systems, and the standards and effectiveness of these systems vary considerably. These will now be considered under the key criteria of regulation as set by George and Button (1997) and Button and George (2006): the 'width, depth, compliance and responsibility' for regulation.

Wide regulation

The first key principle should be that regulation applies to the wider private security industry. There are many sectors in the industry, covering, among others, occupations such as security officers, security managers, door supervisors (or crowd controllers, patron protectors or bouncers as they are also known), close protection officers (or bodyguards), security managers, private investigators, security consultants, installers of security equipment and locksmiths, employed either contractually or in house (staff employed direct by the client organization). As discussed earlier in this chapter there are a variety of differences which mark these occupations out from an ordinary citizen or other occupations. There is also the risk of not regulating the wider private security industry of creating loopholes which the unscrupulous can take advantage of. Many regimes do not regulate in-house security and this provides a major loophole which can be exploited. For the benefits of regulation to be fully felt it should apply to the wider private security industry.

An example of good practice here is the Republic of Ireland where the Private Security Authority (PSA, 2011) licenses employees and firms and it extends its influence over the wider private security industry (Button, 2008). Sectors licensed include the following:

- door supervisors
- suppliers or installers of security equipment
- private investigators
- security consultants
- security guards
- providers of protected forms of transport
- locksmiths
- suppliers or installers of safes.

British Columbia in Canada is another example of a wide regulator where the following require licences: security guards (contract and in-house); armoured car security guards; alarm installers, salespersons, monitors and responders; CCTV monitors; locksmiths; electronic lock installers; private investigators; and security consultants (Ministry of Public Safety and Solicitor General, 2011). At the other extreme are some regulatory regimes which just regulate contract security guarding such as Luxembourg or, as is the case in many US states, contract guarding and private investigators (Hemmens et al., 2001; Weber, 2002).

Deep regulation

The second major principle of regulation is that it should be deep. Regulatory systems vary a great deal in terms of the standards which are set for both employees and firms. For employees, the best regimes mandate standards beyond character (and there is much variation on standards of character set and the extent to which it is investigated, such as through criminal record checks, fingerprint checks, etc.). Standards should also cover minimum levels of competence and staff training and quality-enhancing requirements should apply to the firm as well as the employee. Thus the licensing system should apply to employees *and* firms and mandate quality enhancing standards and this has been called a 'Comprehensive' system, with anything less 'Minimal' (Button & George, 2005). Licensing removes opportunities for corner cutting if both firms and employees are regulated, and ensures accountability is maximized. Putting an employee's or a firm's licence at stake – with some form of sanction for non-compliance – provides a much greater incentive to comply. These two criteria underpin the 'Comprehensive Wide' model of regulation in which regulations apply to the wider private security industry, to both firms and employees, and where the standards set cover quality-enhancing criteria (see Button & George, 2006).

One of the least sophisticated systems is Luxembourg's, which centres on the requirement for a licence for a security firm from the Ministry of Justice. There is no licensing of employees, minimum training requirement or character standards that would bar persons from working in the industry. There are requirements relating to the carrying of identity cards, and collective agreements between the firms and trade unions set minimum working hours and pay (Weber, 2002). In the United States where regulation is a state responsibility many of the regimes have very basic standards. Most of the states have 'Minimal' regulation based upon character checks and of those with minimum standards of training generally have low requirements, with minimum standards of training for unarmed security guards generally around one or two days training (Hemmens et al., 2001; Strom et al., 2010).

A novel idea in South Korea is the creation of different types of security officer in the legislation, with different standards of training that apply. There is the 'special security officer' and 'general security officer', with different levels of training and rights (Button, Park, & Lee, 2006). In the Spanish regulatory system both employees and firms are required to possess a licence and there are standards of character and training for personnel. The training standard for security officers includes 240 hours theoretical and 20 hours practical, with refresher training of 75 hours mandated every three years. Standards also apply on uniforms, weapons, guard dogs and the financial resources of the undertaking. Training standards also apply to managers and, uniquely, in-house security is prohibited, so organizations wishing to employ the equivalent to in-house must set up their own security firm. The law also sets out the activities that the private sector may undertake. Such is the ambition of the Spanish system that it has sought to integrate the private sector in the public justice system as a complementary arm to the state security infrastructure (Gimenez-Salinas, 2004).

A gap in many regulatory systems are standards to enhance security managers (Button, 2011). Security managers are leaders and are key agents in promoting cultural change within the sector. They should provide the model for inspiring junior security officers to aspire to managerial positions. In the National Health Service (NHS) in the United Kingdom there is sector-specific regulation. Under this scheme regulation has begun with minimum standards of training for security managers. Managers must do a training course that lasts about five weeks and equates to a standard at first-year undergraduate study and brings the award of 'Accredited Security Management Specialist'. It is also embedded into higher degree level awards, which are voluntary to achieve (NHS Counter Fraud and Security Management Service, 2003).

Building upon the mandatory

An area which has been under-developed in research on regulation of private security in the past (including the research of Bruce George and the author) is the importance of voluntary or self-regulatory standards which build upon basic statutory standards. These are usually rooted in trade and professional associations (such as British Security Industry Association [BSIA], ASIS, Canadian Security Association), as well as independent standard setting bodies (such as the British Standards Institution, Standards Australia, etc.). Strong basic standards of training for security operatives are very important. However, what is also essential is the more advanced standards beyond that and the measures pursued to encourage aspiration to higher standards than the norm. Regulatory systems need to set good basic requirements below which none fall, but even higher standards, which are voluntary to achieve, also need to be made which are widely embraced.

One of the defining characteristics of the occupational culture of security officers is inferiority and isolation (Button, 2007b; Wakefield, 2003). Symbols of rank are very important in the military and the police in denoting status to peers and the public as in the provision of a career structure with incentives to progress. These are also important in the private security industry where many come from that background and there is generally also a uniformed service culture (Gill, Burns-Howell, Keats, & Taylor, 2007). This provides an opportunity for creating a voluntary structure on top of the mandatory structure which is very attractive for uniformed and other personnel to achieve. In Finland they have recognized the desire for symbols of status, where guards who complete the recognized vocational training are entitled to wear the letter 'A' on their epaulettes (Government Decree on Private Security Services 534/2002 Section 9 (2)). This has proved very successful, encouraging staff to undertake additional training and giving greater status to successful candidates. One must also remember that this is on top of the minimum training for a security guard of 100 hours! Therefore creating officially recognized badges, apparel and designations can be used to enhance the take up of higher training awards.

Another good example is England and Wales where there is the additional framework of the Community Safety Accreditation Scheme established under the 2002 Police Reform Act (ACPO, 2009). These are run by local police forces (although there are national standards) at the discretion of the Chief Constable. Where these are in operation it enables security companies, entities (such as a hospital, shopping centre) as well as local authorities *if they wish* to secure additional powers for their staff, which *inter alia* include the right to confiscate alcohol and tobacco, issue fixed penalty notices and require the name and address of a person. There is a national training course set for this as well as other requirements set by the local police. Successful accreditation, however, entitles the person to wear the 'Community Safety Accredited' badge 'which can be viewed at http://www.securedbydesign.com/pdfs/ CSAS%20information%20for%20private%20companies.pdf'. In the last audit there were a total of 1667 accredited persons from 109 schemes of which 31 were private companies (Home Office, 2010). This is not a huge uptake in terms of the total number of security personnel working in this area. However this partly reflects opposition by some Chief Constables, who need to support a local scheme.

Good practice would be to develop a suite of advanced training standards which on completion enable a security operative to wear an approved badge, armband or epilate (and this should also be confirmed on their licence). It could be as simple as those who have undergone the appropriate training in the use of handcuffs being entitled to wear a badge with a picture of a handcuff on it. This could ensure that in potentially difficult situations it was clear to members of the public that security officers were competent for the task. It should also apply to security managers with higher voluntary standards linked to specific licence titles such as 'advanced security manager'.

Compliance

Another important element of a regulatory system is the degree of compliance. There are significant differences in the culture of compliance and degree of enforcement in different jurisdictions and amongst different occupations (Hyde, 2003; Lister et al., 2001). Therefore, what on paper might seem like a 'Comprehensive Wide' system might turn out to be much less effective when analysed in terms of the degree of compliance. Unfortunately there has not been a great deal of research on compliance with regulation. In the absence of such research all that can be done is to indicate whether compliance is 'high' or 'low', where in the latter there is significant evidence of non-compliance with the legislation. One can also look to the systems of enforcement that exist to try and engender compliance. Clearly the aspiration should be a system that maximizes compliance.

In Canada, Hyde (2003) has explored the issue of compliance and enforcement. Some of his findings included low numbers of staff employed in regulatory agencies with some struggling to cope with the large number of licence applications. Limited or no strategies to uncover non-compliance was also found in many of the provinces, with a tendency to focus upon reactive investigation of complaints, rather than pro-active random inspections. Finally Hyde found sanctions that were in some cases very low and unlikely to act as a significant deterrent. Similar problems were illustrated by Kakalik and Wildhorn (1971) and the National Advisory Committee on Criminal Justice Standards and Goals (1976) in their research on regulatory bodies during the late 1960s and early 1970s. More recent research in the United States has further highlighted lack of compliance. Gotbaum (2005) found in New York that 12 per cent of officers interviewed had had no training; a further 17 per cent had received less than the state mandatory 8 hours, with an average of 19 hours training in 2.3 years of employment. The state law requires a further 40 hours training in the second year and only 6 per cent of officers interviewed had received even this minimum.

The United Kingdom is not a model of regulation to pursue in many of the criteria above. However, in compliance and enforcement there are some positive elements to note. Over 35,000 operatives have had their licences revoked in the United Kingdom since the implementation of the legislation. These are people without regulation who would have been otherwise working in the industry (White, 2010). During 2010–2011 there were 3124 licence revocations, 268 written warnings and 36 improvement notices issued against 360,000 plus valid licenses (SIA, 2011a). The SIA regularly conducts blitz inspections of specific areas. During 2010 there were 770 random inspections with 2387 individuals checked of which 97 per cent were properly licensed – well above the 90 per cent target set (SIA, 2010c). The majority of its 113 staff are also engaged in compliance and enforcement (60) (Better Regulation Executive, 2009). Prosecutions of those who contravene the regulations also occur, with a total of 89 during 2008–2009 including 13 entities (Better Regulation Executive, 2009). Nevertheless White and Smith (2010) found a perception amongst suppliers that enforcement was weak. There is also a gap in the armoury of the SIA in that it lacks an ability (other than revocation) to sanction licence holders and firms through its own system of justice, which other regulators in the United Kingdom do possess, such as the Financial Services Authority (Financial Services Authority, 2010). Criminal prosecution is often reserved for the most serious of cases, so having the power to sanction (such as fines, imposing restrictions, etc.) for middle-range offences without going to the criminal courts is a useful tool absent in most security regulators.

Responsibility

The final criterion to explore is responsibility and there are three categories (Button & George, 2006). First of all there are *monopoly* systems, where all parts of the private security industry are regulated by one body, as the PSA currently does in the Republic of Ireland. Second there are *divided* systems which can be further split between *functional* and *territorial*. As the name suggests, in a *divided* system there is more than one organization responsible for regulation. In the *functional* version, different organizations take on responsibility for regulating different parts of the private security industry. In the *territorial* model, responsibility is shared for the same sectors, but certain responsibilities are devolved to another body in a defined geographical location. An example of the *functional* division is Florida (United States) where the Department of State, Division of Licensing, regulates the manned guarding and private investigator sectors, and the Department of Business and Professional Regulation is responsible for alarm installers. In France and Italy there are divisions between the central government departments and local government responsibilities. The most efficient regulatory model is *monopoly*, as this minimizes organizational disputes over responsibilities and different interpretations over rules and processes (Prenzler & Sarre, 2008).

Linked to this is the degree of independence of the regulator. Pure self-regulation, where the industry is given the power to regulate itself, is counter-productive, as the regulator is captured and serves the interests of the regulated rather than the broader public interest. Similarly giving the responsibility to the police (as is the case in New South Wales in Australia, and several American states), who have a competitive interest in the private security industry, is also counter-productive, as they may begin to regulate the industry with a view to inhibiting its ability to perform certain police functions. It is also important to note that regulating industries is not the core business of the police.

This then leads naturally to independent regulation, where the regulatory body is neutral towards the regulated industry and where the broader public interest is at the forefront of practice. Generally this is achieved with government departments and special boards (although the latter can vary on the degree to which they are independent). The problematic element is the possibility regulation could emerge that is impractical, frustrates the industry and is over bureaucratic. The mentality of regulation is therefore important. Ayres and Braithwaite's (1992) model of 'responsive regulation' offers a way forward. In this model the presence of interest groups is enshrined within the regulatory process, but they do not have ultimate control. The appropriate interest groups are built into the regulatory process, which means that are able to help shape the regulations, but not to determine them. The benefits of this model are not only that it is likely to result in the creation of more practical regulations, but that such regulations are more likely to be complied with. The regulatory body should therefore formally integrate the key groups representing the regulated industry (both employers and employees via trade unions), the purchasers and the public into the regulatory formulation process for consultation (Prenzler & Sarre, 2008).

In the United Kingdom the board of the SIA has no formal representation from the industry (i.e., a trade association), and the majority of the board have had no prior connection to the industry. To address this lack of representation the SIA has a wide-ranging stakeholder engagement strategy that encompasses a broad range of different strategies, including the use of the media, the Internet, research, surveys and periodic meetings (SIA, 2007), but there is no formal structure that brings all these groups together and enables two-way debate between the regulator and the stakeholders. A consultative council with the key stakeholders represented could do this. In Finland, for example, the regulator is a government department in the Ministry of the Interior, but a key part of the regulatory structure is an advisory board composed of representatives of the security industry (employers and employees), the business world and consumers of security (Section 51–2 of the Private Security Services Act 282/2002) who have a formal role in advising the regulator (Section 52 of the Private Security Services Act 282/2002 – Unofficial translation). This advisory board can bring a positive influence to bear on the regulator by ensuring that restrictive regulations are avoided, without actually dominating it. From the regulator's point of view it also provides invaluable advice. This provides an example of very good regulatory practice.

Another good example is the Republic of Ireland's PSA, which is an arm's length body appointed by the government. Unlike the British SIA, however, the board of the PSA incorporates considerable industry expertise. Of the nine board members, five come directly from the private security industry (two employers, two employees and one member from the Security Institute of Ireland), with the rest either from the police, the government or independent representatives. The author's position is that the industry should not have a majority on the board, but it does mean that there is expertise at the 'top table'.

From 'pimp' to 'fag'? The demise of English regulation and lessons for other countries?

With the passage of the 2001 Private Security Industry Act in England and Wales a consensus emerged on the benefits of regulation, and debates were only concerned with the details of the Act (White, 2010). This was shattered by the Conservative/Liberal Democrat coalition in October 2010 when a review of Government quangos (arms' length public bodies of which the SIA is one) was published in which it stated next to the SIA, 'No Longer an NDPB – Phased transition to new regulatory regime' (Cabinet Office, 2010). Worse, security journalists had received a press release the evening before suggesting the SIA was to be abolished completely, with the industry deregulated. This was then quickly changed to the statement above (SMT Online, 2011). It was only saved by the intervention of a hastily arranged organization called the 'Security Alliance' (SA) (consisting of the BSIA, the Security Institute, UK ASIS Chapter and the Worshipful Company of Security Professionals, another association for managers focussed more on raising funds for charity). The SA had lobbied Ministers and MPs and managed to secure a reprieve for the SIA until after the 2012 Olympics. Thereafter, the 'new regulatory regime' was to be created. What is all the more surprising, however, is that the decision to seek to abolish the SIA came from the Government with no pressure to do so. There had been no serious industry calls for deregulation, no campaign, not even calls from back-bench politicians. It was a complete surprise.

Serious questions were raised about this review of quangos from many quarters. Some found it strange that with the same criteria to assess regulatory bodies as to whether they should be retained, the SIA was for 'the chop' whereas the Gangmasters Licensing Authority (a body that regulates those who supply labour in various industries) was to survive. As the coalition dominated House of Commons Public Administration Select Committee in its report on the review was to comment (2011, p. 3):

This review was poorly managed. There was no meaningful consultation, the tests the review used were not clearly defined and the Cabinet Office failed to establish a proper procedure for departments to follow.

The finer details of the new regime are yet to be published. However, the broad principles have been set out by Baroness Neville-Jones, one of the Home Office Ministers responsible. These include the following:

- The transition to a new regulatory body, subject to new primary legislation, to give statutory force to the new regime.
- The introduction of a new regulatory regime focused on business registration, with robust sanctions to exclude businesses that do not meet the registration conditions, and an approach and fees that recognize the particular position of smaller businesses.
- Allowing registered businesses to play a greater role in the checking and registration of individuals, in certain circumstances, while maintaining a national register of individuals and access for those not directly employed by registered companies (SIA, 2011b).

It is also been made clear the final pieces of licensing included in the 2001 Act to be activated – private investigators and security consultants – will not be implemented. There is much detail to emerge before proper comment can be made. Nevertheless, it would seem the new regime will shift considerable power and responsibility to the industry. The new regulatory body will probably have a much greater representation from the industry, if not control it. This will be dangerous in a market where cost is still very important, as by giving greater responsibilities to firms, some will no doubt be tempted to cut corners to win business. The ability of individual licence holders to be held to account will also probably be weakened as well, if it's the companies rather than the regulator, administering the Act.

Zedner (2006) has described the SIA as the industry's 'pimp' based upon its promotion of the security industry. The stay of execution secured for the SIA by the industry and likely future shape could risk the new regulator (if it occurs) moving from a 'pimp' to a 'fag' (the term used in British public schools to describe junior pupils acting as servants for their elder pupils). Regulation is likely to increasingly be used to service the industry's interests, rather than the public's. The devolved nature of the UK state at least means the provisions will only apply to England and Wales. Early indications from Scotland and Northern Ireland (where the ruling parties are different) are that there is little appetite for the 'new regulatory regime'. It must also be noted the current coalition government has developed a habit of u-turns, so it would not be a surprise for the current proposals to be further reformed or even 'shelved'. Nevertheless, the English experience is a warning. The expectation amongst some observers on this subject is not necessarily the case – that the trend on regulation is deeper and wider based upon the experience of other countries. Neo-liberal tendencies can still resurface, even if there is a consensus for the status quo and even when there has been no crisis to trigger a change. Regulation of private security is not a natural form of intervention by the state as it is for industries such as banking. It is a policy that needs to be fought for, justified and regularly defended.

Conclusion

This chapter has argued that the regulation of the private security industry is an important factor in optimizing security. It has set out the case for regulation and why the private security industry is not just any other industry. The chapter then explored four key criteria for assessing regulatory systems. These included the width, depth, compliance and responsibility for regulation. In doing so, it illustrated good and bad practice from around the world. Finally the chapter considered the case of England and Wales and the proposals for dismantling some of the minimal regulation there. It used this as a warning for other countries, that regulation of private security is not a natural order. It is something for which a case needs to be made. It needs to adapt and be responsive to meet the changes in the private security industry, but it should also face the regular challenge of balancing consumer, industry and public interests. There is much to learn from around the world, and this chapter has offered many examples of good practice to aid that process.

References

ACPO. (2009). *Community safety accreditation scheme private sector companies.* Retrieved from http://www.securedbydesign.com/pdfs/CSAS%20information%20for%20private%20companies.pdf.

Ayres, I., & Braithwaite, J. (1992). *Responsive regulation.* Oxford: Oxford University Press.

Better Regulation Executive. (2009). *Security Industry Authority: A hampton implementation review report.* Retrieved from http://www.sia.homeoffice.gov.uk/Documents/reviews/bre_hampton_report.pdf.

Bushman, B. J. (1984). Perceived symbols of authority and their influence on compliance. *Journal of Applied Social Psychology, 14*, 501–508.

Button, M. (2007a). Assessing the regulation of private security across Europe. *European Journal of Criminology*, *4*, 109–128.

Button, M. (2007b). *Security officers and policing: Powers, culture and control in the governance of private space*. Aldershot: Ashgate.

Button, M. (2008). *Doing security*. Basingstoke: Palgrave Macmillan.

Button, M. (2011). The Private Security Industry Act 2001 and the security management gap in the United Kingdom. *Security Journal, 24*, 118–132.

Button, M., & George, B. (2006). Regulation of security: New models for analysis. In M. Gill (Ed.), *Handbook of security*. London: Palgrave Macmillan.

Button, M., Park, H., & Lee, J. (2006). The private security industry in South Korea: A familiar tale of growth, gaps and the need for better regulation. *Security Journal, 19*, 167–179.

Cabinet Office. (2010). Untitled. Retrieved from http://download.cabinetoffice.gov.uk/ndpb/public-bodies-list.pdf.

CoESS/UNI Europa. (2004). *Panoramic overview of the private security industry in the 25 member states of the European Union*. Retrieved from http://www.coess.org/pdf/panorama1.pdf.

Crawford, A., Lister, S., Blackburn, S., & Burnett, J. (2005). *Plural policing*. Bristol: The Policy Press.

Financial Services Authority. (2010). *FSA implements new powers granted by the Financial Services Act 2010*. Retrieved from http://www.fsa.gov.uk/pages/Library/Communication/PR/2010/123.shtml.

George, B., & Button, M. (1997). Private security regulation – Lessons from abroad for the United Kingdom. *International Journal of Risk Security and Crime Prevention, 2*, 109–121.

George, B., & Button, M. (2000). *Private security*. Leicester: Perpetuity Press.

Gill, M., Burns-Howell, T., Keats, G., & Taylor, E. (2007). *Demonstrating the value of security*. Leicester: Perpetuity Research and Consultancy International.

Gimenez-Salinas, A. (2004). New approaches regarding private/public security. *Policing and Society, 14*, 158–174.

Goold, B., Loader, I., & Thulma, A. (2010). Consuming security? Tools for a sociology of security consumption. *Theoretical Criminology, 14*, 3–30.

Gotbaum, B. (2005). *Undertrained, underpaid, and unprepared: Security officers report deficient safety standards in Manhattan office buildings*. A Report by the Public Advocate of the City of New York. New York: Public Advocate for the City of New York.

Hakala, J. (2007). *The regulation of manned private security: A transnational survey of structure and focus*. Retrieved from http://www.coess.org/pdf/article_on_regulation_survey.pdf.

Hemmens, C., Maahs, J., Scarborough, K. E., and Collins, P. A. (2001). Watching the watchmen: State regulation of private security 1982–1998. *Security Journal, 14*, 17–28.

Hobbs, D., Hadfield, P., Lister, S., & Winlow, S. (2003). *Bouncers: Violence and governance in the night-time economy*. Oxford: Oxford University Press.

Home Office. (2010). *Community policing*. Retrieved from http://tna.europarchive.org/20100419081706/http://www.police.homeoffice.gov.uk/community-policing/citizen-focused-policing/community-safety-accredit-scheme/index29f9.html?version=9.

House of Commons Public Administration Select Committee. (2011). *Smaller government: Shrinking the Quango state.* Retrieved from http://www.publications.parliament.uk/pa/cm201011/cmselect/cmpubadm/537/537.pdf.

Hyde, D. (2003). *The role of 'government' in regulating, auditing and facilitating private policing in late modernity: The Canadian experience.* Paper presented to In Search of Security Conference, Montreal, Quebec, February 2003.

International Alert. (2005). *SALW and private security companies in south eastern Europe: A cause or effect of insecurity.* Retrieved from http://www.seesac.org/reports/psc.pdf.

Johnston, L., & Shearing, C. D. (2003). *Governing security.* London: Routledge.

Jones, T., & Newburn, T. (1998). *Private security and public policing.* Oxford: Clarendon Press.

Kakalik, J., & Wildhorn, S. (1971). *Private police in the United States: Findings and recommendations. Vol 1.* Washington D.C.: Government Printing Office.

Lister, S., Hadfield, P., Hobbs, D., & Winlow, S. (2001). Accounting for bouncers: Occupational licensing as a mechanism for regulation. *Criminal Justice, 1,* 363.

Loader, I., & Walker, N. (2007). *Civilizing security.* Cambridge: Cambridge University Press.

Ministry of Public Safety and Solicitor General. (2011). *Security industry and licensing.* Retrieved from http://www.pssg.gov.bc.ca/securityindustry/statistics/index.htm.

Murray, C. (1996). The case against regulation. *International Journal of Risk, Security and Crime Prevention, 1,* 59–62.

National Advisory Committee on Criminal Standards and Goals. (1976). *Private security. Report of the Task Force on Private Security.* Washington D.C.: Government Printing Office.

NHS Counter Fraud and Security Management Service. (2003). *A professional approach to managing security in the NHS.* Retrieved from http://www.nhsbsa.nhs.uk/SecurityManagement/Documents/sms_strategy.pdf.

Prenzler, T., & Sarre, R. (1999). A survey of security legislation and regulatory strategies in Australia. *Security Journal, 12,* 7–17.

Prenzler, T., & Sarre, R. (2008). Developing a risk profile and model regulatory system for the security industry. *Security Journal, 21,* 264–277.

Prenzler, T., Baxter, T., & Draper, R. (1998). Special legislation for the security industry: A case study. *International Journal of Risk, Security and Crime Prevention, 3,* 21–33.

Private Security Authority (PSA). (2011). *Licensing information.* Retrieved from http://www.psa.gov.ie/psa/psa.nsf/agentvw?Openform&vw=psaLicensing.

Reiner, R. (2007). *Law and order.* Cambridge: Polity.

Rigakos, G. S. (2008). *Nighclub.* Montreal: McGill-Queen's University Press.

Sarre, R., & Prenzler, T. (2005). *The law of private security in Australia.* Pyrmont: Thomson.

Security Industry Authority (SIA). (2007). *Stakeholder engagement strategy.* London: Security Industry Authority.

SIA. (2010a). *The impact of regulation on the security guard sector.* Retrieved from http://www.sia.homeoffice.gov.uk/Documents/research/sia_sg_impact.pdf.

SIA. (2010b). *The impact of regulation on the door supervision sector.* Retrieved from http://www.sia.homeoffice.gov.uk/Documents/research/sia_ds_impact.pdf.

SIA. (2010c). *Annual report and accounts 2009/10.* London: SIA.

SIA. (2011a). *Enforcement activity*. Retrieved from http://www.sia.homeoffice.gov.uk/Pages/enforcement-activity.aspx.

SIA. (2011b). *Update from our Chief Executive*. Retrieved from http://www.sia.homeoffice.gov.uk/Pages/future-update.aspx.

SMT Online. (2011). *The SIA's future: How the private security industry was nearly 'quangoed'*. Retrieved from http://www.info4security.com/story.asp?sectioncode=10&storycode=4125992.

Stenning, P. C., & Shearing, C. D. (1979). Private security and private justice. *British Journal of Law and Society, 6,* 261–271.

Strom, K., Berzofsky, M., Shook-Sa, B., Barrick, K., Daye, C., Horstmann, N., & Kinsey, S. (2010). The private security industry: A review of the definitions, available data sources, and paths moving forward. Washington D.C.: US Department of Justice.

Wakefield, A. (2003). *Selling security – The private policing of public space*. Cullompton: Willan.

Weber, T. (2002). *A comparative overview of legislation governing the private security industry in the European Union*. Retrieved from http://www.coess.org/pdf/final-study.PDF.

White, A. (2010). *The politics of private security*. Basingstoke: Palgrave Macmillan.

White, A., & Smith, M. (2010). *Security Industry Authority: A baseline review*. Retrieved from http://www.sia.homeoffice.gov.uk/Documents/research/sia_baseline_review.pdf.

Wood, J., & Shearing, C. D. (2007). *Imagining security*. Cullompton: Willan.

Yoshida, N. (1999). The taming of the Japanese private security industry. *Policing and Society, 9,* 241–261.

Zedner, L. (2006). Liquid security: Managing the market for crime control. *Criminology and Criminal Justice, 6,* 267–288.

Index

Note: page numbers with *f* indicate figures; those with *t* indicate tables.